WILLIAM FAULKNER
AND JOAN WILLIAMS

WILLIAM FAULKNER AND JOAN WILLIAMS

The Romance of Two Writers

Lisa C. Hickman

Foreword by Richard Bausch

McFarland & Company, Inc., Publishers
Jefferson, North Carolina, and London

LIBRARY OF CONGRESS CATALOGUING-IN-PUBLICATION DATA

Hickman, Lisa C., 1959–
    William Faulkner and Joan Williams : the romance of two
writers / Lisa C. Hickman ; foreword by Richard Bausch.
        p.   cm.
    Includes bibliographical references and index.

    ISBN-13: 978-0-7864-2599-0
    ISBN-10: 0-7864-2599-7
    (softcover : 50# alkaline paper) ∞

    1. Faulkner, William, 1897–1962—Relations with women.
2. Williams, Joan, 1928– —Interviews. 3. Williams, Joan,
1928– —Correspondence. 4. Faulkner, William, 1897–
1962—Correspondence. 5. Novelists, American—20th
century—Correspondence. I. Title.
PS3511.A86Z7873   2006
813'.52—dc22   2006030655

British Library cataloguing data are available

Cover photograph: Joan Williams and William Faulkner
(courtesy Joan Williams)

Manufactured in the United States of America

McFarland & Company, Inc., Publishers
    Box 611, Jefferson, North Carolina 28640
        www.mcfarlandpub.com

In loving memory of our son, James,
September 16, 1980–May 20, 1999.
Your spirit guides us every day.

And for Jess.

Acknowledgments

First and foremost, I wish to remember Joan Williams—for her friendship, cooperation, and her beautiful legacy of words.

My family, especially my husband, Jesse W. Bunn, our son, Jeffrey, and daughter, Jordan; my parents, Patricia Arch Jacobs and Jerome C. Jacobs; and my mother-in-law, Martha W. Bunn, for their inspiration and support.

My friends who have been a wonderful source of encouragement and help. A special thanks to Memphis attorney Mike Roberts and Memphis author Cary Holladay for their early and sustained assistance; Richard Bausch for his insightful foreword; photographers Murray Riss and Arlie E. Herron for their generous contributions, as well as, Ezra and Dawn Bowen; Judith Rutschman for sharing her many talents; former *Memphis Magazine* editor James Roper for publishing my two-part article on Faulkner and Joan; *Memphis Flyer* book editor Leonard Gill for being a wonderful editor and literary critic; Susannah Northart for her intellectual savvy and for compiling my index; Sandra Baldwin for her incredible ballet classes; and Francisca Devine, for all you do. Also, Tom Mendina and Kay Kroboth for inviting me to discuss Joan Williams' work for Friends of the University Libraries at the University of Memphis. Dr. Linda Kay Myers and Steve O'Dell who so enriched Joan's life, especially her later years, through their friendship.

Dr. Daniel E. Williams for welcoming me into the Ph.D. program at the University of Mississippi; Dr. Robert Hamblin, director of the Center for Faulkner Studies at Southeast Missouri State University, for his faith in this project; and my Ph.D. committee at the University of Mississippi: Dr. Donald M. Kartiganer, Howry Professor of Faulkner Studies, for reading my material as it evolved; Dr. Thomas M. Verich, professor and former university archivist, for contributing an important Faulkner letter; Dr. Benjamin F. Fisher IV, Victorianist and Poe scholar, and Dr. Joseph R. Urgo, former English department chair, Cather and Faulkner scholar, for their expertise and guidance.

A heartfelt thank you to all.

Table of Contents

Foreword
by *Richard Bausch*

It was January 1992, and I was touring my novel *Violence*, for Seymour Lawrence and Houghton Mifflin. I began the tour in New York, then went on to Florida, and the West Coast, before flying to Memphis, and the mid-south part of the tour. My friend Richard Ford, who was living in Oxford, Mississippi, then, picked me up at the airport, and we drove together down there, to Sam Lawrence's house, just up the street and within sight of Faulkner's Rowan Oak. Joan Williams had been with Sam for almost ten years at the time, and it was at Sam's house that I met her. I thought she was pretty, and that her staccato way of talking was charming. I knew she had written books—I had read *The Morning and the Evening*, in fact, and liked it very much—and of course I knew of her history with Faulkner, because I had read the biographies and also knew some of the people who had been around then. I remember that I was a little surprised at how ingenuous she seemed with me. I mean there was a deference she assumed that I was sure I hadn't earned or merited. I marked it as a form of politeness.

We spoke about the tour so far, what the crowds had been like in Florida and out west. Joan served some finger food, some cheeses and wine. It was all very cordial and all colored by the fact that although this was my seventh volume of fiction I had never done a book tour, and my publisher was the legendary Sam Lawrence. Sam had stories to tell about his other authors—the famous ones—and about the industry in general. He told me that he had started out in this neck of the woods, as a textbook salesman, back in the late fifties. At some point Joan asked if I would like to go tour Rowan Oak. I said I would, very much so.

It turned out that Ford and I walked down there first—later that same afternoon. Joan had excused herself and gone into the other room to take a nap. Sam had some business to conduct; so Richard and I walked down

1

there. The place was shut up—it was dusky late afternoon by now. We looked in the windows. He and I walked around in the yard, and then we went on back to where Richard and Kristina were living that year.

I read to a large crowd at Square Books that night, introduced by Richard, with Sam and Joan in the audience. I recall that Barry Hannah also turned up, and we all went out to dinner afterwards. It was a fine night, and Joan was good company, talking about the people of Memphis and environs that she had known most of her life. We never spoke of Faulkner once. The name never came up.

At one point Joan expressed interest in taking a fiction workshop with me—and again I felt no small amount of surprise at the apparent deference in the thought. This woman had, after all, been nominated for a National Book Award the year *before* I entered high school. It seemed so odd to have her eyes turned upon me in that way, as a creative presence from whom she might gather nourishment. This sounds a little precious to say it that way; but that is the only way to describe the feeling of those exchanges.

In the three or four other times that we were together after that, this same deference came through, and there were several more expressions of interest in studying with me. For some reason she thought of me as teacher, and herself as student. She gave me a long story that she had written, a wonderful novella, that I helped get published, and her gratitude made it evident that she attributed the story's publication to my influence. Of course, nothing could be further from the truth. The merits of the story were all hers; the virtues of the prose line, the truth in the images, the felt life in every scene, were all uniquely hers, and there was a canniness in all the gestures that was clearly the product of her own shrewdness as a story teller—as a story *writer*.

I think it was about this time that I began to see how the only thing necessary in life and circumstance to silence a writer is something to break that writer's confidence in her way of working. This had happened to Joan, I believe, and for years she had been casting about for a way to believe again. She had written memorably and gracefully about things that mattered. I think the fact that she was Faulkner's last love hounded her even when no one spoke about it, but not in the ways you might be thinking: she had lived her life fully and to the hilt always and she had a passion for her art, and he was a part of her history. But others were often too willing to remember it, or try pointedly to ignore it. It must have been annoying to her, when it wasn't hurtful.

But she was with Seymour Lawrence now, and she was reasonably happy and wanted to do her work. She was perfectly fine company, very smart, very direct, with a keen eye for social nuance and with a sociologist's cold eye for how things were in her culture.

As a writer, she had somehow come to having no idea how good she really was. Her critical sense regarding her own work had grown faulty in the extreme the other way—that is, her good lines, her good scenes, her good stories, looked too clumsy and too willed to her, and she de-valued them all, thought they weren't good enough. Because she was an instinctive writer, she didn't feel completely in charge of her material, and this troubled her far more than it should have—troubled her exactly the way it troubles the inexperienced and the newborn among writers. This was the curious thing about her: she had a wonderful ear and an impeccable eye, and a large gift that had already been mined well and used well, and yet it was as though none of it had ever happened and she was back to the very beginning, a bright spirit wanting to write. A beginner wanting to take a creative writing class.

I knew quickly enough that I could never teach her a thing, but only try to tear away some of the layers of misconception that had accumulated over the years; that all she needed to do was put pen to paper and begin, as she had always done before, and the good things will happen. She came to this anyway—good writers usually do—and it had finally nothing to do with me, except that I urged her to submit that one novella, and it was taken, and she was on her way again. And even so, she occasionally called me and asked if it might be all right if she came and sat in on a class or two.

That first trip to Oxford, I did go inside the Faulkner house. I went with Joan. The attendant there was a young writing student who recognized her, and knew my name, and so we were allowed past the guard-screens and into the rooms. Joan and I walked around in the study, and took some books out of the shelves and looked at them. She talked a little about the layout of the house, and how the people of the town saw Faulkner. I stood for a long time and stared at the scrawl on the wall above the desk, the famous notes for A Fable. She stood with me, and shook her head. I think she may have wanted to find in it something of what she perceived as his certainty concerning what he was about. I said something to that effect, anyway, that I wished I could plumb through the notes to what he might've been thinking. She said, "It's pretty desperate. Writing on a wall." And I laughed quietly. "You mean he wasn't any more in charge of it than we are?" I said.

She smiled. "I don't know." But she did know, and she nodded at me. We were two writers standing in the study of one other, and we understood that we were not different in kind, anyway, than he.

Outside, the attendant was sitting on the front step. I sat next to him, and Joan leaned against the porch railing on the other side. I bummed a cigarette off him, and we smoked. It was January, and growing toward dark, and there was a chill on the air. I made a joke—told the boy that I was so happy about his trusting us with the house that I took it upon myself to wash all that scribbling off the walls in the study. He gave me a knowing look, but didn't laugh. Joan laughed. It was such a pleasant sound in that winter dusk. We walked back up the road together, and in her quick-speaking way she told me she'd like to have a solid year just to write and read, and not think about anything else. I spoke, rather pompously I now realize, about how writers generally have no material ambitions; all they really want is time and the space to work.

"Well, that's what I want now," she said. "That's for sure."

Richard Bausch holds the Lillian A. and Morrie Moss Chair of Excellence in the Writing Program at the University of Memphis and is the author of sixteen volumes of fiction, including Hello to the Cannibals, The Last Good Time, In the Night Season, The Stories of Richard Bausch, Wives and Lovers, *and* Thanksgiving Nights. *He also is the current chancellor for the Fellowship of Southern Writers.*

Preface

I met Joan Williams in 1993 while working on a magazine article about two Memphis psychiatrists who treated William Faulkner in the early 1950s. She was living part of the year in Oxford, Mississippi, across the street from Faulkner's home, Rowan Oak. I called her in hopes of a phone interview and she invited me to Oxford. She even arranged for Faulkner's nephew, Jimmy Faulkner, to come to her home as well. Mr. Faulkner, at seventy, bore a striking likeness to his uncle. He was inordinately kind to my twelve-year-old son, James, who was with me. Mr. Faulkner called him "Jimmy" and told him he was the "main man" because they shared a first name.

Joan and I stayed in touch after that meeting, and in 1995 she returned to Memphis, her hometown. By then I was reading her novels and short stories and we talked off and on about her friendship with Faulkner. Usually, she would insist she already had told their story, in a slight essay for the *Atlantic Monthly*, "Twenty Will Not Come Again" (1980), and in her 1971 novel *The Wintering*. Published nine years after Faulkner's death, *The Wintering* recreates many important instances with attention to emotional nuances. Yet even with her essay and novel, the context of the relationship remained elusive. The more we talked, and especially after she shared her letters to Faulkner and the hundreds of letters she had received from him, I knew nothing existed that captured the complexity of this relationship.

Eventually, Joan and I agreed that I would write their story, which would focus primarily on 1949–1953. For Faulkner, these years marry professional triumphs and personal disappointments: the Nobel Prize for Literature and an increasingly unlifting depression. For Joan, these years were a tempest of youth and a burgeoning literary career. We spent hours studying and discussing their correspondence as I recorded the interviews. The project took shape through a melding of letters, interviews, Joan's published and unpublished material, and existing biographical and scholarly resources.

I wanted to more fully develop this story through primary sources; to go beyond the premise of an aging artist meeting a lovely young woman who admired him. No doubt Faulkner was attracted to Joan, but their shared personality traits formed a deeper union. Both were nonverbal people comfortable with a companionable silence and their letters record chronic bouts of depression, loneliness, and unrest. They sympathized and understood as only those can who know the pain of depression. Joan, new to the craft of fiction, agonized over the hard work, yet she saw Faulkner, with all of his success, struggling still. She learned firsthand that the labor and uncertainly of writing never abates.

The present volume then began to evolve. It would not be a book of correspondence, a biography, or a literary analysis in the traditional sense. I decided to let the letters, interviews, and whatever context I might supply determine the narrative flow. I also determined to remain as objective as possible. Readers may interpret the relationship as they will. Faulkner and Joan both were driven by motives beyond simply wanting to spend time together. Over and over Faulkner pressed for a sexual union, stressing his need for a fresh, beautiful woman to serve as muse. He insisted as well that Joan would not develop as an artist until she freed herself of conventional Southern mores. This was very problematic for a young woman in the early 1950s educated at Miss Hutchison's School for Girls. Joan believed she wanted a mentor, not a lover, and her letters generally sought instruction or advice from Faulkner. His, on the other hand, encouraged personal paths. Still, when she noticed Faulkner's interest flagging, her tone shifted. Her letters would take an impassioned turn, promise more time together, or remind him of a satisfying interlude.

My interviews with Joan introduced another layer of interpretation. She downplayed Faulkner's fervent sexuality. If she could recast the story, the affair would have remained unconsummated. Faulkner would be pining while Joan learned what she could from the master. By and large, Faulkner's role in Joan's artistic development was more of example than writing teacher or editor. As she returned to these issues so many years later, contrasts and ironies emerge between what she said in the interviews and what she wrote in her letters. Such is the nature of time and reflection.

Using the exchanged correspondence was a natural approach to this book, especially when the affair often seemed more alive and significant in the letters than in any other form. Faulkner himself envisioned an epistolary novel about their friendship and prodded Joan to write such a book. At one point he arranged a desk and typewriter for her in his New York suite at One Fifth Avenue for motivation. He encouraged Joan to recreate the first letter she sent him—one he regretfully felt he had to tear up and throw out the car window—and he often returned her letters to her for material. He even went so far as naming the novel's protagonist Laurel Wynn. A pretty name, he thought. And while that character name eventually surfaces in Joan's fiction, the protagonist for *The Wintering* is Amy Howard, a self-absorbed often-insecure young woman who has captured and invited the attentions of Jeffrey Almoner, a well-recognized author. Labeled by some a roman à clef, there is a strange and persistent detachment in *The Wintering* despite the polished prose. Joan said often the book is an accurate reflection of those years she shared with Faulkner. The detachment might be attributed to the challenge of taking an essentially biographical story and attempting to recast it as fiction.

Joan's interest and belief in my project remained strong after she moved from Memphis to Charlottesville, Virginia, in 1999. Her death on Easter Sunday, 14 April 2004, casts a lingering sadness. A year after her passing, I contributed Joan's narrative and an attempt at a complete bibliography to the Mississippi Writers Page sponsored by the English Department at the University of Mississippi. It was rewarding to record the many influential publications and authors who reviewed Joan's books (five novels and a short story collection), and the writers who followed her life and career. Her literary contributions extend far beyond her six books and are duly noted in this bibliography. Joan often, and rightly, felt she struggled more for recognition because of her relationship with Faulkner, that her talent somehow was dismissed because of their association, despite the fact that her oeuvre, with the exception of two published short stories, evolved after 1953.

I do know an author as gifted as Joan Williams will continue to find a receptive audience and I hope this book leads new readers to her fiction and encourages others to revisit her work. She would appreciate that. She also would be pleased with this fuller recounting of her friendship with William Faulkner.

Introduction: Middle Years

When Nobel Prize–winning author William Faulkner met Memphian Joan Williams both lives were forever changed. Their complex, touching relationship is both love story and Künstlerroman. Any student of Faulkner's life knows he fell in love more than once, but his relationship with Joan Williams, encapsulated in the years 1949–1953, and detailed in hundreds of letters exchanged between the two, carries a significance others lack. Only in this relationship with Joan Williams did Faulkner's personal desires comingle with an opportunity to mentor a talented young writer. Their relationship united Faulkner's urgent need for romantic love with the opportunity to play Pygmalion. His Pygmalion would not create a cold and beautiful statue to fall in love with; his Pygmalion would take his love for Joan and create a poet out of her.

Part of the wonderment of this relationship was Faulkner's commitment to nurturing Joan as a writer, and Joan's commitment to a recognizably difficult attachment. That they developed and maintained a very real emotional bond for many years speaks to their perseverance. Why, when it was at times so hard to see Faulkner, when meetings required secrecy and deception, when she felt nothing but pressure from him, did Joan persist? Her answer was simple: "Because he was Faulkner."[1]

Joan's backward glances at those years access nuances of Faulkner's personality that may surprise. Such memories also reveal Joan's maturation as writer and as an individual. Faulkner is widely known for his ability to pursue, create, and develop new facets of his personality. Over the years he assumed many roles—Boy Scout leader, postmaster, down-and-out house painter, wounded World War I RAF veteran, young man abroad in Europe, off-and-on undergraduate at the University of Mississippi, New York bookstore clerk, bank clerk, New Orleans house guest, Mississippi landowner, hunter, fisherman, commoner, and Virginia gentleman who enjoyed fox hunting—all of which embellished and contributed to his most important persona—American author.

After almost a decade of work on A Fable, he completed the novel in November 1953, with his four most productive and intense years paralleling the beginning and end of his affair with Joan. Outwardly, these same years signaled success—a host of accolades including the pinnacle of literary achievement—while inwardly Faulkner's depression was profound and sustained. He wrote Joan in 1952, "I am too unhappy here now, never in my life have I ever been so unhappy and depressed"[2]

In 1946, a Faulkner resurgence occurred due largely to the efforts of New Republic editor Malcolm Cowley and publication of The Portable Faulkner. As readers put his work into a broader perspective, Faulkner enjoyed a new critical appreciation. Several publications followed Cowley's edition: Intruder in the Dust (1948), Knight's Gambit (1949), The Collected Stories (1950), and Requiem for a Nun (1951). Always productive, the difference during these years for Faulkner would be the attention paid to his new books and his personal regard in the literary community. Intruder in the Dust not only sold well, but it also was adapted to the screen in the fall of 1949. During the summer of 1950, the American Academy of Arts and Letters awarded Faulkner the Howells Medal for Distinguished Work in American Fiction; in the fall of 1950 he was recognized by no less than the Swedish Academy; in March 1951 The Collected Stories garnered the National Book Award; in May of that same year the French Consul bestowed upon him the Legion of Honor Award; and in November 1952 the Ford Foundation traveled to Oxford to make a short documentary film about the author.

Contrarily, his personal life often involved severe depression and serious bouts with alcohol. Between 1949 and 1953 Faulkner was hospitalized frequently—four times alone in Memphis, Tennessee, for back pain and alcoholism. At the same time, his discontent with his wife, Estelle, increased.

When they met in August of 1949, Faulkner was fifty-one years old and Joan was twenty. Both their birthdays would occur a few weeks after that first meeting: Faulkner's, 25 September; Joan's, 26 September. Until his death on 6 July 1962, Faulkner remembered Joan's birthday with a telegram: "HAPPY BIRTHDAY. I LOVE YOU. BILL."

An excellent article by Elizabeth Mullener for Dixie magazine published thirty-three years after Joan and Faulkner's initial meeting records Joan's vivid assessment of Faulkner's state of mind as he reached his middle years:

> "At the time I knew him, he was tired," Williams said. "He was tired period. He was tired of writing and tired of feeling neglected and tired of being around people who didn't appreciate him. He just kept talking about getting rid of the house and everybody and just leaving everything behind

and getting out from underneath it. He needed love and affection and somebody to feel that what he had done was worthwhile and to keep saying go on. He felt he was surrounded by people who didn't appreciate his work and didn't care about it.

"It's odd to think that people now have so much awe over someone I knew who, at the time, was so neglected. Back then, we would go around and nobody ever spoke to us or ran up and wanted an autograph.

"He wasn't locked in his room being melancholy, but I don't think he was very happy. I think during the period I knew him, he knew that his greatest work was over. He was not fired up as a writer, the juices weren't flowing with the passion of youth and real creativity, and he was just sort of stopping midstream and saying 'Well, I've done all this work but I don't have anybody to share it with. I don't have a person who belongs to me.'

"He was lonely. He just wanted to be connected with somebody—somebody he felt understood him and whom he could really love.

"I don't think most people feel his last novels were his best.... I mean, the man was just written out. I know he was. He said so in his letters to me. He said, 'I know I'm getting to the bottom of the barrel. A little trash is coming up. It's time to break the pencil.' And of course I always said: 'Oh no, you've got to go on' and all that. But he knew his great things were written. A writer knows."[3]

———

What Faulkner felt he needed and wanted with Joan was a redemptive and rejuvenating love affair; what Joan hoped for was a close friendship with an author she greatly admired. They frequently experienced the anguish of two people pulling in different directions. Faulkner's ardent desire often received a cool reception, making their romance far from a mature coupling. For Faulkner, Joan's youth was also a bane. She was immature and hesitant to embrace him as a lover. The thirty-year age difference loomed large for both. Joan's beauty and talent attracted suitors her own age whom she dated throughout her years with Faulkner. Faulkner in turn responded with jealousy and anger.

Beyond the obvious—Faulkner the famous author and Joan the youthful protégée—deeper and more profound personality traits held them together: they felt a sense of loneliness that haunted them their entire lives; they experienced depression and felt keenly the suffering of others; and they shared a love for their kindred South. She was, as he once told her when she asked why he liked to be with her, "his countryman."[4] "I think we both felt that we were each other's countryman and that there was just a basic bond between us."[5]

In *The Wintering*, Joan writes: "Having nothing to say, it was understood, they would say nothing. With that situation they were comfortable.... Suppose she said, Think of rain falling in places we'll never see. He would understand and know she was thinking how lonely they both had been. Turning, he seemed to ponder, too, the enormity of this moment in which no longer were they lonely."[6]

———

Despite what some might consider a privileged background with expensive private schools and colleges, Joan searched persistently for self-confidence. Born 26 September 1928, Joan, an only child, was sandwiched between her hard-working and hard-living father, P.H. Williams, and her mother, Maude Moore Williams, who chose a much quieter existence—playing bridge, reading, and shopping. Her father was a bigger-than-life figure who discovered the use of dynamite in the formation of levees. This greatly boosted his income as a dynamite salesman. In 1936 the United States government commissioned Williams to flood farms in Cairo, Illinois, preventing high waters from flooding the entire Mississippi River Valley.

P.H. was a self-made man with an eighth-grade education who made his reputation shooting off dynamite himself, often by removing the cigarette he was smoking to light the fuse. When Joan graduated from Bard College, he agreed to attend her graduation but would not talk to her professors because "he didn't know how to talk to people like that." (Joan returned to her father's life in 1966 with the publication of *Old Powder Man*. This powerful novel meticulously recreates the days of levee camps and her father's imposing figure.)

Almost always on the road, P.H. could not be reached at his hotel the night Joan was born. It was a resentment Maude held all of her life. Their marriage was strained and P.H. indulged in drinking episodes not unlike Faulkner's. Joan felt alone and overlooked, especially by her father. Faulkner keyed into this issue, often referred to himself as the father she never had. Joan confirmed there may have been some truth to Faulkner's identity as her missing father: "And also, there was something of wanting a father mixed up in there, too, because I didn't have a father who was close to me. And I was looking to an older man and wanting to make him my father."[7]

Later in life Joan discovered she shared more with her father than she imagined. He told her that he coped with all the traveling by making up stories as he drove. Joan felt that was his way of telling her he also had wanted to be a writer.

———

Eighteen years after Faulkner's death, an *Atlantic Monthly* editor approached Joan with an idea. Would she please write an article about William Faulkner? Joan was a well-published author by then with three novels; her essay, "Twenty Will Not Come Again," is a sparse, tender tale of her time with Faulkner. At the essay's conclusion, she comes to a personal awakening—"I had seen the last; and if I had not seen the real first, I had seen a beginning of another kind, in his middle age. Someday, Joan, he said, you will know that no one will ever love you as I have."[8]

> I guess what he mostly helped me with, as time has passed and I've had a hard time writing and things like that. I think of him and his struggle and I think if he could go through that, through the years of unrecognition, then I could keep on. He taught me tenaciousness and not to expect a lot of fame from the beginning and just to keep working. You might think that Faulkner just sat down and wrote those books. But there's a letter from him that says something about the difficulties of being a writer. He says people think you're odd and there's the loneliness. But the main thing is the work—how hard it is to write. He worked hard and he must have done a lot of revisions. Just to have sent out short stories for 13 years and never to sell one and not to have given up in all that time is amazing.
>
> He had this one effect on my life: that I feel I met the only genius I will ever meet and I can't be awed by anybody else. I know I've met somebody far superior to anybody else I'm ever going to meet. I guess he was the last of my heroes. Nobody could ever be a hero to me again.[9]

In her article "Faulkner's Advice to a Young Writer," Joan eloquently acknowledges how profoundly her intimate glimpse of Faulkner's life as a writer clarified her own career path: "He was at the height of his fame ... but continued to struggle and worry. And this was what I learned mostly about writing from Faulkner, that it was never certain and was always hard work, without his ever being aware that had been his message, without his knowing my observation had been all the while it was a life's process that entailed a lonesomeness of spirit."[10]

I

1949—An
Afternoon Recalled

How William Faulkner and Joan Williams met may be attributed to something as simple as young people in search of an afternoon outing. At least that is how Joan's first cousin, Regina Moore Holley of Oxford, Mississippi, explained it.

One August afternoon in 1949, as the last days of summer passed slowly, the idea of meeting the South's preeminent author took hold of two young Memphians. Joan Williams, winner of the college fiction contest, had just experienced her first literary success with the August publication of her short story, "Rain Later," in *Mademoiselle* magazine. Her friend and fellow literary enthusiast Kenneth Orgill Jr.,[1] also home from college, suggested they travel to Oxford and meet Faulkner. Earlier that summer, on Orgill's recommendation, Joan read *The Sound and the Fury*, and was swept away by the intensity of Faulkner's novel. It was her landscape, the kind of people she knew, and the emotions she experienced. Though by nature a shy individual, Joan had to agree with Orgill that with Faulkner a mere seventy-five miles south, it was a trip worth undertaking.

Joan hoped that Regina, recently married to John Reed Holley of Oxford, might smooth the way for an impromptu visit to Faulkner's home, Rowan Oak. Even though her maternal aunt, Ethel Moore of Senatobia, Mississippi, had warned Joan away from such a meeting, Joan persisted. Ethel Moore advised Joan that her knowledge of the Faulkner family convinced her that "Faulkner was irresponsible, a drinker, and someone to avoid."[2]

Regina, an Oxford resident since her days at the University of Mississippi, said that the trip to Rowan Oak came about in part because they were restless. "It was a rainy, summer afternoon and we'd been in the house quite

15

a bit and my husband had talked on the phone to Mr. Bill, as he called him, and we were told that Mr. Bill was going to the lake. To Sardis. But we assumed, John and I, we looked at each other, and we assumed this was Mr. Bill's manner of saying 'I really don't care to have company.' So John Reed just said, 'Let me drive you by and let you look at the house.'"

With the Holleys' year-and-a-half-old son in tow, the four set out on a sight-seeing mission not as presumptuous as one might think. Mrs. Holley said that John Reed grew up in Oxford down the street from the Old-ham home, Faulkner's in-laws. Holley played in and out of the home and was on a first-name basis as children with Estelle Faulkner's children from her first marriage, Malcolm Franklin and Victoria (Cho-Cho) Franklin. John Reed recalled Miss Estelle as very pretty and remembered Mr. Bill for the Halloweens when he would tell the story about the death of a Civil War soldier who pined for his lover. The children would sit outside and listen to Mr. Bill tell this story. "They believed it," Mrs. Holley said. Thus, John Reed Holley was well known to Mr. Bill and Miss Estelle. Regina's husband described the Oxford he knew as a young man as "free of distinctions." That he was friendly with the Faulkners seemed a natural result of growing up in the same community. When Mr. Holley, John Reed's father, died, Faulkner and Estelle were among the many to send their con-dolences.

The memories of that particular afternoon evoke feelings of awkward-ness and amusement at Faulkner's response to his uninvited guests. "I remember sort of being embarrassed," Mrs. Holley said. "I didn't ask John this question but I feel like he and I shared a bit of embarrassment. If he felt free enough to drive up in Mr. Bill's yard, even though it said 'No Tres-passing,' and you must understand John has told Joan what Mr. Bill has said, 'he's not going to be there, he's out on the lake.' No matter what you think, an afternoon with a young man and a young woman out of Mem-phis, you need some entertainment. John said, 'Let's go riding.' And when we pulled up you cannot see from the roadside, and I think if my husband had the audacity, it was not audacity, he felt as if Mr. Bill would not have minded if he nosed the car up to let the friend see the house. And it was rather a hidden embarrassment that he and I shared, but we never talked about it because it was over too quickly. The fact that we could see and he could see us what else do you do?

No matter what anybody makes of it, this was no infringement on Mr. Faulkner's privacy. And it so happens that we laughed heartily, and mostly laughed, because when we were by ourselves, John said, 'Do you know what Mr. Bill said when I got to the fence?' He said, 'What does she want to meet me for, to see if I have two heads?'"[3]

As chronicled by Faulkner biographer
Joseph Blotner, John Reed phoned Faulkner
twice that day, the first time after lunch
(Faulkner had plans to go sailing), and
again around three in the afternoon when
it started drizzling. Faulkner still maintained he planned a trip to Sardis Reser-
voir just a few miles from Oxford. Finally
about five, they drove to Rowan Oak, glid-
ing in the turn-around drive past the
NO TRESPASSING sign. Just as he made
the turn, John Reed spotted the author in
a pasture with the horses. Faulkner was
casually dressed in khakis and a tee shirt.
John Reed parked the car and walked
toward Faulkner. Harkening back to their
friendship, John Reed told Faulkner he
would appreciate it if Faulkner would
speak to Joan. The two men stood in
the drizzle near the car and Faulkner
spoke briefly to Joan, Orgill and Regina.

Joan Williams as a Bard College student in 1949, the same
year she met William Faulkner
at Rowan Oak, his home in
Oxford, Mississippi (courtesy
Joan Williams).

Faulkner was probably surprised by Joan's youth. At twenty, soon to be
twenty-one years, Joan was an attractive girl with red hair, freckles, and
brown-green eyes.[4]

Joan shared the Holleys' embarrassment and felt it more keenly as she
had hoped for a satisfying introduction. Mortified by their intrusion, her
first response was to write Faulkner a letter of apology, and without that letter Faulkner's brief glimpse of Joan in the turn-around of his driveway most
likely soon would have faded. Instead, a letter intended as an apology served
as a much more intimate introduction than Joan could have mustered in
person. Not only did the letter strike Faulkner's fancy, but it also ignited
an intense and sustained body of correspondence that would cease only
with his death in 1962.

Faulkner told Joan during one of their first tentative meetings that he
reluctantly had torn up her first letter and had thrown it out a car window.
Rewrite that letter, he would tell in her in 1951. Write a novel about us and
our meeting—"soul mates" and some reason we met and "spun round in
orbit together a while," he said.[5] When Joan settled down to recreate her
first letter, it was for her third novel, *The Wintering*, published by Harcourt

Brace Jovanovich in 1971. Faulkner appears as Jeffrey Almoner, and Joan as Amy Howard, in this highly autobiographical tale of an older, artistic man in love with his apprentice:

> Dear Mr. Almoner:
>   ...I am unhappy and I know you are unhappy too. I wanted to tell you you shouldn't be unhappy and lonely when you have done so much for the world. There were so many things I wanted to ask you because I know you have thought and felt and suffered everything I ever have and I wanted to ask you the reason for suffering. Why some people have to and others don't? In the end do you gain something from it? ... Could I come again by myself? You don't have to worry as I know all about your drinking and that doesn't make any difference to me. My father drinks too. So don't worry or be embarrassed....
>
>   Sincerely,
>   Amy Howard[6]

Joan's working draft of the letter for *The Wintering* offers more insight about the actual meeting with Faulkner than what appears in her novel:

>   End of August
> Dear Mr. Almoner
>   I know that you do not remember my name. I am the girl who came this afternoon to your house to meet you even after you had told my cousin over the phone not to bring me there. And having done that, I know that I should not be writing you now and bothering you again. But I had to let you know, in case it should make any difference to you, that I did not come for the reason I was afraid you would think I came, for the reason I knew you thought as soon as I saw your face.
>   I came only because of what they said, the poems, and not so much because of the words themselves as because of what was behind them, because of the kind of man I knew it must be who had written them. Because, after taking them up, I was filled with so much wonderfulness and I knew that even though we were not the same age, had been through different things, lived in different places, known different people, underneath it was all the same, and you would understand, for I was sure that you had asked yourself the same questions, suffered, laughed and cried for the same things, for the whole world, not just for yourself, because of the lostness, the sadness of it all, the too lateness, the things gone and never to return again. And I knew that you must have found something, that you must know something, and I had to come just to meet you, perhaps even to ask you.
>   Everyone told me that you would not see people who came, but I thought that if I could just stand there and say~I read them and I know what you mean for I have felt that too~that perhaps it would mean something to you to know that, that somehow perhaps you would be glad. I just a girl, who somehow, I do not even know, took up one of your books and even through

the ache of the poetry itself, the lostness of it, felt a deep down well of happiness that it existed, that you did.

But it was all so terrible, all turned out so much the wrong way. Now it is all ruined, but I had to tell you anyway the way it was so that you would know. I went to my cousin's house because he said he knew you, living there in town always and your family and his, and I said—I must meet him—and he laughed because, as you know, you do not mean anything to them, living right there among you all these years, never realizing a genius is among them, and he called you to tell you and you said you would not be at home all afternoon, making it clear that whether you were going to be at home or not, you did not want to meet his cousin. Then he said—well, we could at least drive by his house—because I had come all the way in the rain. And then we were in your driveway, going over the mud-ruts between the trees, and he said—there he is—and I looked and there you were, standing in the small rain pulling branches out of the tree, or whatever it was exactly you were doing, and somehow that seemed right, as if the rain did not make any difference to you.

When he went over to ask you to come back to the car, I did not want him to for I knew by then how it was going to be. And that is why I could not even shake hands with you because I felt it would be doing it just to say afterward I had done it. And I did not want you to think that. There was that one moment when you mumbled an acknowledgement of the introduction and then it was all over and there was nothing we could do or say except drive away again. And then my cousin said it—he thought you came to see if he had two heads or something—and I wanted to cry all the way home for I knew that was what you thought and that was not the reason at all and how it was too late to tell you.

Perhaps you will never even see this letter for I do not imagine that you yourself would go and take them up and read them. I can only hope that if someone else reads them for you, they will give it to you. Probably they will only throw it away with others like it, but just as I had to come, I have to write this now. I wish so much that I had just walked into the yard by myself and when you turned there in the rain and looked at my face, you would have known too.

Again, I am sorry that I bothered you and I am sorry too, if you ever read this, if even this letter is just another mistake. But I had to write it for so many reasons, for all the things we cannot do anything about, for all the remembered things, for the lostness, because of all the people who never understand each other, and for a lot of things that I probably couldn't tell anyone even if you would have listened to me.[7]

Joan must have been surprised to receive a prompt reply—31 August 1949—from Faulkner addressed to her at her parents' Memphis home, 1243 E. Parkway South. In this first letter to Joan, Faulkner reprimands himself for his habit of inattentiveness, writing that he had paid little attention to John Reed's request, and that he thought at first she was a Mrs. rather than a Miss—"a grim beldame of 40 or 50 summers, president of some limited literary circle, come out of curiosity."[8] He dismisses the idea of another visit to Rowan Oak. Because they are strangers and will probably remain so, he won't give her a reason for discouraging a second visit; and because her letter deserves honesty, he also won't give her lies: "Something charming came out of it, like something remembered out of youth: a smell, scent, a flower, not in the garden but in the woods maybe, stumbled on by chance, with no past and no particular odor."[9]

> The discovered flower is already doomed for the first frost; until 30 years later a soiled battered bloke aged 50 years smells or remembers it, and at once he is 21 again and brave and clean and durable. I think you know enough now, already have enough; nothing to lack which a middle-aged writer could supply.
>
> But I'll do this: write me the questions as they occur to you, and sooner or later I will answer them.
>
> William Faulkner[10]

For a young woman with literary aspirations, Faulkner's promise to "answer" her questions was an offer Joan hardly could refuse. By the time Joan wrote her second letter to Faulkner, during the fall of 1949, she was back at Bard College in Annandale-on-Hudson, New York.

In an address for the Memphis Friends of the Library, Joan said: "I went to Bard as a junior saying I wanted to be a writer because I was embarrassed to say I wanted to be a movie star. My advisor said if I wanted to be a writer then write a short story and enter it in *Mademoiselle* Magazine's college fiction contest. He knew the editor and knew they had not found yet anyone they wanted to be the winner. I wrote 'Rain Later' without any instructions whatsoever about how to write a short story. I knew none of the things I learned later.... I wrote instinctively and just as instinctively about the small place in Mississippi I visited. Wrote out of what Katherine Anne Porter has called, 'a useable past.' It was rewarding as a writer that thirty-four years later that first story stood up on its hind legs and was included in my collection *Pariah and Other Stories*...."[11] "'Rain Later,'" Joan was fond of saying, "just came out right."[12]

During high school, Joan's literary bent, albeit secondary to her initial aspirations as a movie star, blossomed along with an early and sustained friendship with Louise Fitzhugh, niece of Southern author Peter Taylor. Fitzhugh later would write the children's classic *Harriet the Spy*. Following Miss Hutchinson's, Joan and Fitzhugh decided on a local college, Southwestern at Memphis. Despite Fitzhugh's companionship at Southwestern during her freshman year, Joan felt limited by attending a hometown college and transferred on her own to Chevy Chase Junior College in Maryland.

It was evident by the close of her sophomore year that Chevy Chase—in too many ways a "finishing "school—wasn't the answer. Likewise, Fitzhugh also was ready for a change. The two young women sought the advice of Peter Taylor, then teaching English at Kenyon College in Gambier, Ohio. Taylor told them that there was really only one college he felt would best develop their writing careers, and that was Kenyon. Unfortunately, at that time Kenyon was an all-male college. With Kenyon out of the question, Taylor recommended Bard College. So in 1948, as college juniors, Joan and Fitzhugh began what would be a very satisfying experience at Bard. (One of Joan's early English advisors was Southern author William Humphrey, then a member of Bard's English Department.) It probably is a testament to the progressive nature of Bard and the quality of its English department that Joan writes Faulkner, "many times i have heard people remark that you are the only person writing to day worth reading."[13]

On Bard College letterhead stationery, Joan types Faulkner a second letter—all lowercase beyond the salutation—in a girlish and awestruck tone. Of particular interest in this early letter is Joan's attempt to raise Faulkner's self-esteem and self-awareness. Perhaps attributable to the negative, sometimes harsh comments made by her own relatives about him, Joan believes Faulkner absorbed these denigrations and noticed this dismissiveness. She urges him not to feel "worthless." Did it strike her as odd, even audacious, to not only assume to understand Faulkner's emotions but also to administer advice and solace? The immaturity of the style belies her surety:

tuesday

dear Mr. Faulkner~

when i got your letter it was a feeling of so much wonderfulness inside as i haven't felt for a long time. i hope that in some way it will help to make you a little happy to know that just your writing me a letter has given me a certain faith in things. i immediately wrote you an answer but then my mother said you will bother him to death writing so much so then i stopped to think and naturally i didn't mail it. because if i had ever stopped to think in the first place i would never have written you the first time. then several times i have written you again but each time i thought about what i was saying and then i tore them up and i wondered inside, does he think about the fact that i haven't written or is he glad not to be bothered. almost everytime [sic] it rains i start a letter, but now i know that the only way i can write to you is not to think but just to say what i feel inside. that is another thing i have been afraid about that i would become too much in what i have to say but i read once:

adoration is a universal sentiment: it differs in
degrees in different natures

which is not profound but says what i want you to know; altho adoration is not the word i want. but i do have to be somewhat emotional about the whole thing.

that's what i thought. i wonder if by just telling you i can make you know that you are not only what you think you are. i understand how you feel that those people there do not read your books, but do you know how many there are who do? perhaps not as many as have read forever amber but then you know about that and is not what you want anyway. but you see there are so many like me who would never think of writing to tell you. how many times i have heard people remark that you are the only person writing to day worth reading. you see this is the thing i am afraid of that you are irritated by my saying all of this but i think you need to know and believe in it. you have not been worthless although what ever you have done aside from writing ... has been done to you. but you must feel something to know that your writing can inspire so much impeople [sic] that i write to you like at eleven i wrote to movie stars and now i feel silly.[14]

When Faulkner writes back, 15 October 1949, his letter goes some way to extinguish the depiction of their friendship as silly or immature. That letter, Joan remembers, arrived "too early" in their relationship and was "surprising and scary." "I think it was too early for him to have said some thing like that ... because there was always the implication that this was going to be a love affair which I had never thought of." Perhaps Joan's lowercase typescript or her own use of the word "silly" prompted Faulkner's bold response. Joan's questions, he writes, are best asked of a man in bed, and not the first time the couple is together, but after several times. And while he appreciates her fretfulness, Faulkner actually encourages Joan to embrace the grief she feels over her problems and questions: "These are the wrong questions. A woman must ask them of a man while they are lying in bed together. Not the first time but after several, and when they are lying at peace or at least are quiet or maybe on the edge of sleep so you'll have to wait, even to ask them."[15] "You may not find the answers even then; most dont.... I'd like to know if you ever do. Maybe you will tell me; that can be a good subject for the last letter you will need to write me.... The kindest thing the gods can give people at twenty ... is a capacity to ask why, a passion for something better than vegetation, even if what they get by it is grief and pain.[16]

Faulkner relents at his letter's end, writing that he'll be flattered by Joan's questions even though they both know he is the wrong one to give the answers. (He has some questions of his own. Is she twenty years old? Did she tell him that or did he assume that, just as he has assumed full knowledge of her after her two letters? He wonders if her eyes were as blue as he remembered. Was she a smallish woman, perhaps plump?) "Meanwhile, get Housman and read him again, read him a lot."[17]

However surprised she may have been by Faulkner's letter, Joan's reply reflects her talent for answering without answering: She does, however, confirm her age. Perhaps Joan and Faulkner found their kinship strengthened by their side-by-side birthdays:

...you have answered the one, the main question. in one line, which took me so many to say and even then only in half-formed thoughts:

the kindest thing the gods can give to people
at twenty is a capacity to ask why, a passion
for something better than vegetation, even if what
they get by it is grief and pain.
thank you. i will not forget.

yes, i told you twenty in the first letter ("twenty will not come again, and take from seventy springs a score, it leaves me only fifty more") but since then it has become twenty-one ("when i was one-and-twenty I heard a wise man say-) but i am listening and will continue to listen so do not go away but stay awhile.

i have been reading about the "intruder"[18] opening in the commercial appeal[19] and i wonder so at the things you are thinking about all of that....

i have never read any of your poetry.... i do not mean to write to you too often or bother you and if there are no letters from you for a long time i will understand. i wish i could tell you about the feeling when there is one, though. It is strange because I am so far away from the last time i got one. do you see. i still do,-the two rows of trees and the house and the left-over rain and that was summer and now the leaves snow, so circling slowly they loosen from the trees and fall when the wind blows. only the dried brown ones are left and a few yellow. they rustle when you walk and whisper at the unfairness of dying when it is only the middle of october. they said in the paper you are going to start on another book in nov.[20] and then i know there won't be time for letters. is there time to write when you are growing up? there is so much i want to write but then living everyday through seems to take up all of my time and i have not worked out how you really begin to write although you think this and this and then where do you start? what, a little, is the new book about.

is the happiness of knowing the things you think and the things you know which no one else knows enough to make up for the unhappiness of knowing them ... we walk together.

Joan [handwritten]

not so blue as that ... sometimes grey or green.[21]
what else should i read?[22]

Surely Faulkner must have been struck by the novelist detail of Joan's letter—"...and now the leaves snow, so circling slowly they loosen from the trees and fall when the wind blows. only the dried ones are left and a few yellow. they rustle when you walk and whisper at the unfairness of dying when it is only the middle of october"—though he makes no mention of such. He is, however, throughout the entirety of their correspondence, very attuned to the tone of her letters.

With just these few letters between them, certain themes of their relationship already were evident. Over and over Joan would try to define the relationship as a mentorship, hesitating, postponing and oftentimes rejecting Faulkner's strong impulse for an entirely different kind of union. "I always had this kind of sense I think with him," Joan said, "that I was being rushed into something. I am not sure he meant that. I just don't think he knew he was so much older and more experienced. Obviously, he wanted another affair."[23]

And it was part of Faulkner's personal history to want a new, young woman in his life, someone to write not *to* but *for*. Thus Joan figured as both muse and object of Faulkner's sexual desire. Such a conflict might have been more than most twenty-one-year-old women could handle. Joan felt trapped by her middle-class Southern morality; not "sophisticated" enough for Faulkner's expectations. As their correspondence advanced, Joan and Faulkner would agree to meet on occasion in Memphis or Holly Springs, Mississippi (roughly halfway between Memphis and Oxford), and the difficulties of their friendship became evident. Faulkner's marital state loomed large in Joan's psyche and their clandestine meetings often were unsatisfying for both.

———

Besides a budding acquaintanceship, Faulkner's life during the fall of 1949 was rich in developments: the film adaptation of *Intruder in the Dust* debuted in October; *Knight's Gambit* was published 27 November; and rumors flew that Faulkner would receive the 1948 Nobel Prize for Literature. The long list of candidates started with such literary icons as Steinbeck, Hemingway, Pasternak, Sholokhov, Mauriac and Camus; it then shortened finally in Faulkner's favor. Yet the decision came too late and the 1948 Nobel Prize for Literature was not awarded.[24]

On 11 October 1949, *Intruder in the Dust* premiered at the Lyric Theatre in Oxford, Mississippi. Not an easy person to understand, Faulkner rejected his hometown's hoopla, and literally was forced into attendance by his Aunt Bama, probably the only relative still capable of making the author behave. Hearing of her nephew's decision not to attend the opening, she called him the day of the premiere and told him he would be her escort that night. The previous day his demeanor and tone at a press conference left much to be desired. Faulkner appeared before the press looking "aloof and annoyed." His answers to questions were abrupt and "after each response he would fall silent and moodily swirl the ice in his glass of club soda."[25]

How to account for such behavior? On the one hand, it could be argued that Faulkner should have been more gracious, larger than the moment. Yet perhaps he felt annoyed that his hometown would respond so affirmatively to his success after years of neglect or downright dislike. It might have troubled him that it took a movie to catch Oxford's notice while his novels generally were overlooked. Certainly such indignations would sting any other writer, but Faulkner knew all too well the lure of movies. For many years, especially in the 1940s, Faulkner's primary financial sustenance came from writing movie scripts in Hollywood. This time, for *Intruder*, Faulkner received a lucrative fee—fifty thousand dollars—for the screen rights for his own novel.[26]

Such dichotomies were often at the core of Faulkner's emotional responses. Having been both author and script writer, Faulkner might have taken real pleasure in seeing a successful adaptation of his novel and his town's fervent reception. Instead the MGM publicity shot for *Intruder in the Dust* shows Faulkner "wearing a tweed jacket, a T-shirt, and a three-day growth of beard" holding a copy of his novel.[27]

Even though she was far from Oxford when *Intruder* premiered, Joan also was caught up in the excitement, having viewed the movie in a New York City theatre. As is especially true of the initial correspondence, her letters can be maddening in their randomness. Here she flits from the movie debut to receiving what would be the first of many signed, first-edition copies of Faulkner's books to suggesting a second meeting. Tacked on at the end is a question fit for a graduate seminar:

Dec. 26, 1949

Dear Mr. Faulkner~

I came home Wednesday and all before I left I tried to write you and thank you for the book[28] and all since I came home, but I never could until tonight when there is small rain. The feeling when they handed me the package and I saw from whom it was and that was still the same feeling of humility and of wanting to do something for you. But there is nothing I can do except if I do write another story it will be because I want to work hard because of you. I had one published this summer but I haven't written any since then.

I think that you didn't send the last letter[29] because it was criticism of mine, but if that is why please send it because I do not mind that. I want you to. I want you to send it whatever it says unless you really cannot.

I am going away again about the fifth of January [1950]. I would like to see you but I would not come again unless you said yes. It does not have to be at your house if you don't want that~it will not be at all if you don't want that and it will not change things. What do you think?

I have not yet finished Knight's Gambit. It is not the Sound and the Fury; it does not make me feel the same way~you know~but I like it still. I saw Intruder in the Dust in N.Y. and the lights were eight stories tall, bigger than any others and I felt very proud and wished you could see them and I thought the movie was good only missing some of the meanings in the book. And I wanted to say to the usher, the ticket seller, the woman in front of me--I know him in some ways, and he's a great man--but of course I couldn't.

Thank you again for giving me the book; it is something I will keep always.

Joan

I would not bring any other people.

Do you have a certain conception of what you think a short story should be?

The critics seemed to be in some agreement with Joan as far as *Knight's Gambit* was concerned. While the *New York Times* and *Chicago Tribune* praised the stories for their suspense, intrigue, plotting and style, Edmund Wilson described it as "'very inferior Faulkner' in *The New Yorker*, and for Irving Howe, in *The Nation*, the stories were second rate.'"[30]

Discussions regarding Faulkner's conception of the short story would have to wait; and when such answers came, Joan often found them indirect: "He didn't talk about himself and he didn't talk about his work to me and at that time I hadn't read much of it and I was too young to know enough to ask him questions. But he wouldn't have told me anyway. He would have given me maybe some kind of answer but it wouldn't have been a definitive answer. It would have been some kind of quip. It wouldn't have been a straight answer."[31]

———

Possibly one of the best indicators of Faulkner's interest in Joan was the quick response her letters received (as time went on he sometimes would write her with such intensity that dates were replaced by time of day). Her 26 December 1949 letter is affirmatively answered on December 29. Yes, Faulkner writes, he also wants to see her; had almost driven East last fall with that thought in mind. But he feels meeting in Oxford is wrong, it will be full of repercussions—"a bad taste in the mouth."[32] They will have to meet elsewhere, which, he frets, might also leave a bad taste in the mouth. The answers Joan wants will come at a price, Faulkner warns. Perhaps, he advises in his closing line, it would be best for her to think about it, or maybe, better, forget it.

Another letter dwelling on finding the nicest possible place for their meeting quickly follows that hesitant letter. On New Year's Eve, 31 December 1949, Faulkner suggests an outing on a friend's houseboat anchored at Sardis Lake. He assures her that the chance of using it on a weekday in winter should be good. Faulkner includes a bus schedule and specific details (even recommending appropriate attire for Joan). That winter outing did not come about, but during the summer of 1950 Faulkner, his wife, Estelle, Joan, and her college boyfriend, Brandon Grove, would spend an afternoon on Faulkner's boat, the *Minmagary*.

Just four months after their introduction, it was evident neither Faulkner nor Joan could give up on their new friendship. Over the next four years it would dominate much of their lives with emotional pitches ranging from euphoria to despair. Its texture of complexities and sadness suited their personalities and temperament, even had they wished differently.

II

1950—A Courtship
of Letters

That Joan Williams was seeping into Faulkner's consciousness beyond their direct correspondence was evident in a 10 January 1950 letter. Writing Professor Dayton Kohler of Virginia Polytechnic Institute, Faulkner thanked him for his article "William Faulkner and the Social Conscience," appearing in the December 1949 issue of *College English*: "I agree with it; I mean, re Faulkner's aim. You and Cowley have both seen it ... and one twenty-one-year-old Tennessee school girl...."[1]

While Faulkner's oblique reference to Joan certainly would mean nothing to Professor Kohler, it demonstrated how surely she had captured his attention.

Faulkner's outpouring of letters to Joan during 1950 served many purposes: they evinced a concrete relationship; they inched toward familiarity and intimacy; they reinforced her significant role in his personal and professional life; and they substituted for physical encounters. They reveal also a need for intrigue (some of his proposed rendezvous with Joan border on the ridiculous) and a rich fantasy life. Joan insists that Faulkner's letters depict a sexual union more imaginary than actual—that "much of it was made up." And after their relationship finally took the turn he desired—he had waited three years—Faulkner's letters, while sometimes giddy with happiness, often lapsed into petulance. Joan still was not giving enough—sexually or emotionally. Of Faulkner's sexual prowess, she offered simply, "Well, he wasn't eighteen."[2]

Prior to Joan's acquiescence to a sexual union, Faulkner's letters are singularly focused. If Joan is to succeed as an artist, she must leave her Southern provincialism and inhibitions behind. Faulkner's evident tendency toward manipulation occurred to Joan even at the time, but she believed she withstood his efforts.

I don't think he ever manipulated me. You'd have to gather that from your own reading of the letters. I never sat around thinking "Oh, Faulkner's manipulating me" ... A lot of those letters he would write, I would think, he was trying to make me angry or jealous. I just didn't feel any of that. It didn't make a difference to me very much.[3]

I wasn't passionately in love with him. There were just too many hangups: too much age difference, too much worry about people finding out, too much worry about my family being embarrassed, too much worry about being out with a married man. I couldn't break through all those barriers. I think in a lot of ways I didn't allow myself.... I felt a lot of affection for him, which I think is part of love, and it's something that doesn't die as quickly as love.[4]

He was just as hung up about the thing as I was. He was worried about his wife finding out. Being a writer, he was at home all of the time. So if he wanted to come to Memphis for the day to see me or something, he'd be afraid because he couldn't think of an excuse for saying where he was going.

He never suggested that we go to a hotel or a motel or anything like that. So you see, he had his own peculiarities or hangups. Propriety meant a lot to him. And he was also very afraid that he would cause me harm. This was part of his romantic nature. In some ways, he probably liked it the way it was. He probably wanted this ... I don't know whether to say this *flower* ... to protect, this young girl.[5]

Yet when the conversation turned to Faulkner's writing advice, Joan conceded a sense of disquietude. "See this is the way I guess the word is manipulative. I always felt like he was saying 'if you do what I want you to do, I'll help you write.'"[6]

Joan said that Faulkner taught her tenacity—to never, ever give up—but what she may not have realized was that she already possessed that attribute. The easiest and most predictable role to assume for someone in Joan's position would have been that of acolyte. She, however, rejected that, as well as Faulkner's attempts to rewrite her prose. She persisted in developing her own subjects and style.

He didn't really teach me a lot ... I think he could have, but maybe not. Maybe most really good writers are probably not really good teachers. Mostly he would take things and rewrite them and then I would feel it wasn't mine. You see, he couldn't tell me what to do: he could just rewrite it. But he could have taught me more than he did. Or he could have tried. He could have told me about writers like Eudora Welty and Willa Cather. He could have told me about writers like that who were women, for one thing. I don't think you can say that men and women don't write differently because they do. Maybe not in style but in the way they perceive things.

I came from that same South that Faulkner and Welty were writing about. My stories have got that sort of country flavor to them and they're about country people. And just to know that people were writing about that and that it was OK to write about that.... Why didn't he say to me what Sher-wood Anderson said to him: Look, don't leave that little postage stamp of native soil. That's where all your material is. Go there constantly and look around and listen. I don't know why he didn't tell me those things.[7]

In person, Faulkner never talked much about writing techniques, though eventually would say I had not used my time with him enough to learn about point of view. Though what he never seemed to realize was, I didn't know enough about writing to ask questions.[8]

———

Stylistically, Faulkner's letters are a direct departure from his prose. He tends to be direct and rarely treats Joan to the complex, adjective-laden style of his fiction. He has a fondness for the F word, and uses sexual language and images in some letters, but according to Joan, those words and ideas were not orally expressed when they were together. This parallels a remark by Meta Carpenter, another young woman from the South whom Faulkner pursued; she was certain he loved her "by looks, by touch, by the poems and the letters, only seldom by what he said to me."[9] Even Faulkner's more vividly erotic letters to Joan are conservative compared with those he penned to Meta,[10] in which he describes her as "my heart, my jasmine garden, my April and May cunt; my white one, my blonde morning, winged, my sweetly dividing, my honey-cloyed, my sweet-assed gal."[11]

If anything, his persona drifted toward an old-fashioned courtliness with occasional British affectations. Reflecting back on their correspondence and times together, Joan said, "It's in people's minds a lot more than it was to me a romance.... What I wanted was the mentor sort of relationship and no matter what he always turned it on a man and woman relationship.... I always think I thought that everything he always said was trying to ... was about sex."[12] "He wanted me to be madly in love with him in a romantic sort of way. But I was always very truthful. I went out with other people and he knew that. I didn't feel guilty. I mean, I couldn't just give up my whole life because I saw William Faulkner occasionally."[13]

Though her letters are more sparsely preserved, Joan proved an adept correspondent. Faulkner returned several of her letters for "Laurel," the name he envisioned for the protagonist of Joan's epistolary novel about their relationship. Quite often Joan would make a copy of her letter to Faulkner before sending it. While it is not something she elaborated upon, the mere fact that Joan preserved the correspondence, even making copies, shows that she understood almost immediately that this relationship was highly significant. Her belief would have been advanced by Faulkner's very early emphasis upon their letters and the nature of their letters. He told her once that it wasn't her face that caused him to fall in love but her first letter to him.

Retrospectively, Joan said, "When I read those letters I was surprised by them myself.... I don't even remember writing them as effusively as some of those letters are. I cared a lot about him but I knew I wasn't going to marry him. He was so much older and that played a large part in my thinking, that he was so much older." Faulkner perhaps inadvertently advanced Joan's concern, "writing [her] incessantly about being old."

At times Faulkner pointedly would blame his alcoholic episodes on Joan and the difficulty of the relationship.

> When I wouldn't go to bed with him or something like that. I didn't know he had a whole, long history of all that so I accepted the blame. But it wasn't my fault because he'd been having alcohol problems like that long before I met him.[14]
>
> I never saw him drunk except when he was so drunk you had to take him to the hospital ... It wasn't some long thing. It seemed to me that he didn't drink for very long before he went to the hospital. He'd usually pass out in his hotel room and then you'd go and find him and have to take him to the hospital. He was never publicly drunk when he was with me. I always thought his drinking was sort of overemphasized. He could go out and have drinks at night. Now a true alcoholic can't drink at all. If you have drinks at dinner and then have to get up in the morning and have a drink~that's an alcoholic to me. But he could handle liquor perfectly sometimes.
>
> Also, he took Seconal at the time that he drank. That's a sleeping pill or something. So the combination is what put him into a worse situation than just drinking.
>
> One time I took him from the Algonquin Hotel [in New York] out to a taxi cab and the next day he didn't remember it. He didn't remember walking out of the hotel. But he asked me if he looked all right. In other words, he wanted to know if anybody had stared at him and said there goes William Faulkner drunk. But he looked fine. I mean, I had him by the arm but he walked out.
>
> The binges were always bad enough that he had to go to the hospital. They would keep him and put him on~in those days they used paraldehyde. It's something they gave him to make him not want liquor. It kept you half-drugged, though. It kept you in a semi-comatose state. My father had these drinking binges so I was prepared for that kind of thing.[15]

Thirteen years prior to Joan and Faulkner's meeting, Faulkner was admitted to Wright's Sanitarium in Byhalia, Mississippi, on 31 January 1936 to recover from an alcoholic episode. And it was at Wright's Sanitarium that

Faulkner's death occurred. Faulkner frequented this sanitarium (which has long since ceased to exist) as well as the Memphis Gartly-Ramsay Hospital when his condition was beyond the care his family could provide. His treating psychiatrists at Gartly-Ramsay, Dr. Justin H. Adler and Dr. D.C. McCool (a 1928 University of Mississippi graduate), were two of the three earliest practicing psychiatrists in Memphis. The doctors remembered their famous and enigmatic patient vividly in a series of 1993 interviews.[16]

McCool, even as a freshman at Ole Miss in 1924, was aware of Faulkner's stature as a writer. Faulkner turned 27 that fall, and his first book, a poetry collection, The Marble Faun, appeared just three months later. Faulkner had been publishing poems, reviews, and articles in the college newspaper, The Mississippian; the town newspaper, The Oxford Eagle; as well as The Double Dealer, a New Orleans literary magazine. He already had a national publication, a forty-line poem, "L'Apres-Midi d'un Faune," in The New Republic (6 August 1919). "I think that those who knew of him at all, like me, were interested that he was a writer and had had things published," McCool said.

In spite of his writing accomplishments, Faulkner's reputation among students was as "a sort of character. Most students like me rarely saw him. He was a recluse, sort of. He was at that time as far as I can recall a loner; I never saw him with anyone." McCool's first glimpse of the young writer and postmaster seemed to confirm Faulkner's eccentricity. "I was standing in the student union university post office one day, Faulkner being the postmaster at the time, assistant postmaster in charge of it at least. There was a student assistant in there at the time and no one else was in the place and we were chatting and he looked up and he said, 'Do you see that fellow coming across campus?' and I said, 'yes.' He was dressed in an outfit that you would probably think of as a karate thing, sort of loose-fitting short pants, belt with a rope, and short above his ankles, and sandals, [shirt] open at the chest, the hairy chest, unshaven, hair uncombed, and I remember the student said, 'Do you know who that is?' and I said, 'no.' He said, 'That's William Faulkner. He lives over there in that little fraternity house, and they call him Count No 'Count, and he'll never amount to a damn.'" Years later the Ole Miss freshman who attended Faulkner as a prominent neuropsychiatrist appeared to relish the student assistant's ironic prophecy.

Adler met Faulkner as a patient during an April 1949 stay at Gartly-Ramsay. Adler remembered that the treatment of his important patient coincided with the birth of his daughter, Susie, on 14 April 1949. At one point during his hospital stay, Faulkner suggested a trip to the circus, so Dr. Adler and his son, Michael, accompanied Faulkner, Estelle, and their

Dr. Justin H. Adler (left), the fourth psychiatrist to practice in Memphis, and Dr. D.C. McCool, Memphis's third psychiatrist, stand at Rowan Oak in front of a portrait of William Faulkner, whom they both treated in Memphis during the late 1940s and 1950s (courtesy Murray Riss).

daughter, Jill. At the circus, Adler was struck by the "averageness" of the author, noting that no one seemed to notice Faulkner. "He was quite fond of the circus. He got a great kick out of it. We just carried on polite conversation without any particular significance. I remember both his wife and daughter didn't say very much. I think they talked more to my son, who was six years old." Adler noted a tension between husband and wife that he attributed to "his [Faulkner's] inclination to have a girl friend." While Adler believed that the girlfriend in question was Joan Williams, Faulkner would not even meet Joan until August of that same year. If the couple was estranged it was not because of Joan. The confusion probably was the result of Faulkner's later references to Joan. He once asked Adler to mail a letter to Joan from the hospital, and she received letters on Gartly-Ramsay letterhead stationery. Adler was not sure if Mrs. Faulkner and Jill returned to Oxford after the circus, but Faulkner went back to the hospital.

Both McCool and Adler recall Faulkner's vulnerability and ordinariness. They regarded him as quite the opposite of grandiose. His physical appearance was, according to Adler, "rather unshaven, kind of rough. He always wore old hand-me-down clothes which were not very impressive. One thing I remember particularly—he always carried his satchel with him, a canvas satchel with a little bit of leather embellishment around it. That was his traveling bag. It was kind of an ugly satchel, something like I would visualize in the past that a carpetbagger would carry."

McCool found him a "shy, sensitive, dedicated person. Self-abnegating even." He believed the notoriety of the Nobel Prize affected him contrarily, the "opposite of giving him any big head." Adler concurred, citing Faulkner's "apparent indifference toward his reputation" and "his friendliness which seemed sincere." He enjoyed talking with Adler, especially recounting colorful tales of his service in the Royal Air Force during World War I.[17] This favorite topic of Faulkner's was enhanced because Adler was in World War II for four years, serving with the U.S. Medical Corps as a psychiatrist from 1942 to 1946, and spending more than two years in Europe.

The war entered another discussion as well. Once, during a session with McCool, Faulkner recounted a disturbing dream, "...a wild, hallucinatory nightmare he had. He was in a cemetery in France where at each grave there was a head of a German aviator and they all looked at him and said, 'You and your friends shot me down.'"

According to Adler, Faulkner would "express his feelings and attitudes the way he felt them, not colored by puritanical conventions." Faulkner's treatment at the hospital focused on the immediate task of achieving sobriety. When Faulkner gave his history, McCool said, he was sincere and cooperative. "He was really a forthright individual. He would just want to do what I wanted [him] to do to get to go home." Normally, his Oxford physician, Dr. Chester McLarty, would have referred Faulkner to McCool. (Adler would assume his care if he was the attending doctor.) After talking with McLarty, McCool would oversee the necessary arrangements for Faulkner's admittance and ensure that a room would be reserved. "He'd been drinking heavily, which was a problem prior to my seeing him and long after, I guess," said McCool. "That was the diagnosis as far as I remember—acute intoxication." (Adler confirmed that Faulkner would have been taking Seconal as well as drinking.) "We'd take him off of alcohol and give him vitamins, feed him as much as he'd eat, and give him what sedation he might require."

An average hospital day for Faulkner, according to Adler, would have included "sleeping, reading, and conversation with the personnel and with the treating physician." McCool said there was no specific routine. "There was no treatment other than the medication he was receiving with his meals, and they probably gave him some physical treatment, massages, and so forth." Faulkner's visits with McCool each day "might be five minutes, fifteen, twenty, thirty, depending on what he felt like. He was an aloof person. A very private, very sensitive man. And unless he made some overtures to talk I certainly did not initiate conversation with him." During their sessions together, Faulkner would do most of the talking, some of which centered on Oxford and Ole Miss, since that is what they held in common.

While Adler speculates that Faulkner might have profited from ongoing private consultation, he was not optimistic. "People of such strong minds don't like to relinquish even part of their self-determinations," he said, adding that "most intellectuals at that time did not think too much of psychiatrists."

Whether or not Faulkner wrote while a patient in the hospital was a source of speculation. Adler believes it "quite possible, but somewhat less likely in view of the sedative medications he probably took at the time." McCool "assumed he did no writing. [He] wouldn't have been in the mood to write." Whatever Faulkner was working on during his various hospitalizations "never came up," at least to McCool's knowledge.

Physically, Faulkner "was in pretty good health considering his self-abuse with alcohol," said Adler. "He kept on drinking; he didn't give a damn." Part of Faulkner's vitality involved women, and their reaction to him. "A man like that with so much strong masculinity—women flocked to him. His name meant something." The latter part of Adler's assessment certainly applied to Joan's attraction to Faulkner, a fact Joan acknowledged: "I said to him one time ... if you were an insurance salesman I wouldn't be wanting to know you. He said, 'I know it.'"[18]

———

That two writers—one established, one a fledgling by comparison—should best communicate through letters seems almost natural. Key to their body of letters is realizing that the significant dialogue occurs here. Over and over Joan stressed that the "important" issues are in the letters, and even though there are hundreds, the evident themes ebb and flow. As in most relationships, problems are rarely completely resolved. Faulkner's preoccupation with his age and his conception of Joan's upbringing led him to conclude that he was the father Joan never had; that it was part of his job to build, develop, perhaps restore her self-confidence. Yet this belief was never verbalized. "No, we didn't talk about these things. Anything that comes out is really in the letters. Well, I must have told him something about my childhood because he always had this feeling that I had had this terrible childhood."

The theme of the substitute father clearly is one Faulkner embraced as he circles back to it at the end of their affair. It dominates a late December 1953 letter from Faulkner to Joan. "I think I was—am—the father which you never had—the one who never raised his hand against you, who desired, tried, to put always first your hopes and dreams and happiness."[19] This notion intrigues him further because it introduces the taboo of incest, writing Joan that it is not just love that unites them. They have committed what the moralists call a mortal sin. This bond compounds their love and holds them close in both spirit and remembering.[20]

This letter is reproduced as dialogue between Jeff and Amy in *The Wintering* as, in reality, the affair was winding down:

> He moved onto his own bed and stared at her seriously. "No matter what course your life takes, there are some things between us that can't change. There's a bond that nothing can break. There's been love between us, but sin. No, I'm not talking about morality. I know I was the father you wanted. We've committed incest, then. That alone will always hold us together."[21]

Faulkner's fascination with incest in his literature is well recognized, but attaching this taboo to his relationship with Joan introduces all kinds of speculation. More unusual and striking is Joan's attention to incest in her late short story, "The Contest," published in 1995. The story, told from Mary Virginia's viewpoint, weaves past memories through present-day events to force fearful clarities:

> Something dead had come back to life. Another memory surfaced she thought long gone and knew now it never had been. Hands holding her child's thighs went creepy-crawly up in a way she knew even then was wrong. "Don't, Daddy," she had said, wobbling above the crowd. The fingers went up, touching the biting, elastic edges of her lace panties. She had to wear her best ones going out, her Mother always cautioned. "You might be in a wreck and lay dead showing dirty, old underbritches." A thick finger separated with a scratchy hangnail, probing toward the warm, soft, moist, pink hole belonging only to her self, offering comfort in the night. "Your girl-self," he whispered up.
> There was a sluicing sound and a low, guttural, deep growl that was not his own. "You like it," he said. "She-devil. Minx."
> "I do not. I hate it," she cried. "I hate you."[22]

In interviews, Joan did not suggest that Faulkner's reference to incest was influential in her fiction. She said simply that, as far as the story's protagonist of "The Contest" was concerned, "It only happened once."[23]

———

During his November 1952 hospitalization in New York City where he was diagnosed with depression following an alcoholic spell, Faulkner asked Joan to read him a letter from his daughter, Jill. That helped Joan recognize that "Obviously she [Jill] had a background very similar to mine." In her letter, Jill, then 19 years old (just four years younger than Joan), pleads with her father to be "nicer to Momma" and expresses her hope "that when he comes home for Christmas things will be better." "That," Joan said, "was exactly what I was escaping from with my own parents, and what I wanted to say to them."[24] Joan's father frequently would go on drinking binges like Faulkner's, and her mother drank as well. Joan said it would be evident by dinner time her mother had been drinking, although she doubted a stranger would have noticed.

Like the Faulkners', the Williams' marriage was troubled. There was the alcohol, P.H.'s long absences, and other women. Thus, Joan's situation mirrored Jill's with the exception of their fathers' diverse occupations.

Even though Faulkner told Joan that he and Estelle never argued in front of the children, Joan found that unlikely: "I think at the time I didn't think that was true. I think they grew up very much with this terrible situation around them."[25]

Faced with a budding relationship with a man not only years older but more worldly and sophisticated, letter writing suited Joan's purposes. Responding to Faulkner through letters allowed for great flexibility—she could answer as directly or indirectly as she chose. If Faulkner pressed too hard with sexual references or if he portrayed them more as lovers than friends, those passages rarely found an echo in Joan's letters of reply.

Toward the end of her Christmas break from Bard College, Joan and Faulkner had their first personal meeting since they were introduced at Rowan Oak. The problems associated with meeting are detailed in a letter to Faulkner from Joan:

> friday morning
> of course. but where? there is getting to be little time left so we must decide in the next letter, or if you want to call me ... I didn't know about calling your house.... Would you want to come to Memphis: I can meet you at the bus or train station or wherever you suggest__.
> In Oxford it would have to be someplace easily found since I know nothing about the town.

or Holly Springs if you know enough about it to suggest a place.
You decide. It seems like a long time since August and now that I know
I am going to see you I don't know what to talk about.
Joan

Faulkner's 2 January 1950 telegram from Oxford assured Joan that he
would arrive in Memphis by the 10 a.m. Southern Trailways bus. The most
vivid recollection of that meeting—a meeting that would set precedence for
those to follow with its random and secretive nature—occurs in Joan's 1980
Atlantic essay, "Twenty Will Not Come Again":

At ten a.m. the Southern Trailways bus emptied, its passengers scattered.
A small man was left, bundled, belted into a trench coat wearing a brown
Tyrolean hat. I moved forward. Mr. Faulkner?
Miss Williams.
As pressing as where to meet was then where to go? He knew nothing
about the city [Memphis] and had no ideas; the only object was not to be
recognized. He had something to take to a typist in the Peabody Hotel.
Would I drive him there? I would drive him there.
Is it a book? I asked as we moved along, and he replied, I hope so. Ignorant of the capriciousness of creativity, editors, publishers, and the public,
I wondered what he was talking about. Was it a book or not? The Peabody
had been part of my upbringing, yet I was momentarily uncertain when he
said to take him around to the carriage entrance. I assumed he meant to
drive beneath a portico where cars came closest to a door. Courtly manners,
willfulness toward the old-fashioned, would strike me many times, and he
was still calling me Miss Williams. I didn't think Faulkner was so old as to
have come to the Peabody in a carriage.... Waiting, I thought about getting
into something I had never expected. I had expected to see Faulkner as
Faulkner, but his need for secrecy had turned the situation into my seeing
a married man.... By the day's end, driven almost beyond endurance by cold
and aimlessness, I took him to see my mother: the house being both warm
and stationary was the only reason. I told no friends about the meeting, for
I felt they would either see no significance or make a joke.[26]

This meeting in Memphis, like those to come, served more as footnotes
to the evolving relationship forged by their letters. Faulkner and Joan passed
most of their time together in silence, but in their letters exchanged lofty
ideas about life and literature. Letters were the source and facilitation of
their friendship, a means for expressing anger, jealousy, insecurities, and
affection. "Because," Joan said, "it was not my nature to have talked intimately
... and it was not our nature to talk. We sat in those [Mississippi] woods and
every place a lot, just saying nothing. He [Faulkner] didn't talk that much
either. I think we were the type of people who could pour things out on paper
that you couldn't say. In those days, I don't think people were ... what do
they call it now days ... being in touch with your feelings or something ...

and all that jargon they've got. I don't think people did discuss things the way they do now."[27] "Even though we didn't talk a lot, it was important just to be together. And we knew, like, that we were sharing something by not even talking."[28]

Joan attributed part of her silence to not knowing what to say, to not knowing the right questions—especially technical—about writing to ask. One day when they met in the woods, she told Faulkner she felt she should come with a lot of questions, and Faulkner said, "There's not enough silence in the world and most people are embarrassed by it."[29] On a later attempt, Joan appeared with a pad and pencil. Faulkner waved her away, "saying what I got from the moment was enough, the silence of woods, a butterfly lighting on his hand with no idea of death or knowledge of fear."[30] "He said I was getting something from the solitude of the woods, more than his talking to me about his literary work, answering questions. He said he could do that with any interviewer anywhere."[31]

Removed from those summer afternoons in the Mississippi woods by a number of years, some regret lifted for Joan when she realized Faulkner might not have believed writing could be taught. "I do know that Faulkner thought if I wanted to be a writer, I shouldn't be in college. He would have had me quit except I was in my final year."[32]

Whatever Faulkner's true belief about the possibility of teaching writing, his role as writing instructor and Joan's role as apprentice offered a socially acceptable premise for the burgeoning relationship. Upon her return to Bard in January 1950 for a six-week term, Joan found two letters from Faulkner, with the same 7 January postmark, one short and one long. The long, typed letter opens with a sentence proclaiming his desire for a love affair, and the difficulty of writing about literature "because when he looked at the blank paper he wanted to write a love letter."[33] The language sandwiched between strikes a balance: Faulkner as cheerleader and Faulkner as coach. He harkens back to something he told Joan during their first meeting in Memphis—"If I had lived in the New York Bowery, I would still have written Faulkner. I mean by that, that what is worth it in Faulkner would have got itself written regardless. Of course, if I had been the Bowery bloke, I would not have been Faulkner."[34] "...So will Joan W. get itself written, provided it is worth it ... You are worried because it is slow, because you think you are wasting time. All right. Here is the idea: let's try if I can get the Joan W. written quicker. I dont mean, collaborate or rewrite it, nor even just get it printed whether it's good or not. Not to teach you to write creditable stuff as you teach a dog a trick, but, the two of us together ... to get the good stuff out of Joan Williams."[35]

This early letter advances the Faulkner as Pygmalion theme "creating not a cold and beautiful statue, in order to fall in love with it, but Pygmalion taking his love and creating a poet out of her—something like that. Will you risk it?"[36] What was at risk, Faulkner felt, was Joan's capacity for privacy and silence, though not her capacity for truth. Yet he already proclaimed a victory of sorts; she had let him penetrate, if only a little way, her privacy and silence. His final line suggests complicity; he will sign his letters better when Joan tells him how they should be signed.

Also postmarked 7 January is a handwritten letter. This doesn't count, he writes Joan, because it doesn't answer anything she wanted to know or anything she doesn't already know, just the oldest thing men have always been writing to girls.

———

A week later another letter. In the direct style that dominates his letters, Faulkner tells Joan he can come up in February, that in fact, he is coming to see her. If that news disarmed her, Joan must have been pleased with the letter's second paragraph. Faulkner found and read her short story in the August 1949 *Mademoiselle*:

> I read the piece in Mlle. It's all right. You remember? 'to make something passionate and moving and true'? It is, moving and true, made me want to cry a little for all the sad frustration of solitude, isolation, aloneness in which every human being lives, who for all the blood kinship and everything else, cant really communicate, touch.[37] It's all right, moving and true; the force, the passion, the controlled heat, will come in time. Worry because it's~you think~slow; you've got to worry; that's part of it: the suffering and the working, most of all the working, the being willing and ready to sacrifice everything for it~happiness, peace, money, duty too if you are so unlucky. Only, quite often, if you are really willing to sacrifice any and everything for it, everything will not be required, demanded by the gods.[38]

Perhaps feeling a bit overwhelmed by all Faulkner suggests, and a little guilty at not having answered his letters more promptly, Joan writes a long letter telling Faulkner finally that he must sign his letters to her the way he sees best. For the first time, Joan addresses him as "Bill."

Jan. 17, 15950

Dear Bill,

   I am sick in bed and do not feel too much like writing but it has been such a long time since your letter that I was afraid you would think I just didn't want to write.

   Your letter was strange, a combination of two people. I shouldn't have started this; I am too tired to write and I don't know what I want to say. It is very lonely here. Very few people, bleak and bare and cold and only the mountains in the distance are still beautiful. I like being alone only too much is bad, and then I become selfish thinking too much of myself, or become depressed and restless with no where to go.

I have been reading Chekhov; his notebooks and letters are very interesting. In one he advises someone to read don quixote.

I didn't understand one thing in your letter:[39] you said, Only you want to write the Joan Williams, don't you? Then added in pen— I'm the one to. What does this mean? Yes, I'm the one to but I don't know when it will be. It would be good to work as you suggested; I guess I will always have to be pushed! Now I feel that I am living, and when I have lived some will then be ready to stop and write it, only am I really living?

When I went home I wrote down a lot of the things you siad [sic]; it took a long time because we talked a long time, but I am glad that I did because so much of it was so worth remembering. Not (as you are afraid) because you "know how to punctuate a little" but because you are one human being talking to another, saying something, something real, worthwhile, that means something~which is hard to find in people.

there are different kinds of love letters: I do not know the kind you might mean to write. Our letters will never be the same as before I talked to you, but I hope they will be as we talked.

I know that you have not lost the sadness that was with you that day, but I hope that you are not too unhappy. I feel that in this letter I am failing you, probably disappointing you also. Will you let me know if I have?

Pygmalion cannot create a poet out of his love or anything else unless it is already there. to unfold, help, flower it is possible. I might be nothing but a dreamer. Once I would have been like the Henry James character[40] who thought all his life that he was destined for something different, and finally died just as he realized that the only thing different about him was that he had never done anything, was the only person to whom nothing had ever happened. But I know now you must live day by day unafraid to live it, to take what is there when it is. Of course I am thinking about the future, but you know what I mean.

what are you thinking?

When the trees fell down in the icestorm it was like the enemy being conquered, as if being paid back for the time they have laughed in their strength at our weakness and refused to help us.

do not feel loneliness because of this letter. They aren't the little girl anymore, they grew up, some anyway.

You must sign the letters the way that you think; the way that they are meant. With hope that you understand the way that this is said.

with love[41]

There is, Faulkner answers Joan, only one kind of love letter, even if no love letter has ever matched those of Donne and Cyrano. And if she is sick "I would be the sickness too, the air you breathe, the clothes you wear, the bed you sleep in, all the thinking and feeling that goes on behind your eyes."[42] Finally, despite his concrete plans for an early February trip to New

York where he will see Joan, he imagines a more successful union for them "by the ocean all bleak and winter and cold, beyond a window."[43] Faulkner reminds Joan that his very first plan to meet her involved water—an outing on a boat—and he imagines a Freudian would find much to analyze in his desire. His own theory he likes best: purity and a wind from Samothrace or Cnydos blowing up April.[44]

As was the case with many of his stays in New York, Faulkner attended a literary dinner party; this time, however, Joan accompanied him. Their host was Random House editor Robert Haas. Joan remembered meeting Albert Erskine (a Random House editor originally from Memphis who would replace Saxe Commins as Faulkner's editor) who was "One, very handsome, but ... I was so impressed because he had been married to Katherine Anne Porter."[45] The parties Joan remembered as unlike Memphis parties where people talked about local things. There were many eminent editors from *The Saturday Review* and Random House, but she never met any famous writers. (Later, while in New York, Joan introduced Faulkner to Dylan Thomas.)

At one such party a woman asked Joan how she met Faulkner. (In *The Wintering*, Amy replies, "He's a friend of my aunt's really."[46]) Another time, as they were joining a group at a table, Faulkner turned to someone who was already seated and said, " 'I'm William Faulkner.' And whomever that woman was, she said, 'I know who you are.' He was always on the surface very modest seeming. And something came up about Shakespeare—people were trying to think of something—and Faulkner just started quoting this Shakespearean sonnet that was somewhat obscure."[47] At such parties, Joan found Faulkner relaxed and comfortable. "He liked being in the big city. It wasn't so much that he liked New York but that he liked the change from Oxford. He liked to go and, as he said, play literary lion. When he went to parties, when people gave parties for him, he realized that he was the star attraction."[48]

Joan's youthfulness, attentiveness, and quiet demeanor pleased Faulkner. He would reminisce about a party at the Haases' in later letters, complimenting her pretty, white, girlish slip.[49] Faulkner's sexual attraction to girlishness is evident far beyond the literal fact of his fifty-two years in relation to Joan's twenty-one.[50] From what he remembers as a visible white slip to describing her handwriting as a splashy girl hand, Faulkner clearly relishes the idea of courting, perhaps corrupting, a young woman (girl). This becomes more confused as Faulkner frequently adopts a paternal role. Joan compounds this complexity by stating that she both thought of him as a father figure—was searching for a father figure—and then retracts such statements: "He would always say ... that he was the father she [Joan] never had. That's not true. I didn't think of him as a father."[51]

––––

The Haas party also is recreated in *The Wintering*—"Never before had she been to a party where women wore long dresses, unless it was a dance. She was so much the underdressed female at the party that she forgot to worry about her appearance"—and from the moment Amy [Joan] enters the room, her youth and innocence receives notice. Haas, fictionalized as Alex Boatwright, greets Almoner and Amy. "She went across the room between him and Almoner feeling safely maneuvered, occasionally nudged, like a little boat between larger ones." Curiously, Boatwright repeats her order of a martini to the waiter, adding only "for this young lady." "She wondered why, with a little smile, Mr. Boatwright had repeated her order. Holding her glass, she stood between them like a child with something to pacify it, while they talked across and above her head.... As they went from group to group, he [Almoner] sometimes touched her elbow, guidingly. Irritated that she was so inadequate, she felt annoyed by his possessive touch."[52] Boatwright compliments Almoner on finding Amy, and Almoner tells her, "Amy, you were charming. And you are modest. Not many women are that way any more."[53]

For the first time in New York, at Faulkner's hotel room at the Biltmore, Faulkner kisses Joan. "When she turned, at his touch, he put his lips briefly on hers. 'There, he said, did that hurt?' There had been no more pressure than a flower but there was none in return."[54] The New York visit is significant as Faulkner credits the idea behind *Requiem for a Nun* to something Joan said over drinks at the Biltmore.[55] Joan, however, has no memory of the exact exchange. "He always said that something we were talking over at the Biltmore gave him the idea. But what it was I don't know and I have never gone around saying 'Oh, yeah, I gave him the idea' because I don't know if I did or not. It probably came as much from him as me."[56]

––––

After their first public appearance in New York they returned to letters. Even before Faulkner's train arrived in Oxford from New York, he had written a three-page draft of *Requiem* on Hotel Algonquin letterhead stationery. At the bottom he tells Joan to pick up the thread where he left off and includes a brief synopsis. Joan should start work where, in the draft, Nancy refuses to say "not guilty." "You can begin to work here. This act begins to tell who Nancy is, and what she has done. She is a nigger woman, a known drunkard and dope user, a whore who has a jail record in the little town, always in trouble. Some time back she seemed to have reformed, got a job as a nurse to a child in the home of a prominent young couple [Gowan Stevens and Temple Drake Stevens]. Then one day suddenly and for no reason, she murdered a child. And now she doesn't even seem sorry. She seems to be making it impossible for the lawyer (Gavin Stevens) to save her."[57] At the end of this act, he writes, everybody is against her. The community believes she deserves to hang; they are void of sympathy, even her own lawyer.

Faulkner draws a line (literally) separating the play material from his personal message of closing. His tone conveys an abrupt transformation. He thanks her for her sweet letter he received that morning in New York, and he tells her it was not her face that day at the Memphis bus station—for in fact he would not have recognized her if she hadn't known him—but the very first letter she sent him that told him he would fall in love with her.[58]

Realizing he must keep a steady and vibrant exchange of letters alive, Faulkner foists his hopes on the developing play. Faulkner instructs Joan in a 14 February letter (which is not, he writes, really a letter, doesn't really count) to send only plain envelopes—no Bard College letterhead—and no return address. His mail at home is never safe. He also encourages her to hurry and finish her college thesis so her involvement with the play can match his. He has destroyed her last letter but kept the violet, her moving, delicate, and true gift.[59] Violets become an important symbol for them. Faulkner even wrote Joan once that he carried one she sent him in his wallet. "That was something he started," Joan said. "I don't know how. Oh, he said my eyes were the color of violets."[60]

In her reply to Faulkner's draft and note, Joan composes a detailed, two-page, single-spaced letter, with the first part focused on the play, in which she proposes some solid strategies to develop Nancy's character. It is unfortunate Faulkner didn't adopt her suggestions, as Nancy's enigmatic character is one of the play's central flaws. Her contribution demonstrates a thorough reading of Faulkner's draft and also an adept assimilation of the play's essence, especially Joan's understanding of Nancy's impossible though prescribed role in this Southern drama.[61] (Later, Joan distanced herself from *Requiem*, writing that at "twenty-one my heart was not in trying seriously to rewrite Faulkner."[62])

The letter then returns to more personal matters and ends with a rather unexpected declaration of love from Joan:

monday

....

It has snowed all day in very fine swift flakes; it is so
beautiful and clean. I have felt very lonely and wished you were here.
In the letter I could not read something. You say—"I told

you once you can have only one_?_." Do you remember the word? And was this right~ "I'm proud to have what you once called a 'great man' to offer the face in homage." If that is what it said I am not sure I know what you mean.

I wish that you could have come Sat. I wish it now more than I did then. I have been haunted ever since I left you by a sadness, something of fear~ and also an eagerness at the idea of us working and creating a play~a living thing. If we can and if we do it. If only we were together I would have no idea of our not succeeding, but being so apart and having other demands such as studying, which I must meet, makes it hard and I am sorry~I am afraid you will work hard and I will fall behind. I do hope we can spend a lot of time spring vacation and doing actual writing. Do you, but then I'm sure everyone does, become eager sometime to look into the future. What is to be in even three years.

I hope we will always be able to have our talks.

May I offer my congratulations about being nominated for the Nobel prize. I hope that it makes you happy.

Oh, Bill, this is all such a wonderful wonderful part of my life. To have found someone, embodying so many things I've looked for, in so strange a way, under strange circumstances. I guess I have felt I wanted to cry because it was all so wonderful and means so much to me; that is why it is hard to tell you about because it is so close to me and means so much.

Bill, I do love you.

joan

Faulkner's letter of reply spans three days. On Monday afternoon he attempts to assuage Joan's uneasiness by explaining what she couldn't read in his last letter. She previously had written that when he talks of love, it doesn't make her too happy; that it means they won't be friends. He answers in this letter that anything he has is hers and that he will try to be whatever she wants him to be, a friend if that is her desire, though he was "capable not only of imagining anything and everything, but even of hoping and believing it."[63] She also questioned his motives—asking if maybe it was the way she looked or her age that attracted him—and not Joan herself. Faulkner insists that there is nothing to worry about. If he is in love with her, it can't be helped. And that the last thing she should be is unhappy about it. He believes she should be flattered that the bloke whom she called "great man" has offered her the homage of love, whether to her twenty-one years or her face.

Wednesday night

I dont know anything about the Nobel matter. Been hearing rumors for about three years, have been a little fearful. It's not the sort of thing to decline; a gratuitous insult to do so but I dont want it. I had rather be in the same pigeon hole with Dreiser and Sherwood Anderson, than with Sinclair Lewis and Mrs. Chinahand Buck.[64]

His letter closes with a detailed account of Thursday and Friday in New York, missing her and walking off a hangover, and then a final desperate thought of coming to Bard on Saturday. A coal strike that closed the trains saved not Joan but the work she needed to finish.[65]

About the Nobel matter, Joan said, "...he felt that Pearl Buck didn't deserve the Nobel Prize and that these people did. It just shows that he cares about these writers and he was sorry they got passed over. And he would have rather been in their company than Pearl Buck's."[66]

———

Meanwhile, Faulkner's optimism about the promise of their relationship and their collaboration collides with Joan's sense of being overwhelmed and depressed:

Feb. 21, 1950

It is all the same again; all the people are back [Bard College], screaming, laughing, calling and I do not want it.

Your letter confirmed what I was worried about and that is that it is really going to be your play. If I were there we could really work on it together and I would be proud and know that I had done my part of it, but I won't let you do it and then say that we did it. But I do not know what to do on this end; I do not know what changes you have made and there is nothing I can write on it. Are you planning on doing some, sending it to me and letting me go on for awhile or what? I cannot ask you to put it off until spring and this way seems not too good. Do you really believe that I can do anything. Please tell me because to fool me about it would be more hard than not to consider me at all. Had you rather just have it for your own?

Aside from this there is nothing to write about except the deep snow and the cold.

What a terrible time in life this is. I would like so much to give up all I am doing and devote everything to trying to write on the play with you. I have in fact been very tempted to do that but one doesn't when one has spent three and a half years working toward something and is this close to the end. And one doesn't spend one's family's money for that long for something and then just throw it away, cannot disappoint the family. I am so tired too of having those kind of responsibilities, owing things to people, having this to do and that and doing it just to pass the time, get it over with.

I am nothing now. Neither woman nor girl, not myself yet, not free and yet not, as when I was twelve or so, a child with no mind and no definite way. So what do I do now, just go on and then reach a period when I no longer feel this way? And yet it is wonderful too, because I am full of promises and faith in myself and my ability and haven't found out yet if I am just fooling myself. I have much I tell myself now and it makes it easier even if it turns out I am fooling myself. Do you know?

Today I received Go Down, Moses and Man's Fate[67] from Random House, from Mr. Haas I guess and that is such a nice thing for him to do and remember; and it is nice that you have friends who like you so much that they take pains to be nice even to your friends. A wide vista has opened through you and I hope that I am capable enough to enter.

j~

Another of a similar vein follows that letter shortly:

Sunday after noon[68]

I don't think this feeling is ever going away~the one I wrote about last time. I am very unhappy, not the feeling sorry for one's self kind but just dissatisfaction, unrest, wanting, but not knowing what. To feel something, anything; I almost want to be hit, beaten, just to feel something. I know I should make myself sit down and work and keep my mind occupied and not think about myself but keep busy but that is easier said and besides that I don't want to do any of the things I would have to do if I were to work.

Bill, how very often I've thought that: the great man offering love and friendship to me but I have not wanted to say it again because I did not want to embarrass you by calling you that again. And was afraid you would think it was only the "man who can punctuate a little" when it is not the writer mainly I am referring to by great man but the man by the river, the man in the hotel room, the man at the party, the man who talks to me, the one in the snow by the old barn.[69]

I think that you were answering the college stationary [sic] letter in the last I received from you and not the one on this kind of stationary [sic] in which I asked about the play—that is, isn't it really now only yours and can it be mine, I mean is it possible? Of course I want to see it and work on it but only the way I said in the last letter, not just claiming it because you will let me do that. If you sent the first draft is there anything I can do to it or is it the way now that it has to be. Do you want to send it? I don't know what you can tell her.[70]

.... I have very probably looked at you in the way you say I look at B.[71] Knowing things about you as I do him, understanding so much, knowing what you are thinking, sometimes going to think, what you feel often and why, about the past. seeing something of the future, respecting, feeling secure with, happy with, not afraid to say do think act as I feel and knowing that you know the same things about me, and loving for these reasons.

Very small fine delicate snow is beginning, adding to that which is already here, so small that it is not even the kind you can hear so that unless I watch it I am not aware of it, like I am, without being able to see, that you move about the yard sometimes, that house, the town, the square, the streets with the memory of another life lived far away which no one knows was and might be again and some parts of it definitely anyway. with love

joan

Joan's letter receives a quick reply. What she is experiencing emotionally, Faulkner labels a serious letdown resulting from the closeness of their few days together in New York. They were much closer, he professes, than other people who had only been together once before. While her malaise, he predicts, will diminish, he is not about to let her give up on their play: "...the play is yours too. If you refuse to accept it, I will throw it away too. I would not have thought of writing one if I hadn't known you." The notes she sent are "all right, so all right there is no need to comment on them.... You will help, you will do your own work too of course; that should come first: you do that, and I will keep on the play until you can take up on it; no hurry."[72]

Faulkner continues to exhort Joan, telling her that a little less humility is called for, and that he believes in her ability to be a good writer, possibly quite good one day, or else why would he choose her among all the others he might have? She is very possibly his last chance, his last cast. Does she think he would waste it? He assumes a position of authority in his last paragraph. She also must do her school work, hate it, but do it.[73]

Oddly, though Joan found herself unhappily in the role of other woman, she had considered the competition. "I always felt that he certainly could have had other women, you know, girls too.... There certainly were more sophisticated women in New York who would have liked to have gone out with Faulkner. And he told me about some. He said, 'don't you know there was some girl from'—now if I say Alabama I'm not sure that's what he said—'who was always writing to him.' I've often wondered if that could have been Harper Lee.[74] But I have no idea. I'm not even sure he said Alabama. He didn't mention any names. But you certainly felt that he could have picked—that there were plenty of people—who would have wanted to know Faulkner."[75]

Just as Joan would learn that his severe episodes with alcohol were a pattern of behavior long before she entered his life, so too was his womanizing. "At some point and time, long after we were not seeing each other anymore, he wrote Saxe[76] or somebody and said he hadn't done anything but dull outdoor work for a long time or he hadn't been writing. And it must be time for him to find another young woman. I think he needed intrigue. I mean he had it all his life. He was *incurable*."[77] Nothing could more definitively corroborate Joan's assessment of Faulkner's need for intrigue than his own letters, especially those outlining convoluted travel plans and schemes to meet.

———

Beyond the novelty of a new relationship, the letters from 1950 trace the development of *Requiem for a Nun*—"By 1950, he conceived the idea I'd learn about writing by helping him write a play ... the idea of one having come from a conversation between us, anyway. The idea would be, as in all writing, to make something that wasn't here before us, and wouldn't be here except for us."[78] "But we must do it," he said, "for the simple pleasure, ecstasy. Otherwise, it won't be worth the trouble."[79]

While Joan laments that she did not learn what she might have from Faulkner about writing, in actuality he was teaching her firsthand the process: uncertainty, desire, and perseverance—qualities one also might apply to a love affair.

In a handwritten letter, Faulkner tells Joan that this first draft may in no way resemble the final draft. And whether it is by her hand or his hand, let it later change, but get something written. "Anything we do in this first draft may have no connection at all with the finished one. Let it change itself in either your hands or mine while we are getting it on paper; we expect that. So herewith is not only a few pages of play, but (as I see it now) a kind of synopsis of it. I wont remind you of your school work again; I'll just leave it with you to work—think—on the play when you feel you can. Rewrite that first scene if you want to, write any of the rest of it; this is just *first* draft; all we want is to get something on paper to pull apart and save what is good and right."[80] Finally, what he wants from Joan in actual words— in her sweet, splashy, little-girl's hand—is reassurance that she knows he would never deceive her.[81] Faulkner's fondness for all things girlish consistently appears in his letters: from Joan's handwriting, to her white slip, to insisting that Meta Carpenter[82] wear ribbons in her hair during lovemaking.[83] According to Meta, "His [Faulkner's] sexual key was the image of a young woman, fresh, fragrant of skin beneath her summer cotton dress, tremblingly responsive to his desire."[84]

From the outset, Joan felt the play collaboration was merely a means to spend time with her.[85] "The only way you could say you were going to do a play together was to sit down at a table and talk about it first. It was already his idea, his everything. And his characters."[86] And when those drafts would arrive, she felt "that there was nothing I could do ... I didn't see anything I could change. If I had been a different person I maybe would have ... It was all finished. If he sent just ideas or something like that it might have been different."[87] Though she tries to feign enthusiasm for the idea of collaboration after receiving another insistent letter from Faulkner, Joan's actual misgivings dominate this early March 1950 letter:

> Your letters did help so much, and I feel better. I do believe~in you and that the play will be ours~someway and someday. Almost definitely I will arrive in Memphis on April 5 (Monday) & be there till the following Tue. or Wed. Together we will be able to do something that will make it mine too. Alone I cannot do too well~ talking to you things come that are good

enough to write down. Looking at it here it is such an alien piece of paper. Can you understand how that is?

I believe all you said in the letter~ & I did not mean that you would tell me something you didn't mean or believe in the sense that you would lie about it, but out of sheer kindness, love & sympathy.

In early March, Joan also received a letter from one of Faulkner's Random House editors, Robert Linscott, whom Joan met at the Haases' dinner party. Linscott's letter demonstrates a great attentiveness to and regard for Faulkner. Since Faulkner obviously is interested in Joan, Linscott obtained the August 1949 *Mademoiselle* in which her short story appeared. He compliments her story and tells her that one day he hopes to read her novel.[88]

That same March Joan writes Faulkner that Bard is looking for a literary "lion" to speak (one year later, Faulkner will grant her wish and speak to Bard College students and faculty):

I wish you could be here now~they want a literary lion to come and speak-~you could be that for an hour and then we could work together, talk and think.

A letter from Mr. Linscott came saying he had read the Mlle. piece & thought it good (but he wouldn't say bad anyway).

Almost every day I read the play~there is something about Temple[89] that doesn't seem completely right. I am looking forward to April so much~will it work out about seeing each other and being able to work steady? love,
Joan

Surely Faulkner was pleased and no doubt encouraged, when he received this note in the form, almost, of a poem:

sunday march 12
the flowers came yester day, surrounded by their
leaves made into a bouquet and tied with
lavender ribbon. And it was snowing outside;
this seemed so strange~the warm flowers and snow~
later I walked and I could still smell the violets
it seemed. Thank you so very much~ they are here
now to remind me, help me to remember, be happier.
with love

———

Faulkner's insistence that they collaborate on *Requiem for a Nun* fueled his hope that the mentor-student portrayal would mollify not only Joan but his wife as well. By 1950 Faulkner had known Estelle Oldham most of his life and had been married to her for twenty-one years. In order for his friendship with Joan to advance it was imperative that Estelle accept Joan as his student, though Faulkner knew such acceptance on his wife's part unlikely. He writes Joan in a 22 March 1950 letter that Estelle often imagines more than the facts provide. He hopes they will be able to meet over Joan's spring break from Bard for work on Requiem—"We should be able to meet twice, anyway. Your family will want most of your time probably, but maybe you could come down here one day, and I will come up one day. That is, we will do one or the other as soon as you are home. Talk, lay out work, then you can work, telephone me when you need, until the last day of your visit, then we will meet again and plan how to carry on when you are back at school"[90]—and his letter includes detailed advice on how she should behave around Mrs. Faulkner. Probably just acting twenty-one will be enough, he assures her, but that should be bolstered by calling him mister and sticking to one fact— Faulkner as the great artist and Joan as the earnest student come to worship at his shrine. They must stick also to the task at hand, collaboration on the play.

The kiss he sends her in his letter, twice used, leaves no mark, is airy and intransigent, like a violet. He remembers her lower lip trembling slightly that night in the Biltmore hotel and he wonders what it signifies, the tremble lighter than violet. He determined it was deliberate so he would touch both of her lips, if only for a moment.[91]

Both Joan and Faulkner realized shortly after her brief trip home to Memphis that their expectations were too high. Joan never traveled to Rowan Oak nor had she ever had any intention of doing so. Instead, they met in Memphis and experienced another day of random driving without a specific destination. Once again the reality of an actual meeting proved unsatisfying. Faulkner's discouragement spilled over into his writing.

With the simple notation "Tuesday," Faulkner begins his letter proclaiming that Requiem isn't a play: "It's not a play. I begin to think I cant write one. But it's good stuff. I think it will be beautiful."[92] He is beginning to believe Joan probably will have to rewrite the whole thing. Then he turns again to how much he misses Joan and their unhappy meeting in Memphis with too many people crowding them. They are not free and he cannot communicate what he needs to tell her. Finally, disgusted, he writes that it is a rotten letter, that he is tired from working hard and steady at the play. He ends by sending her an imaginary kiss and an imaginary violet, and asks a question, will she accept them?[93]

While she would have intuited Faulkner's distress, Joan probably would not have directly addressed their shared disappointment in her next letter had he not broached the subject:

letter May 5, 1950

Dear Bill~I had not written you because I was not sure you would want me to; I was not particularly nice in Memphis, and as you said, the whole environment is different, but also my week at home was a very terrible one in a family sense and it carried over into our meeting. I, furthermore, got nothing decided about next year but I am going on and make plans anyway; a lot could depend on Haas merely in the sense that it is something concrete with which to confront my family. Do you remember Katherine Rosin[94] who was at the party? She gave me her name and number and told me to get in touch with her when I began to look for a job so do you think it would be all right if I did? May 29th is the deadline for work on the thesis so these days are filled with nothing but work on it. We have had only about one day of sunshine and just everything put together it's depressing. I feel ready soon to try to write another story, and then I hope so much that this summer we can do something. If only we didn't have to be in Memphis! Whatever happened to the job you were going to take at some writer's conference this summer? If only things could be simple; last summer was a complete waste of three months of my life, among the last three months that I will be young, can be silly, have no responsibilities that tie me down; this summer the same thing, and I hate to waste it: I don't want to play bridge, go to the Peabody, swim at somebody's club, and to the movies!!! I know you had the same feelings and that you did something about it and now? are you still glad. This is terrible of me to inflict my feelings like this on you when you have so much of your own at home, but when we start working together maybe we can be happier. Yes, I accept the violet and thank you, and the kiss too, if it is given on the cheek. Please forgive me for not writing any more often or any better than this; the disconnectedness of this is characteristic of my mind these days. But I hope you will write to me. I think of you often and regret the day in Memphis as time lost in which we could have come to a closer understanding; I should have told you the family things that were worrying me. love,

joan

Though Faulkner's relationship with Joan was far from ideal—he envisioned a sexual affair with a young woman eager to develop and sustain an emotional and physical attachment—these same years of personal frustration brought him his greatest recognition and critical acclaim. In a 6 May letter enclosed with several pages of draft material on *Requiem*, Faulkner nonchalantly mentions that he is to receive a literary award on 25 May (later he refers to it as "the medal thing"[95]). If he does come up to receive the award, will she have time to see him?

The award is noted in passing but his feelings for Joan receive much more. He tells her twice he loves her and how much he misses her: misses hearing her heart beat, her breathing. He hopes when they are together it will be a quiet, private time, without talking. It is wrong to talk too much.

Just how much his personal concerns eclipse the professional are starkly presented. He is lost; working isn't enough, even when the work is going well, as it is now (with *Requiem*).[96]

Passages in *Requiem* emphasize ideas expressed in Faulkner's letters. In one of Temple's narratives, she attempts a description of "ideal" love that is very reminiscent of his letters to Joan: "If love can be, mean anything, except the newness, the learning, the peace, the privacy: no shame: not even conscious that you are naked because you are just using the nakedness because that's a part of it...."[97]

And there is a long discourse, again Temple's passage, on the desire for a listener; an emphatic assertion that what a woman (a person) really wants and needs in a confidante is the mere ability to listen: "Somebody to talk to, as we all seem to need, want, have to have, not to converse with you nor even agree with you, but just keep quiet and listen. Which is all that people really want, really need...."[98]

———

The William Dean Howells Medal, dismissively referred to as the "medal thing" in Faulkner's letter to Joan, was from the American Academy of Arts and Letters. This prestigious award, given every five years, recognized "the most distinguished works of American fiction published during that period." After some vacillation, Faulkner declined to personally receive the award. His explanation to the Academy rested upon his seasonal duties as a Mississippi farmer and that he "doubt[ed] I know anything worth talking two minutes about."[99] Calling upon his identity as a Mississippi farmer who would have to scramble for something of interest to discuss belied his literary persona. Even when he chose to play the common man, the complexity of his mind almost invariably overshadowed this artifice.

With Joan, he would take many roles—suitor, lover, artist, mentor, father, failed poet, farmer, hunter, and horseman. His ability to shift in and out of roles—at times living a near imaginary life or one with merely tangential aspects of realism—enhanced his life. The same was true of this new relationship. In his mind, Faulkner already had invented much that was not there, and the elaborate plans for various rendezvous provided the suspense his daily life lacked.

This pattern of behavior reached back into his childhood. Faulkner's family conceded early on that his imagination outstripped most others, blurring lines between honesty and dishonesty. As early as the third grade he claimed his lineage as an author, stating, "I want to be a writer like my great-granddaddy."[100] Faulkner told his cousins and playmates fanciful stories as they completed his tedious chores. According to one cousin, "'It got so that when Billy told you something, you never knew if it was the truth or just something he'd made up.' Perhaps the real world and the world of the imagination have never since that time been really separated in Faulkner's mind...."[101]

Jimmy Faulkner described his uncle as a deeply private man who grew up in a house rich in oral storytelling. He said when Faulkner was young there were as many as three or four generations living in one home, with the older generations telling stories to the younger. Faulkner maintained this oral tradition with his children, as well as drawing on the people and incidents in the Oxford area for his fiction. "Nothing he made up was completely from scratch," he said. Mr. Faulkner didn't believe people in Oxford were angered by the stories and descriptions in his uncle's literature. "The Snopes," he said, "are not any specific people, but a type of people."[102]

———

On 9 May Faulkner returns to the issues raised in Joan's 5 May letter. He advises her on pursuing Mrs. Rosin's offer of help along with assistance from Robert Haas. As far as her question about summer and his involvement with a writer's conference, he asks her to imagine the trouble she would have explaining it all to her family—her accompaniment of him to a writer's conference—and to likewise imagine the problems he would have with his wife.

This brush with reality evokes the emergence of another theme: how to be an artist among middle-class Southerners. Faulkner hopes that Joan is beginning to see the near hopelessness of such.[103] In "Faulkner's Advice to a Young Writer," Joan reasserts his concerns found in this 9 May letter: "So from the beginning, he warned me about what would be required for me to be a writer: 'If you cannot resist the middleclass unaided, you do not have it in you to be a good artist.' He thought I would 'save my soul' anyhow, unaided, but he wanted to save me 'some of the lacerations and abrasions' he knew. 'They didn't hurt me,' he wrote. 'And I never considered myself especially tough. They were no fun, but I was a better man than they were.'"[104]

It is evident in this letter that Faulkner also is discussing his own situation: "You can see now how it is almost impossible for a middle class southerner to be anything else but a middle class southerner; how you have to fight your family for every inch of art you ever gain and at the very time when the whole tribe of them are hanging like so many buzzards over every penny you earn by it. Queer business."[105]

This insult was repeated to Joan both in letters and in conversation.

"He told me ... that he could be writing and they would ask him if he would go to town and get some coffee or something because he was the only one in the house who supposedly wasn't doing anything. Now I believe that. That kind of thing. I said in the Atlantic article[106] he sent out stories for thirteen years before anyone ever took one. And he wasn't making any money off his books. So I can see how she [Estelle] could very well wonder what he was ever going to amount to."[107]

Faulkner's sense that his work was not only unappreciated but also misunderstood spills over in other correspondence. In a letter to Saxe Commins, he writes that "she [E.] has never had any regard or respect for my work, has always looked on it as a hobby, like collecting stamps."[108]

———

Faulkner's 9 May letter continues with strategy. He believes Joan's success involves getting a foothold elsewhere, perhaps New York, and using that as a club[109] to hold over her family. This will give her as much freedom as marriage but without a husband who also may be a champion of the middle class. In a near battle cry, Faulkner incites Joan to never vegetate nor succumb to the Memphis or Tennessee middle class.

The kiss she accepted, but only on the cheek, is withdrawn. He can kiss his nieces and daughters on the cheek. He will just have to wait until she grows up (a repeated phrase in his letters suggesting her failure to be sexually responsive), unless he is dead by then or physically distasteful to anyone twenty-one years old. If it is his age, he begs her to tell him so. He wants only a truthful answer. Perhaps he should have demanded an answer to that before because he believes she has never lied to him.[110]

That age would emerge as a nearly insurmountable problem is evident just eight months into their friendship. The fission over age—"there was always that," Joan said. "I remember one time, I had been in Florida and I came up and saw him and then I went back to Florida ... He drove me to Birmingham and there was a delay with the plane and finally the stewardess or somebody came over and said your daughter's plane is here. He said then something like 'I never think of myself as being older than you until something like that happens.'"[111]

Yet that statement seems unlikely as Faulkner's letters are full of misgivings about his age and Joan's youth. Looking back, Joan did not feel Faulkner was old for his age, though in his letters he referred to himself as "Old bloke."

> I was too young to think about all that, but he walked all the time in New York. He would walk when he lived at One Fifth Avenue up to Random House which I think was Forty-ninth or Fiftieth Street. And he was very

conscious of keeping in shape and trim. One time when I stayed the night at Rowan Oak he was very proud to get out his WWII (RAF) uniform. He could still get into it. But he was very small as you know.

I'd always say he wasn't too old ... I [was] not going to deliberately hurt his feelings, and if he hadn't been married, I probably would have married him, but I didn't want to be responsible for breaking up that marriage. I just assumed, also, that at his age he couldn't have had children and I wanted [children.] I mean he probably could have, but what did I know?"[112]

"Another thing I thought about was that I would be taking him away from Oxford because I didn't see how we could go back and live there and I thought, 'I can't take Faulkner away from Mississippi.'"[113]

The issue of their age disparity was less an obstacle in Joan's mind than Faulkner's marital state. "I just felt the whole thing was wrong, going off and meeting a married man. I just wanted to know him because he was a writer."[114] "I certainly had mores for my time and place. A lot of my restraints with Faulkner were just that he was married, it wasn't because he was old, it was because he was married."[115]

By contemporary standards, few eyebrows would be raised should a man as accomplished as Faulkner find a young woman to enhance his life, but in the early 1950s outlooks concerning marriage were different. While the Random House crowd seemed unfazed by the attachment, the reaction in Memphis and Mississippi was quite different. This friendship brushed right up against that same Southern middle class that also threatened artistic development. And Mrs. Faulkner, for one, would assert herself when possible: a visible and fervent reminder that he was indeed a married man.

———

In June 1950, Joan graduated from Bard College and received a letter of congratulation from Faulkner. He told her he had asked Albert Erskine to have a flower delivered to her (an orchid, as Joan recalls). The personal nature of Faulkner's relationship with Random House editors and publishers is striking. He seemed to think little of asking them for favors and, as has been well established, monetary advances. That an editor from Random House should concern himself with flowers for a college graduation seems in keeping with Faulkner's expectations. Much of this acquiescence was due to Faulkner's stature within the publishing world. From the outset of his allegiance with Random House, Faulkner received attention from the very top. Bennett Cerf, who along with Donald Klopfer founded Random House, told Faulkner, "I think we would rather have you on our list than any other fiction writer living in America."[116] To realize his ambition, Cerf added Faulkner to his author list only by buying the publishing firm of Harrison Smith and Robert Haas in January 1936 (bringing out in October of that year *Absalom, Absalom!).* Smith and Haas became associates with Cerf and Klopfer at Random House.

Faulkner's early and sustained friendship with Smith survived various upheavals in the publishing world. After publishing *The Marble Faun,* a collection of poetry with The Four Seas Company, two books with Boni and Liveright, and *Sartoris* with Harcourt, Brace and Company, Faulkner's next four books came out with Jonathan Cape and Harrison Smith: *The Sound and the Fury* (1929), *As I Lay Dying* (1930), which Faulkner dedicated to Harrison Smith, *Sanctuary,* and *These Thirteen* (1931). In 1931 Smith broke with Cape and named his new company Harrison Smith, Inc. While much bigger houses such as Knopf, Viking, and Random House openly courted Faulkner, the author stayed with his friend, a man he genuinely liked and respected.[117] During the fall of 1932 Smith took a partner, Robert Haas, and published *Light in August.* Thus, Random House's acquisition of Faulkner did not involve an upheaval of his personal and professional relationships; Faulkner's long history with Smith transferred with the author. This transfer probably best explains Faulkner's close ties and personal overlaps with his publishing house.

The very same Random House editors—Saxe Commins, Robert Linscott, Robert Haas, Harrison Smith, and Albert Erskine—who became acquainted with Joan also knew Mrs. Faulkner. In fact, Mrs. Faulkner would sometimes mention Joan in letters to Dorothy and Saxe Commins.[118] Faulkner's literary agent, Harold Ober,[119] of the Harold Ober Agency, likewise knew both women, eventually representing Joan (as the Ober Agency does to this day).

———

Faulkner and Joan's meeting in Memphis during that Easter break ushered in complications far beyond a shared sense of disappointment. An Oxford woman reported seeing Faulkner and Joan in a Memphis "juke joint" to Estelle. Suddenly this relationship was front and center in the Faulkner household, and Estelle had yet another battle on her hands. Faulkner writes Joan, comparing the home environment to hell. Estelle is convinced that her husband is in an intrigue. She is drinking and threatening to call Joan's mother or father, "...telling them what kind of (her words) an old goat I am."[120] Faulkner describes himself as simply reading a book in the corner while she commences her harangue. Faulkner's indiscretion came to Estelle through a beauty parlor report from Mrs. Smallwood, an Oxford neighbor. Faulkner reminded his wife that when Mrs. Smallwood moved near them a few years ago, Estelle never called on her. This is Mrs. Smallwood's retribution, or so Faulkner believed.

In a long letter, Faulkner reveals that Estelle has picked up his mail, including a letter from Joan, and plans to write her back to break up this intrigue. The arguments are taking place in front of Jill, now seventeen (who at one point prevented her mother from mailing the letter), and the servants. Again, Faulkner harkens back to Estelle's failure to understand and respect him as an artist. (In Faulkner's mind that apparently involved unassailable personal liberties.) Oddly enough, Faulkner correlates her drinking to her menstrual periods, asserting that her binges follow her *old* menstrual cycle. "She will of course get drunk again, it seems to follow her old menstrual periods, every month. She seems quite crazy except for an inability to do anything successfully—co-ordinate, rationalize—is really capable of anything that will make enough people unhappy."[121] That Faulkner found his wife incapable of doing anything successfully was a notion Joan felt he shared with many other Southern men of his period: "All men felt that way about women back then; that women weren't supposed to have any brains or do anything. Down here any way. But I think he had to be chasing after a younger woman and that's not admirable. It was something he had to do, have in his life."[122] "I think in Faulkner's most productive years, he would have been a difficult husband for anybody ... He was so involved with his work and that was his main interest in life and I'm sure everything else came second. And it was hard for Estelle."[123]

Faulkner's letter continues with an explanation of why he remains in this unhappy union. His marriage, he writes, would have ended fifteen years ago except for his daughter. Here he offers Joan an out. She must consider the implications of her mother or father receiving a letter from his wife and all that will accompany such a revelation. She may write him registered mail and he will answer. They may either go ahead and see what circumstances portend or these letters will be their last.[124]

This letter contradicts the notion that there were no arguments in front of others in the household. Joan felt Faulkner embraced the idea of Southern decorum regardless of actuality: "I think he liked the ... old Southern thing. He told me once they never argued in front of the children, well, you just know that isn't true. And then you heard about all these drunken scenes and everything. I think he liked to keep up this pretense that everything on the surface was all right. He was always talking about Mrs. Faulkner ... and I always felt sympathy for her and I don't think it was all as one-sided as he made things out." Joan believed Faulkner would have been difficult to live with as well.

His strange analogy between his wife's periods and her drinking was, Joan felt, just another fabrication: "Now ... how can he remember that and would it? See, I always had the feeling he made up a lot of those

things. He believed them, but that was just some flight of fancy or whatever."

Mrs. Smallwood certainly colored her story, as the Cotton Bowl Restaurant would hardly be considered a juke joint. It was a popular gathering spot,
mostly a lunch crowd, for college students from nearby Southwestern College at Memphis. "That was the first time he came to Memphis to meet me.
I wrote that we went to the Cotton Bowl that was over near Southwestern
and the Mills Brothers were on the jukebox singing and that Mrs. Smallwood—that amazing name—saw us ... I laughed about the Cotton Bowl
being called a juke joint." That Mrs. Smallwood was extracting her pound
of flesh for Estelle's possible slight seems likely to Joan. "What else is new
about Oxford?"[125]

In "Twenty," Joan writes: "On the nickelodeon the Mills Brothers say
'You Always Hurt the One You Love.' And he [Faulkner] said that might
be for me. But why? Because he was going to fall in love with me, or possibly already had."[126]

Faulkner used Jill as his reason for staying in his marriage during his
previous affair with Meta Carpenter: "It is true in those days the woman,
no matter what, was going to get the child and Blotner's idea was that Estelle
was never going to give him a divorce because she was never going to let go
of the name.[127] But at some point when she got sober and started going to
AA [Alcoholics Anonymous] when they lived in Charlottesville and they were
older, she did offer him a divorce and he didn't want it, didn't take it."[128]

As the Mrs. Smallwood incident gathered momentum, Faulkner writes
Joan a string of letters. Estelle has phoned Joan's Oxford relatives and asked
John Reed Holley for Joan's address. Faulkner believes that those who know
his wife perceive her as jealous and unbalanced.[129] Four days later, Faulkner
proposes they now correspond by Joan addressing her letters to A.E. Holston,[130] general delivery. (Faulkner first suggests Quentin Compson but
decides his fictional character from *The Sound and the Fury* and *Absalom,
Absalom!* would be recognized.) This maneuver follows a marital dispute so
upsetting Faulkner seems shaken himself. He warns Joan and again offers
her an exit: "I dont think you ever will be safe with her [Estelle], certainly
not until she forgets you, finds another object to project her insanity on."[131]
Further, Faulkner writes there are several courses they might take: to not
see each other again but arrange to correspond in secrecy; to end the relationship; or to see each other and manage a secret exchange of letters. It is
Joan's decision now; she must determine if the play and relationship is
worth it.[132]

Faulkner's inability or unwillingness to imagine his wife's dilemma
speaks volumes about his understanding of female nature. One could

conclude that he is insufferably self-absorbed or that he simply does not care at all about his wife's feelings. "All I could think," Joan said, "was that he just really cared so little about Estelle that he just really didn't care." Or perhaps the disconnect lies in Faulkner's later admission to Joan that he is coming to believe he knows so little about women. To not understand the threat a twenty-one-year-old girl would pose to a fifty-something wife suggests a staggering obtuseness.

> It is like he is trying to excuse himself. Why would she do it [contact Joan]? Any female would do that who knew about it. And the older you get the more insecure you are. And I knew she was very insecure about her age. I think she was older than Faulkner to start with. I told you Mrs. Saxe Commins said when she visited Oxford that Estelle had every known jar of cream in her bathroom that had ever been invented for your face to make you look younger and all. But also it is hard to realize that all those years she was an alcoholic. And he sometimes says she was drunk. Of course, he was probably drunk a lot of the time too, and that's going to change your personality. And cause conflict between them. And I am sure he was not a wonderful man to live with either.[133]
>
> He said to me once that critics—after he said this I thought how he was always telling me he didn't read reviews—he said the critics were always accusing him of not liking women. And he said, "I didn't know that I didn't like women." And then Mrs. Faulkner said—I read this somewhere—"I have always been afraid Bill liked women too much." But I always thought in *As I Lay Dying* that he was very sympathetic toward that old woman, country woman.[134]

Estelle didn't believe Faulkner's insistence that *Requiem* was the "reason" for his involvement with Joan. She wrote Saxe Commins about the situation; explaining that her husband had taken an "absorbing interest" in Joan and he is completely enamoured. While he was working on the play, Faulkner told her and Jill that Joan would be his collaborator "we *both* were a little amazed—as Pappy heretofore, brooked *no* interference...."[135]

And in many ways Estelle knew how to keep her husband off balance. She frequently would tell him she had called Joan and her mother, though Joan remembers only one phone call from Mrs. Faulkner when she agreed to meet her for lunch. Faulkner would react very strongly to Mrs. Faulkner's threats, and he never seemed to know if she actually acted upon them or if they remained unfulfilled. These letters, then, are a combination of Faulkner reacting to his wife and trying to keep Joan interested through the promise of the play. He writes that one thing he knows for sure is that they have gone too far with the play to stop now.[136] Accompanying another letter is a picture Faulkner drew of a man, smoking a pipe, behind a plow and mule.

It is his feeling that after Joan reads the enclosed section they can determine what is wrong with Temple.[137]

Again, Faulkner's imagination runs wild. He tells Joan that Estelle
wants her to come to Rowan Oak in order to put an end to the gossip (but
really just to get a look at Joan he concludes). Despite his machinations,
Faulkner accuses Estelle of perpetuating intrigue. He cautions Joan that if
New York and Haas's party should come up, she should say that she was
there with three friends from Bard. "The Haases and Saxe Commins, particularly his wife," Joan said, "those were her friends too. He was pulling
this thing that he was looking at schools for Jill and all that stuff. He's just
making this all up. I didn't ever go. In the first place, I think it was stupid
of him to think of me coming down there."[138] Faulkner then suggests inviting his wife to accompany him to Joan's house while they work on the play.
He believes Joan and her mother will be better able to surmise her character than his letters have allowed.[139]

Neither meeting occurred, though one phone call from Estelle did
apparently reach the Williams household, causing Joan's mother, Maude,
to fear her daughter would be named in a divorce suit. The tone of Joan's
next letter is fearful. There now appear to be some real ramifications and
she clearly is casting about for direction:

july 15, 1950

saturday

dear Bill, I just don't know what to say. I have been so surprised at what has
been happening, particularly because the behaviour is something I can't figure
out. I don't know what she [Estelle] wants, what she is trying to do, to prove,
how she feels. Did you know she called me the other day to meet her for
lunch at the Peabody the next day, and then she called the next morning to
say she couldn't come; I wasn't here and she talked to my Mother. Everything was very pleasant in both conversations. Maybe if you didn't know this
it would be better for you not to mention it because it would only make her
angry that i had "told," and also she would know we were writing. When she
called and then said she didn't, I don't understand, was she afraid to talk
because you were there? I really would like to have kept the luncheon date
and tried to make her see the truth; would it have been impossible. I don't
really [know if] she is going to approach my family, anyway after talking to
my Mother (sic) she knows my family is aware of us knowing one another,
and continuing to write. When I talked to you I guess you could tell I was
unhappy; it was strange the call came just then for at the time I was talking
to Mother about the whole thing, got her assurance that she knew it was all
friendship and very valuable to me. She is afraid that Mrs. F. might get a
divorce and name me or something of that sort, talk about me etc. and she
advises that I discontinue to write, for I cannot risk being talked about in
such a way, for although most wouldn't believe anything, many would.

She also thinks letters are dangerous for they are proof positive. How glad I am that you have destroyed them all along although I have regretted that you couldn't keep them as I do yours, to re-read with pleasure. Bill, I don't want to stop writing you even if there was nothing else but the letters until sometime when we are far away we could see each other. I, too, could not explain a twelve hour absence very well; I do not want to hide letters and meetings from my family and I don't think it would be necessary except that maybe it would be better if not one soul knew about it. There is of course no reason for you to stop writing me and I want to write you, but is this general delivery safe? I would like to continue to write but to let her think we stopped; but then if she found we had lied it would be the worst thing that could happen. I almost do not mind lying to her any more because she won't accept the truth; and then I have to stop and think that if I were a married woman and in her place maybe I would not like this either so it is hard to do exactly what we want. I would like to see you, but where and how without anyone knowing I don't know; I still think maybe just to come to my house would be the best thing, except she might still tell and people would listen. I don't know, Bill, I just don't. I don't know if I can write even any more, I mean stories. I have been reading Dr. Martino and Other Stories[140] and like them all very much. Please try not to worry and to do your work. Now things will just have to go along, you will just have to act like you never think of me or hear or write to me, yet I hope you will, and let me know if you think it is really all right to continue with this address, and Bill, if you get tired of it all just say so and the writing will stop, because worrying about it all can't interfere with your work, since you are there things might as well be as pleasant as possible and the only way may be to stop everything, presuming that she will believe you when you tell her that it has. We can't do much else except write back and forth the same things but I still like to hear from you. Maybe, as you said, things will be better soon.

Joan

———

One afternoon during the summer, the Peabody engagement did occur. Joan met Estelle for lunch at the Black Cat, a restaurant inside the hotel. Joan remembers most Estelle's frailty and seeming vulnerability. She took Joan's arm, almost for support, as they made their way to the table. Estelle directly asked Joan if she wanted to marry her husband and Joan said no. Trying to explain that she wanted to be a writer, and therefore felt fortunate to know a famous writer, Joan posed an analogous question: "'If she wanted to be a painter, wouldn't she want to know Picasso?' 'No,' she said." Mrs. Faulkner believed her husband was going through a male menopause that Joan interpreted as his need for change.[141] The Peabody luncheon did little to foster Faulkner's portrayal of a raving madwoman. Joan met instead a dignified if fragile woman who decided to find out for herself exactly what she was up against.

If Joan's parents were concerned about their daughter and Faulkner, they kept their conversations and worries private. The Williamses already were aware of their daughter's ability to surprise and be contrary. When Joan was seventeen years old, she and a group of friends celebrating high school graduation took a road trip to a small Mississippi town. Once there, they woke the town's justice of the peace so the various couples could be married. Joan had dated her boyfriend, an Irish Catholic student who had attended Christian Brothers High School in Memphis, for the past two years. At the last moment she changed her mind, but her boyfriend drove into the ditch and said that if she did not marry him, he would simply leave her there. Upon their return to Memphis, Joan told her parents she did not want to be married. "They arranged the annulment [and] they didn't say anything about it."[142] Joan and the young man never lived together. Joan writes of the marriage in Pay the Piper that "It doesn't really count."[143]

Maude Williams said in a 1996 interview that she and her husband, Priestly "P.H." Williams,[144] always thought Joan and Faulkner were simply friends. (However, Joan recalls very clearly her mother's warning that she might be named a party in a divorce suit.) "My mother never said anything that I remember about the [Faulkner's] letters. The postman came to your door, so I was probably always there to get the mail before she was, just for that reason. She never said anything about that. In fact, I never really discussed all these kinds of things with her, except I remember that one remark she made. And when I told her you were coming she said, 'What am I supposed to tell her, you had an affair with William Faulkner?' We never talked intimately about anything like that. She never did talk about anything like that."[145]

Mrs. Williams stressed that Joan continued seeing other people at the same time—"friends her own age." She never believed Joan would marry Faulkner. "He [Faulkner] had a wife and family. I didn't think they were serious."

When Mrs. Williams met Faulkner she recalled him as "All right. Quiet and old fashioned. A little gray-haired man." She said she never met Mrs. Faulkner. Her relatives in Mississippi liked Faulkner though she believed that "the South didn't pay any attention to him." What surprised her more than Joan's friendship with Faulkner was Joan wanting to be a writer: "That surprised me, yes."[146]

Her family's failure to warmly and strongly encourage Joan's writing ambitions was quickly absorbed by Faulkner. After his August visit to Joan's home, he writes in part, "Your mother told me in so many words, calm enough, no hesitation, that she did not believe you could write a play. I expected that, of course."[147] Faulkner's visit to the Williams home confirmed his belief that her parents labored under those Southern middle-class conventions that are the bane of artists and writers. He expected that reaction but he was not prepared for the ulterior suspicion. Faulkner takes some satisfaction in both Joan's mother and his wife looking cross-eyed. This, he believes, affirms what his heart is telling him. The problem lies with Joan's face. He reminds her that after seeing her five or six times he suddenly realized it was pretty, and in Haas's elevator (the New York party), he discovered it was beautiful and he wished he'd never laid eyes on it.[148]

Mr. and Mrs. Williams' lack of support was something "he made a big thing out of.... It is like that downgrading all the time, you know, never, oh, well, that's wonderful Joan, just 'she can't do it.'"[149] With this opening, Faulkner positioned himself and Joan against not only his wife and Joan's family, but also anyone who failed to understand artistic temperament. This attitude conferred valiancy and suggested elevated intentions, both of which inspired Faulkner's chivalry. He once wrote Joan that he wished he could borrow a white horse and snatch her from the dynamite salon (a reference to her father's dynamite business) and gallop away[150]—"snatch you up and gallop off forever—provided of course that you would go, and I could find the white horse."[151]

Both Joan and her mother noted Faulkner's courtly nature. "I think he was very old fashioned, still, almost, I don't know, pretentiously isn't the right word, but he cultivated that old fashionedness," Joan said. In his writings "he wanted an older time, he liked the older time. He liked it that I didn't wear nail polish and that I wasn't aggressive."[152]

———

Aug. 2, 1950

Dear Bill,

I have written my version of the first act, 14 pages, and know that it lacks passion. Also still there is just too much dialogue between the three people to be playable; I have thought of a new beginning, however, and am going to write the first part over and then send it to you, straight to W. F., trying to get it mailed Sat. or Mon....

A letter from Chris[153] this morning asking about you and to be remembered to you and also telling of his engagement to a very sweet girl from school, whom you didn't meet.

I think the only way is just to keep writing it and solving the problems and seeing them at the same time. Much will have to be done to it, but I like doing the work and that is all that we are to think of now anyway. I think about these three people all the time. I think, too, that one thing wrong is maybe that the play isn't realistic enough. We shall see, though. You may not at all like what I have done with it, maybe too childish, too lacking. Let me know really what you think. But as you said we can't let it go now, having come so far that at last even I am working, living it. How are you coming?

I am so happy about the one day here and there will have to be others even if it doesn't work out for me to come there, but now there is work, evidence, although there is ten times more to be done.

More and more Faulkner is taking notice of the writer's spirit of Joan's letters. He says of her 2 August letter that it is the way he likes to hear her talk. Their idea for the play is sound and will evolve through trial and error; all they provide is the work. He hoped for uninterrupted work together— for fun, intimacy, mutual inspiration, and to make something between them that wasn't there before. But the idea of uninterruption is a folly though not the continued work: "Art is a little stronger than any human passion for thwarting it ... art takes care of its own. Takes care of those who are willing, capable of, fidelity to it above everything else."[154] He still feels they will break through it all.

Then he shares an important passage from *Requiem* written in the traditional manner of dialogue with italics for explication. He tells Joan this exchange will explain why Temple returns to Jefferson before Nancy is hanged. If this were a movie, not a play, he writes, they could show the California beach as the setting for the conversation. But, as it is a play, Temple probably should tell the lawyer this. Temple and the little boy will be on the beach. She possibly will be reading, the young boy will have a toy shovel and pail.[155] The dialogue as it occurs in the finished play with Temple addressing Stevens is almost an exact replication of this early draft:

> It was that afternoon—the sixth. We were on the beach, Bucky [her son] and I. I was reading, and he was—oh, talking mostly, you know—'Is California far from Jefferson, mamma?' and I say 'Yes, darling'—you know: still reading or trying to, and he says, 'How long will we stay in California, mamma?' and I say, 'Until we get tired of it' and he says, 'Will we stay here until they hang Nancy, mamma?' and it's already too late now; I say, 'Yes, darling,' and then he drops it right in my lap, right out of the mouths of—how is it?—babes and sucklings. 'Where will we go then, mamma?' And then we come back to the hotel, and there you are too [a telegram from Stevens]. Well?[156]

Joan continued to struggle with what she considered the lack of realism in *Requiem* that most likely stemmed from her initial and sustained disbelief in the play's premise. "I never did believe in that, about the woman killing the baby and all that stuff. I still think the whole premise of her maid killing the baby is stupid."[157] Still she carried on with the project though not with the enthusiasm Faulkner would have liked. "You make me sound like a schoolteacher.... Of course you dont need to work on the play when you dont feel like it; have something else to do. It doesn't matter if we ever finish it; what I mean was, the fun of doing it together, getting it done together. The play itself means nothing."[158] That the play collaboration is more of a ruse than an actuality is evident in his letter's close; he is unhappy at not seeing as much of Joan during the summer as he had hoped.[159]

While the play simmered, August of 1950 yielded an important publication, *The Collected Stories of William Faulkner*. A shift in Faulkner readership was signaled when the Book-of-the-Month Club adopted the short-story collection as an alternate fiction selection.[160] The book was greeted with enthusiasm and acclaim.

———

When Faulkner and Joan could meet, albeit too infrequently, it was usually halfway between Memphis and Oxford, in the small Mississippi town of Holly Springs. Joan would borrow her mother's car or take the bus. Once in Holly Springs, they would drive to the woods. Faulkner usually brought beer for himself and sometimes food for Joan. She believes they both romanticized their meetings in the woods, certainly more than those in Memphis, and even in New York where they had freedom. "We finally decided that we didn't want to meet in Memphis. We never knew what to do in Memphis. In New York, he [Faulkner] always had a place to stay. Of course all the people at Random House knew all about this and you didn't have to hide from anybody. As long as he had a place to stay we could always go there or to a restaurant or something. But of course the woods had an aura to them."[161]

Summer was the season Joan most associated with Faulkner and the Mississippi woods the place of most significance. It would be a summer afternoon in Holly Springs when he surprised Joan by giving her the original, handwritten manuscript of *The Sound and the Fury*.[162] Another afternoon in the woods Joan proudly presented Faulkner with her short story "The Morning and the Evening." And once, sitting by the Mississippi River, Joan read aloud a Katherine Anne Porter short story, about which Faulkner said, "That's too many words to tell a story."[163]

Also underlying their clandestine meetings was sexual tension: Faulkner's advances and Joan's reluctance. Besides the looming issue of Faulkner's marriage, Joan simply didn't feel sexually attracted to him, although the promise of sex kept the relationship alive. "I don't think I was as free and all as I should have been. I should have freed myself."[164] "I wasn't a Jean Stein.[165] I can look back and think I wish I had been. I could see why you might think I was childish. But a lot of mine [my reservations] came from the fact that he was married. I didn't worry about people in Oxford talking or all that kind of thing. And nobody in Memphis knew I was seeing him or anything. And I don't think after Mrs. Smallwood told Mrs. Faulkner we were seen together that it was all over Oxford. Nobody would have known who I was. There was never anything saying that Mrs. Smallwood went around telling anybody else. And you know Mrs. Faulkner wasn't going to tell anybody and I don't think the whole town was talking as he insinuates. You know if they had talked they could have talked about him before me. Of course they didn't know what he was doing in Hollywood, but he was never not seeing somebody. I wish I could have been the kind of girl who just spread my legs. That wasn't my make up. But perhaps he responded more to the chaste, than the other, wilder response."[166]

In a remarkable, undated letter, Faulkner chides Joan for running from herself and running from him. He accuses her of wanting a simple world full of compatible friends where she can take and give only what she wants. This is a cool and simple place, but that world doesn't exist for an artist. She must stop being afraid, stop running and accept the heat, fire and sweat of the real world, the world of the artist. She must overcome fears of her father and those persistent worries of disappointing and hurting him. She knew long ago she is an artist and she now must embrace the difficulties that come with it.

To be an artist you must be free, and he promises absolute freedom. He will take and keep nothing of hers. If she kisses him, she still has her mouth. He has no rights over it. If she sleeps with him, her body is still hers. He has no rights over it just because he had sex with her. And if or when he is free, and she agrees to marry him, she may discard the marriage as well. Should she wake up one morning and decide it was a mistake to marry him, he will free her and there will be no reproaches.

The promises made in this letter—that upon a word from Joan he will be able to disengage, that he will respect her artistic freedom as much as he respects his own—are eventually impossible for him to keep. The grandiose freedom purported here runs contrary to the depths of his emotional attachment.[167] "See that was the kind of thing he would write that I didn't pay any attention to because ... I don't know where he got all that." The anger in the letter Joan attributes to her "refusals of him."[168]

———

Fictional treatments of their sexual conflicts appear in *The Wintering*, and in this scene, Amy struggles with her inability to return Jeff's affections.

As was often the case with Faulkner and Joan, Jeff and Amy meet in an iso-
lated, rural location. After aimlessly driving back roads, they notice an abandoned Negro schoolhouse where they spend the afternoon around "what
remained of a pot-bellied stove" drinking the whiskey Jeff provides:

> They sat like schoolchildren themselves, the blanket drawn over their knees,
> whispering in conspiring tones.... In their winter coats, she thought them
> like two cumbersome bears settled side by side for their winter's sleep.
> Against the stove's warm sides, the soles of her feet had begun to burn
> uncomfortably, though the floor beneath her was hard and cold. The two
> inconveniences loomed large in her mind, and Jeff's hand touching her was
> bothersome. He seemed trembly and shaky, like an old man. This time: she
> repeated that to herself over and over.... Must she blame herself that when
> she tried to return his kiss, she felt nothing at all? Reserve, part of her, tight-
> ened her like a rein. Coldly, she removed his hand from her leg. She said
> all the things she always said: she was sorry but she couldn't and she just
> didn't feel that way. Her longing, however, was for abandonment.
>
> Jeff walked to the window with the whiskey bottle and tilted it to his
> mouth. Having recapped it, he said, turning "Poor baby." That struck Amy
> as being condescending, as she looked at him, a little less sorry for having
> refused.
>
> "—who can't melt," he had concluded.
>
> Against the edgeless sun visible at the window, he seemed all the same
> color, hard to distinguish. "You may think too highly of your body, Amy,"
> he said. "It's, after all, flesh and blood. And, I worry that you're never going
> to be able to love anyone."
>
> How ridiculous, she thought, running over in her mind the people she
> already loved, her family despite all the things they had done to her, and
> she loved him, though not in the way he wanted. Could she help that? Old
> shame filled her as she stood and drew up her pants, uncomfortable that he
> did not look away. Not speaking, she gathered things to take to the car....
>
> "I thought I could help," he said. "I know you're not frigid. You only need
> to have something frozen inside you melted. Something your past did to
> you. But I guess I'm the wrong one."
>
> Miserable, she said, "I'm sorry."
>
> "It's not fatal, he said. "It's a momentary sadness like a star falling. But
> we've put so much into this, it seems a shame it's ended."[169]

Later in the novel, when Jeff and Amy spend the night together in New
York, the scene ends again in frustration and dissatisfaction. Amy's immaturity and lack of emotional generosity registers in this fumbling love scene;
she is unresponsive with thoughts far away from the possibilities of the
moment:

> She cried silently. Don't! with her teeth gritted. Her soul and her spirit were
> unmanageable and ungiving.
>
> He said, unexpectedly, "I'm sorry. I'm sorry."

Having been about to move over her, he lay back. Opening her eyes, Amy was not sure exactly what happened. Then she understood nothing had happened and, therefore, she need not feel guilt.

Jeff said, "I had waited for you too long."

Never thinking to brush aside apology for what she had not wanted, and ignorant of anything she could have said or done, Amy slid down on her pillow and, shortly, fell asleep.[170]

———

Joan did continue seeing young men her age throughout the years of her involvement with Faulkner. While at times her other engagements made Faulkner angry and insecure, it seemed a part of him was resigned to Joan's dating. (In a 1953 letter, Faulkner lists one by one all of the young men he has outlasted.) One young man crossed over from being Joan's boyfriend to knowing Faulkner as well. Brandon Grove, a Bard College student, met Joan in 1948 a year prior to her introduction to Faulkner. At that time, Bard College was a small school with an enrollment just slightly over two hundred students. Early on he appreciated the significance of Faulkner in Joan's life. "I saw him [Faulkner] as Joan's literary mentor, not someone taking advantage of a pretty, young girl," Grove said. "He seemed to genuinely come to be in love with her."

Grove recalled time spent with Joan and the author in New York while he was an undergraduate student at Bard and also during his years in graduate school at Princeton. Grove completed his MA in Public and International Affairs from Princeton in 1952 and did post-graduate work there in political science in 1953. These interests were precursors to his career as United States ambassador, an interest cultivated in part by his father's career as a foreign diplomat.

One story Grove fondly recalled involved his 1950 visit to Memphis and an afternoon on Faulkner's boat the *Minmagary*. Yet little did Grove know that this excursion had been in the planning stage since the day Faulkner wrote Joan his fourth letter. One of Faulkner's earliest desires after meeting Joan was to take her sailing, or better yet, to spend a romantic winter weekend by the ocean with the darkness and cold outside. When Joan and Faulkner finally did go boating, it was months after their first meeting in August 1949, and the company that afternoon on Faulkner's boat included Faulkner's wife, Estelle, and Joan's suitor, Grove. A far cry from the sailing trip or winter weekend by the ocean Faulkner first envisioned.

Imagine then the reality of this boat trip falling one year after Joan and Faulkner first met in the driveway at Rowan Oak. Faulkner already had proclaimed his love for Joan, and Grove was privy to all: "I was in love with

Joan, he was in love with Joan, so it was a bit of a triangle." Joan would share with Grove some of her letters from Faulkner as they arrived on the Bard campus. "She would go to the mailbox in the coffee shop. We had these little glass boxes with a brass frame around them and a key. Bard was very small then, slightly over two hundred students. My graduating class was slightly over sixty. I would go there with her and there would usually be a letter from Faulkner. She would keep it to herself and usually show it to me afterward. When she won the *Mademoiselle* short-story contest she really felt that anything could happen to her; that she could get her feet on the ground. She was given a tremendous boost. That had happened and Faulkner was writing to her. She was very happy."

Grove and Joan were "very much a couple" on the campus. "I saw both hurt and melancholy in her, poignant for one so youthful ... we were both distant from our families—mine living in Egypt—and [were] lonely people. She had a great need for love and affection—being held and cared for.... We created, as young people can, a tender and affectionate world of our own."[171]

Grove, fictionalized in *The Wintering* as Leigh, was the kind of real-life reassurance Maude Williams welcomed. In Joan's novel, Leigh dismisses Amy's innocent explanation of the author's visit. Instead, he believes Almoner hopes to realize his romantic intentions:

"And so," Leigh said, "Almoner's coming East to see you." He was meticulous and had made his way carefully through early spring's mud ruts. On the Vermont hillsides, gouges that were ski trails revealed lonesome-looking rocks. Forgetful, Amy had set her overnight case down on wet ground, where in places snow was accumulated and swirled through with dirt. Leigh, swinging her case to the overhead rack on the train, swung it carefully away from his overcoat with its beaver collar.... "Not to see me," she said, looking up. "To see his publishers."

> Leigh fit with difficulty long legs behind the seat in front of them and said, "How convenient. Just when you have a vacation."
> "You sound like some old biddy from home!" Amy said, hissing.
> "Oh, Amy," he said. "Are you really so naive?" He flipped open *Time* magazine to the political section, sighing weightily, with no time now for anything lesser than the world situation.
> "He has to see his publisher," Amy said, slowly and distinctly. How had she even in fantasy thought of marrying Leigh? In that coat and carrying an umbrella, he seemed slightly effeminate....
> Leigh, with some curiosity, looked up and said, "Where are you meeting him?"
> When she answered, "His hotel," Leigh twirled an imaginary mustache and cried, "Ah-hah!"[172]

Brandon Grove and Joan Williams in conversation at a Bard College dance in 1950 (courtesy Joan Williams).

Having met Faulkner earlier in the year in New York, Grove was pleased to see the author again at his home in Mississippi. Grove remembered taking the train to Memphis and meeting Joan's parents. He described P.H. Williams as "a rough-cut fellow, unaffectionate toward her [Joan], remote. I don't recall seeing a kind of father and daughter warmth. But, oh, he loved her. I sensed a sadness in her very early that I think primarily had to do with her family. I think Joan had felt perhaps hurt and rejected quite early on." Between Mr. and Mrs. Williams he noted a great distance. "Mrs. Williams was a lonely, lonely person. She worked hard at throwing a lovely party while I was visiting ... He [Mr. Williams] was one of the boys but she was very vulnerable."[173]

The vulnerability Grove noticed in Joan's mother, and Joan noticed in Estelle Faulkner, is conferred upon Joan in Faulkner's letters. Faulkner sometimes blamed a hurt in her past for Joan's inability or unwillingness to consummate their affair. While both Grove and Faulkner agreed upon some damage to Joan's psyche, Faulkner's letters emphasize a healing through sex.

With all these issues in the air, Joan and Grove left Memphis for Oxford and an afternoon of sailing. Grove said, "I remember Joan was nervous about it. I mean there was tension all over the place. I knew what was going on. It was pure theatre. We went first to his house, Rowan Oak, and I was so impressed by it, a long, straight driveway and big trees. I thought it was a southern mansion. It was sparsely furnished. And inside I saw his type-writer which was old. In his own surroundings he seemed weighed down, restrained, tense. He was a quiet, gracious host."

From Rowan Oak the four went by car to Sardis Lake. Naturally, Grove wondered about the nature of the Faulkner marriage and remarked that Estelle was somewhat in the background. "I remember her only dimly and I was surprised that she was there. She was quiet and not particularly attrac-tive. I found it an odd match," he said.[174]

Mrs. Faulkner provided a picnic lunch and Joan remembers "a huge basket of sandwiches. That's all I remember thinking about how much food there was for us. And we went out sailing. She [Mrs. Faulkner] was very nice to me. I don't know if at that point she guessed there was anything incipi-ent about Faulkner and me. I guess not.[175] I know afterward—I can't remem-ber when—she said to me she didn't think that boy [Brandon Grove] was nice enough for me. I thought she was very maternal. He was nice enough, whatever she said. She seemed like a nice southern lady like I had grown up knowing. She seemed old, but for me she *was* old."[176]

Grove did not feel that tensions existed between himself and Faulkner. Faulkner never explicitly asked Grove about his feelings for Joan and he did not believe Faulkner was jealous. "I did not feel threatened and whether he did toward me I have no reason to think that." Grove believes Joan was "conflicted but also flattered."

Fictionalized, the afternoon on the *Minmagary* is transformed to a day at the Fish-o-rama, a fishing competition complete with a fly-tying contest. *The Wintering* pursues the Fish-o-rama in some detail. At a later meeting, Jeff tells Amy how he enjoyed looking at her slip—"It made you seem so like a little girl. A white ruffle showed"[177]—and Amy responds with horror that she spent all day with her slip trailing. "Almoner longed to say it had not been only the weather that had made the Fish-o-rama ghastly. If only some-day she would look at him as he had seen her glance once at Leigh."[178]

In a masterful paragraph from *The Wintering*, Jeff's worries about Leigh are resolved (though Joan and Grove's friendship continued for some time). Much is made in the novel about the hopes of Amy's mother, Edith [Maude], that Amy and Leigh are serious and that the relationship will lead to mar-riage. As Jeff and Amy stroll around a lake on a lovely September afternoon, a toddler tosses pebbles into the water:

Amy watched enviously the smooth glittering retreat of the fish, to hide beneath rocks. As smoothly had Leigh retreated. She thought perhaps she had treated him as expectantly as Edith and that had been her mistake. The quick, slick glimmer of the goldfishes' backs transferred in her mind's eye, becoming her party, the ceiling transformed into a night sky shiny with tinsel stars. Only, when the lights had come on fully and the last guest had gone, there had appeared instead a somewhat droopy dark blue canvas. By then, too, the hopeful look Edith had worn all during Leigh's visit had disappeared. When he was eventually waving from the departing plane's window, she had said, "Why did he come here? What did he want?"

"To see the South," Amy had said, realizing the truth.

"For God's sake then, why didn't you let him take a Cook's Tour!" Edith had cried. Now, Leigh had gone off to Yale to graduate school.[179]

Grove did notice Mrs. Williams' hopes for something more in their romance and felt that Joan was more inclined for a serious relationship than he, something Joan confirmed. "Well we never talked about getting married. But it was serious on my part in the sense that I wanted to get married so badly, and I wanted that because of my insecurities. I don't think he ever wanted to get married, to me anyway."[180] Grove said that at twenty-one years he was not ready for marriage. "My life was very uncertain. I had to go into the Navy. And I was a little frightened by her [Joan's] dependency."

Though the intensity of Joan and Grove's relationship lightened after his Memphis visit, they still saw each other in New York during Grove's graduate days. On one occasion Joan and Faulkner came to Princeton and Grove "arranged a meeting with Faulkner and a group of graduate students—perhaps forty—in a large room." Grove credited Faulkner's Princeton appearance to Joan's influence, "a favor for Joan." Grove recalled Faulkner's soft voice and composed responses to the graduate students gathered in his Princeton residence. "Faulkner was not prepared but just sat around and answered questions. He was very happy to do it. He spoke to mostly literature students, undergraduate and postgraduate. And in his slow fashion answered questions for two hours. He had no set speech. I was perhaps a little disappointed. I was not quite prepared but I had to make the opening remarks!"[181]

Grove said he and Joan saw Faulkner "quite a bit in New York. When Joan lived in the Village and I at Princeton, Faulkner visited her often. He seemed to me a father figure to her; I never saw signs of sexual affection. He was obviously fond of her—never unfriendly toward me—quite the opposite ... he not only tolerated me, but befriended me, something I deeply appreciated."

One day Grove took his copy of *Soldiers' Pay* to Joan's apartment, and Faulkner inscribed it "with tenderest regards" May 1953.[182] Joan recounted the book-signing incident quite differently. She felt Grove intruded on her friendship with Faulkner by showing up with his book. When she expressed this feeling to Faulkner, he merely shrugged and said, "That's what people do."[183]

What drew Faulkner to Joan? Grove believed Faulkner felt "happiness in being with her. He admired her desire to be a writer and her persistence in developing the relationship, her youth, physical attractiveness, and sweet nature. There was a conspiratorial, clandestine element to the relationship, and there was their kindred Southernness. She was very accepting of him— unchallenging of him as a person, his drinking and marriage. She filled the spaces between his sadness and pain. And there was pride and gratification in knowing she loved him, tender to a man his age."[184] He described his conversations with Faulkner as very relaxed: "We talked about everything." The conversations about writing and literature, however, were generally between Joan and Faulkner. "The writing was something that he and Joan could understand together that I was out of. I once asked him why he wrote in such long sentences. He didn't answer."[185]

———

Faulkner was skeptical of Joan's "outside" relationships—worried she might marry a champion of the middle class—though he seemed to genuinely like Grove. Regarding her search for the "perfect" relationship, "He thought I [Joan] was like him, searching for something that didn't exist."[186] Meanwhile, their times together were limited and unsatisfying. Following the afternoon on the *Minmagary*, Joan writes from her Memphis home:

aug. 30, 1950
Wed.

that day was strange all right, nothing to write about, maybe talk over sometime, one subtle, restrained, hidden, interpreted, silent.
if only we could just go off and sit and look at the sea or the city or anything, to just go and think about, not to make plans, and not because there is no sense or use to doing so since there is no security and perhaps no future but because we just don't have to and don't want to. maybe to write something else, whatever strikes us, or to continue with what we are doing, improving, humanizing, making passionate, real and living, and breathing.
what to do now, where to go, what to care about.
i like your house.
until i hear from you then for now nothing much else to write about. I feel like the day—plain grey.

j—

Yes, Faulkner writes, Joan sounds blue. The day didn't allow for much conversation, but then, they don't need to talk much, do they? The four-paragraph letter, like most others, contains distinct topics: the afternoon on his boat; Joan's letters; the play; and in the final paragraph, a rekindling of affection through a creative reflection of past experiences. "We need 2nd Ave., a Berkshire hill, something like that—snow, a little boot of a bug trying to go somewhere in the snow, God knows where or why, snow in your hair and not making any noise at all like your face, lips, so that even the snow smells like a young girl, woman. You fell down and then I fell down, remember? And the cold windy street and Haas's elevator, and how scared you were and that evening you spent acting like an extremely well-bred, well-behaved child? Hello, Joan, Miss Williams, sweet love. I didn't even have a chance to tell you what a pretty girl-white white—slip, isn't that it?—you had on that day."[187] Of interest regarding *Requiem* is Faulkner mentioning a need to absorb atmosphere. Before he writes the act dealing with the governor and the evolution of Mississippi's capital [Act Two: THE GOLDEN DOME (Beginning Was the Word)] he plans a trip to Jackson, Mississippi. He wishes Joan would join him.[188]

Returning to Joan's desire to write more short stories, Faulkner writes a long, seemingly inspired letter proposing a story idea with a situation clearly paralleling their own. He specifies that the story should be told in third person from the girl's point of view. Joan should recall the day he visited her at Bard and their walk in the snow—what they did, and how she felt.

> .... A young woman, senior at school, a man of fifty, famous—could be artist, soldier, whatever seems best. He has come up to spend the day with her. She does not know why, until after he has gone. They talk, about everything, anything, whatever you like. She is more than just flattered that a man of fame has come up to see her; she likes him, feels drawn to an understanding, make it wisdom, of her, of people, man, a sympathy for her in particular; maybe he will of a sudden talk of love to her. But she will know that is still not it, not what he came for; she is puzzled a little; when he gets on the train, she is sad, probably worried; she does not know why, is uncomfortable because she is troubled. There is something inconclusive, yet she cannot imagine what conclusion there could be between the two of them. But she knows he came for some reason, and she failed to get it, whether he thought she would or not or is disappointed that she didn't. Then she finds out why he came, what he wanted, and that he got it. She knows it the next day; she receives a telegram that he is dead, heart; she realises that he knew it was going to happen, and that he wanted to walk in April again for a day, an hour.[189]

He bemoans one fact at the letter's conclusion: when he gets hot on the typewriter, he can't type.[190]

The story idea struck Joan as gimmicky and it was not something she

tried to develop. Faulkner frequently cautioned her to write from the outside which was not her style. Faulkner told her, "Don't write from the inside
out, well, I've always written from the inside out."[191]

> My writing has always just come when I felt it or ... lived it or something.
> I remember one thing he said about writing [that] was the difference between
> us was that he set out as early as possible to learn as much as he could and
> I hadn't. Why didn't he tell me what he learned? Nobody was telling me
> what to read, what to learn. What did he learn? How was I supposed to learn
> it and why didn't he teach me?[192]
> He was too esoteric for me. The first book he told me to read was–oh, God,
> something by Flaubert. And not even Madame Bovary. It was called Sappho[193]
> or something, about the Peloponnesian Wars. I mean, *nobody* could read it.
> He told me to read Don Quixote and things like that. I know they're great
> novels but they had no relationship to my writing. I was a 20-year-old and
> not a very well-educated one. I mean you can't sit down and read Don
> Quixote at 20.[194]

———

Joan fretted through the fall of 1950. Her job with a Memphis insurance company bored her and her writing was not what she hoped. Faulkner
attests that people need stupidity and that the only tragedy will be if
she can't take it. She has not disappointed or failed him; he is not trying to
compel her to write: "I like you as you are; only incidentally because I believe
that some day you will find yourself, write it, make it." And while it may
have been that belief which drew him in the beginning it also may have been
vanity—"Lucifer's own pride: I dont, refuse to believe that I can take you—
a young woman—into my life, spirit, and not have her make something new
under the sun whether she wills it or not. So dont worry at what you consider wasted time. If I can wait at 50, you certainly can at 20."[195]

> Oct. 18, 1950
> Bill–you are practically all that's left in this ridiculous process of
>   living. The only one who really understands–about the job so
>   perfectly. We're wasting time–this is life to grab while it is
>   here–and I don't want to look back ten years from now and
>   wonder why we didn't see each other when we are so close–.
>   This is a miracle–we two found each other, and understand
>   each other so well. Unless, I assume too much in thinking that
>   I, too, understand *you*–and that this is some relief to you in
>   life. Thank you for your continual faith in me, not yet
>   justified. I want to start on a play now. In some ways I'd like to
>   start fresh–with something new, to build together from scratch,
>   except I don't want to cause "Requiem" to be wasted–from the

material nor the time standpoint. It is a grind, day after day,
but helps set one's mind in order. These days are so beautiful!
I keep thinking of the Oct. after that first Aug. that you said
you stood up in the woods one day and started to come to
N.Y. to see me. I want us to walk through the leaves some
afternoon~ always with love~
                    joan

Faulkner believed that two people out of the teeming millions coming
together—in orbit together—must have a purpose. God at the very least is
a gentleman, and would not waste their union. In *Requiem*, Gavin Stevens
explains or believes he is explaining Temple's attraction to, Pete, Alabama
Red's brother "a bad man":

> And if this is what you meant, you are right too: a man, at least a man, after
> six years of that sort of forgiving which debased not only the forgiven but
> the forgiven's gratitude too~a bad man of course ... destined to bring noth-
> ing but evil and disaster and ruin to anyone foolish enough to enter his orbit,
> cast her lot with his.[196]

And about God's role in Temple's fate, Stevens asserts: "And since
God~if there was one~must be aware of that, then she too would bear her
side of the bargain but not demanding on Him a second time since He—if
there was one—would at least play fair, would be at least a gentleman."[197]
Though the context of this dialogue has little in common with the
specifics of Joan and Faulkner's relationship, it is fascinating to note the
play's diction seeping into Faulkner's letters or vice versa. He would write
Joan that she has cast her lot with his, and his expressed concern that he
might in some way harm or tarnish her could be construed as "disaster" or
"ruin." However, the tone of his actual letter—that their being in orbit
together is a positive for both—dispels such a negative interpretation.
Returning to Joan's 18 October letter, Faulkner declares her that he too
wants to walk in the leaves, but doubts one afternoon would suffice. Despite
Faulkner's long and effusive assurance that they will make something together
one day, whether it is tangible or not,198 Joan's discontent swells.

Oct. 25, 1950

I know so well what you mean about sticking it out to Christmas, but I've
stuck it out two weeks since I've begun to hate it like hell, and finally I decided
it was too much waste so I quit today: it isn't admirable but I know I *could*
have stuck it out, so I don't feel to [sic] badly. I want to wander away—
autumn much more than spring even fills me like this. I am going to N.Y.
to Bard til Thanksgiving. I'll be back then~if I go~you know how it is~a new
smell, the smell of leaves somewhere else~where one Feb. you fell and I fell
in the snow. I will let you know~don't be disappointed in me~I love you
                    Joan

This short note receives an angry rebuttal from Faulkner. She should go then, damn it. People are queer (perhaps in their need for new and varied environments). He grieves at the thought of her being fifteen hundred miles away, yet when she was a mere seventy miles, they still did not see much of each other.[199] Joan remembers his unhappiness at her decision to leave Memphis, but believes that if he had made her understand the importance of her locale for her writing, she would have stayed. "He never said to [stay in my part of the country] for writing. And that I should be exploring all those people. And I think if he had I would have probably stayed. I've always felt he didn't help me as much as he could have. I mean talk. Because when I got ready to leave, and I guess at that point we were driving around Memphis, he said, 'don't leave your own people.' Well, I was supposed to leave the next day. But he still didn't say, 'don't leave your own people because you ought to write about them.' I think if he had said something like that I would have probably stayed home. Which I should have as far as my writing."[200]

Nov. 1, 1950

dearest Bill~

I hope that last letter was not one really of anger~but just an outburst of the same hopeless frustration that I feel. The same frustration at not being able to make my mother stop drinking, of not being able to talk to my father, not even being able to get up the courage yet to ask him if I can go, just quietly making my few simple plans, which might be dashed about my head when finally I have to actually stand before him and say "I want...."

Oh hell, Bill, hell hell hell—— I want to see you too. I want to somehow reach you, lose my restraint, timidity~all the things that keep us from being close. I would give anything to be somewhere alone, to do, think as we pleased.

As much as I'd like to see you, talk to you, mainly have you talk to me, a meeting of an afternoon in Memphis isn't particularly happy sounding~ you know what I mean~and I certainly want you to come since that seems to be the only way we can manage. If I go it will be a week from tomorrow and I will return by Thanksgiving.

How often I have wanted to send for you, or go to you~: have wanted to say leave all of them and I'll leave here and we'll go to California and live forever~not giving a damn what anyone else says. But we never will, Bill, I don't think, do you? It doesn't work out in storybooks when people don't care anything about any other people~much less in real life.

I have tried so hard to write the story about us~I don't think I can write. All the spontaneity has been finally drained I feel, after years and years of living in this family.

Today I looked all over for violets but no one has any~they come later, they said, and I hope you won't mind waiting until then.

I never forget you~
Joan

"Every letter from you is a violet," Faulkner replies, "and everytime I think of you is one, the color of your eyes, your hair, the shape of your mouth, the shape (imagined) of your body under your clothes, girl woman of course but not screaming at you as most are...."[201] She has retained her modesty unlike thousands of other women. Then, seeming to contradict the beauty of innocence and modesty, Faulkner reminds her again that she has not matured. He is waiting for that even as he realizes no one can help someone mature any more than they can help someone get born.[202] Maturation becomes a mantra—a subliminal message for sexual adjustment and accommodation—and another form of pressure in Joan's mind. Much as he admonished Joan to free herself from the petty Southern middle class, so too does he write her to hurry and grow up. "People need trouble, fret, a little of frustration, to sharpen the spirit on, toughen it. Artists do; I don't mean you need to live in a rathole or gutter, but they [artists] have to learn fortitude, endurance.[203] Happiness, he concludes, belongs only to vegetables.[204]

A decline of modesty surprised Joan in relation to the 1950s. "So long ago I think of people as being modest still. I don't think we went around dressing sexily. But then I don't see how he could have thought of all that." How to explain Faulkner's interpretation that women's bodies are screaming at him? "You could get down to the point of thinking maybe Faulkner was afraid of women. I think he had something of an inferiority complex about having been as short as he was. That might have been something when he was young. Dating, going around with everybody. I think he was very handsome, but he was short."[205]

———

The rumor of the Nobel Prize Joan mentioned in her mid–February letter to Faulkner received confirmation in early November. After a private phone call announcing his selection, Faulkner hung up without even telling his wife and daughter the news. Faulkner's reception mirrored that of the Howells Medal for Fiction when he told the New York correspondent for the Stockholm newspaper, "I won't be able to come to receive the prize myself. It's too far away. I am a farmer down here and I can't get away."[206] Faulkner's reaction was of course less about farming and more about state of mind. The unhappiness of these years and the despair he wrote of to Joan resounds in his response to the idea of the Stockholm trip: "There just isn't enough gas left in the tank to go all that distance."[207] Instantly members of the Faulkner household engaged in tactics similar to the premiere of Intruder in the Dust in Oxford. The net was cast much farther this time, involving phone calls to and from the American embassy. One way or another, Faulkner personally would receive the 1949 Nobel Prize for Literature. Oddly, his decision finally to go was probably colored by his wife's willingness to stay home. Joan knew the trip was an uphill battle from the start: "They had a hard time getting him on the plane and all to Stockholm. I know he didn't want to go and they got him to go. I have always thought that was very kind of her [Estelle] to agree not to go if he didn't want her to or something."[208]

Nov. 9, 1950

I wanted so much to call you—I started to several times yesterday and today, but every time I was afraid to—afraid the time was wrong—or that it would undo something we had tried hard to set up. I am leaving tomorrow (Friday) at 9 a.m.—After I saw about the Nobel Prize I wanted to call immediately to tell you how proud I am—and to wonder if maybe you would be coming to N.Y.—but thought you would let me know.

Hope that when I return I'll have something for you to read. I have missed you terribly lately.

Write me at 100 Bayard Lane, Princeton, N.J. If there is anything I can get you in N.Y. (the special tobacco) do for you—please let me know.

Until I see you—

Joan

When Joan hears from Faulkner it is clear that the reality of the prize is settling in at Rowan Oak. Faulkner describes it all as uproar and hurrah. He thanks her for the violet she sent and reminds her that he is going hunting the next day.

Princeton, N.J.
Monday
Nov. 13, 1950

Dear Bill—

I wish you were here to see this fascinating town; it is really picturesque, quaint, and atmospheric. Also cold. I was in New York only briefly and not long enough for it to have time to creep into my blood again, after being away so long. I think quietness is really what I want anyway, although I don't know what I want really I don't think. Not much to write about, but didn't want you to think I would forget to write. Of course I have been confronted with you at every turn with your picture all over every front page. I am so proud about the prize and I hope that it makes you happy. I am enclosing the write up from the Times in case you might not have it and might be interested in having it.

I will be home for Thanksgiving.

Joan

The hunting trip came off as usual with lots of bourbon and camaraderie. Faulkner was slipping into a serious alcoholic state, and when he replies to Joan's letters, his barely legible handwriting confirms his deteriorated condition. The letter, though riddled with errors, misspelled words, and strike-throughs, conveys strong feelings. He has been wanting to call Joan, but when he returned from hunting and her name came up, so too did all the stink.[209] "I don't know when I will see you, but you are the one I never stop thinking about. You are the girl's body I lie in bed beside before I go to sleep. I know every sweet red hair and sweet curve on it. Don't forget me. I love you."[210]

No one will ever know for sure what persuaded Faulkner to make the trip. Biographers portray it as Estelle's coup de grace. She claimed she did not want to go to Sweden but believed this was Jill's one opportunity to travel abroad. Faulkner adopted this explanation, saying finally, "the trip will be a success if Jill enjoys it."[211] What is the likelihood that Mrs. Faulkner would not want to travel to Sweden to see her husband receive the Nobel Prize? Did she intuit that her presence would deter her husband from making the trip?

The intricacies of this marriage, coming as it did at the end of a difficult and circuitous relationship, cannot be overstated. As a young boy, Faulkner lived only two houses from the Oldhams, and by the time he was seventeen years, he was writing poems for and about Estelle. On 19 March 1915, the Oxford paper mentioned Faulkner's attendance at a masked ball hosted by Major and Mrs. Oldham.[212] Mr. Oldham stood out in the community as a staunch Republican but his family lineage and that of his wife was good and they were able to integrate themselves into the better Oxford social circles.

Even with Faulkner and Estelle's long history as hometown sweethearts, they were unable to capture an early future together. When the time came for marriage, Faulkner was undone by his uncertain future. He was not the suitor one would conjure for a young socialite from a prominent Oxford family; after all, Faulkner was a high-school dropout drifting from one low-paying job to another. The Oldhams were less than enamored with the prospect of William Faulkner as son-in-law and they refused to entertain the idea. They feared Faulkner's inability to provide for their daughter and believed the Faulkners to be too "democratic" in their assessment of class strictures.[213]

During those years of courtship, Faulkner watched Estelle vacillate between her love for him and her desire to take the expected path: a marriage to a successful man from the right family. When Estelle "found" herself engaged to Cornell Sidney Franklin in 1918, she declared herself "surprised." Franklin represented everything Faulkner was not. He was a lawyer, a major in the National Guard, and hopeful of a judiciary career. With the encroaching wedding, Faulkner faced a very real depression.

"Mixed with his pain and sense of loss was his bitterness toward Estelle. Somehow, he felt, she could have resisted the pressures to marry a man she didn't love."[214]

With Estelle and Franklin's marriage behind him, Faulkner did not reluctantly release Estelle as his muse, but instead he produced an eighty-eight-page volume of poetry titled *Vision in Spring* written for her. When he presented this gift to Estelle in 1921, she was in her third year of marriage to Franklin and a mother. Such was the ongoing commitment Faulkner felt for Estelle, for despite her marriage and motherhood, he stayed very much in the picture when she would visit her parents. On 20 June 1929, just two months after Estelle's marriage to Franklin dissolved, she and Faulkner married. In addition to a wife, the author had a new family: Estelle's seven-year-old son, Malcolm, and her ten-year-old daughter, Victoria, or Cho-Cho as she was called.

One would think that having at last secured his longtime sweetheart, Faulkner would settle into something close to happiness. Instead the couple got off to a tumultuous start. The Oldhams still resisted the marriage, even though as a divorcée with two small children Estelle probably felt socially ostracized. Faulkner, on the other hand, imbues the union with intrigue and secrecy. He writes his publisher, Harrison Smith, for $500 in immediate funds: "I am going to be married. Both want to and have to. THIS PART IS CONFIDENTIAL, UTTERLY. For my honor and sanity—believe life—of a woman."[215] Faulkner's sensational explanation continues: "This is not bunk; neither am I being sucked in. We grew up together and I don't think she could fool me in this way; that is, make me believe that her mental condition, nerves, are this far gone. And no question of pregna[n]cy; that would hardly move me...."[216] Joan felt that this letter confirms Faulkner's penchant for a "frantic kind of intrigue. I never have known what that letter meant. That kind of stuff strikes me as something he made up. He liked to be dramatic."[217] "I think of him as being a very unhappy man. Now that might have been his nature to be unhappy. I think you always get back to the essential thing: Why did he marry Estelle? He certainly never seemed happy with her."[218]

The bizarre quality of that letter carried over to the newlyweds' Pascagoula honeymoon, where Estelle, wearing an extravagant silk dress, walked into the Gulf in what has been described as a suicide attempt. Estelle's perhaps desperate cry for attention followed a night of heavy drinking.[219] A disturbing and destructive pattern of behavior was established just weeks into their marriage. The Mississippi Coast vacation also was disrupted by work: Faulkner proofed *The Sound and the Fury* manuscript on his honeymoon.

What Faulkner chose to relate to Joan about his wife was conveyed mostly in his letters. He wrote "about her drinking and her not understanding what he was trying to do and that kind of thing. And he told me about her throwing the manuscript [*Light in August*] out the car window."[220] The emotional estrangement, Faulkner was quick to relate, affected his physical relationship with his wife, or so he claimed. He once told Meta Carpenter that he and his wife had not been intimate since the birth of his daughter in 1933, and Joan agreed this might have been possible.

Equally possible would be the desired effect such a statement would have on a potential lover. An interview with Albert Isaac "Buzz" Bezzerides contradicts Faulkner's claim to Meta. Bezzerides, an author and scriptwriter, became friends with Faulkner when they both worked in Hollywood, and in 1944 and 1945 Faulkner frequently would stay with the Bezzerideses. The Faulkners reciprocated in the late 1940s and Bezzerides and his wife spent the night at Rowan Oak.

> We all sat around talking, getting tipsy. Soon we went to our various bedrooms. I was always very aware of that sliding door that separated Faulkner and his wife, lying in their bed from us lying in ours, but there was no sign of embarrassment by anybody. But, on this night, I awoke about two or three o'clock in the morning, and I heard this fierce, vicious whisper of Estelle's voice: "Don't touch me, Bill. I don't want you to touch me. Don't you touch me." I woke up my wife and she heard Estelle protest, and in the middle of all this, there was a sound I'll never forget: that sharp, intense striking of a hand against flesh. He had apparently slapped her face. Just to hear that slap inflicted pain; and then silence. Shortly after that, we became aware of a sexual encounter on the other side of the door.... Next morning, Estelle was as cheerful as she could possibly be when we sat down to eat with her and Bill.[221]

Naturally, Joan heard only what Faulkner wanted her to hear, and the state of his marriage, though evidently difficult, was still something he was reluctant to abandon. "There was a point when they thought Mrs. Faulkner was going to die, and I thought, if she dies I will marry him, but I never said that to him. See, that's what I mean about not talking. I didn't say 'Oh, if she dies I will marry Bill.' I didn't want to be responsible for breaking up that marriage. I think that the point ought to be brought out that as much as he talks about not liking women and not liking marriage, in his books and things like that, he never ever freed himself. When I was in college why didn't I say, 'Well, get a divorce and then I'll talk about marrying you,' but it never occurred to me to do something like that. The only person it seems who ever wanted to marry him was Meta Carpenter and he never seemed to want to marry her."[222] "I think that is the interesting thing, that he could have had another wife, but he didn't want to when he could."[223]

———

Perhaps believing the introduction of yet another woman in his life would hasten Joan along the path he desired, Faulkner's letter to Joan from London following the Nobel ceremony makes an oblique reference to such. Writing Joan that he loved her and missed her, he also tells her that he discovered in Stockholm he wasn't quite as old as he thought he was.[224] His remark, Joan believed, was an attempt to make her jealous.[225] The woman in question was most likely Else Jonsson who, like Joan, was a redhead with "violet, blue-grey eyes."[226] Else's deceased husband, Thorsten Jonsson, was an admirer and friend of Faulkner's. Else seemed a calming influence during the Nobel ceremonies and during his last day in Stockholm Faulkner took her to lunch.

Just days before Christmas 1950 two letters are exchanged. Joan's—part poem, part reminiscence—assumes a dream-like state:

Dec. 20, 1950

Will we ever ever
Eversuch as before
Walk the streets in anonymity.

Now? Not now, no
There is nonesuch
Left for you and me,

Who, however, never
Tread alone ever
Except in heart.

Can we then? Can,
Must, Will, together
Go all the way,

Handdistant or near.
For knowing you once,
I am with you forever.

That is what it was ... just waiting
in a kind of suspended state, not even of unrest, quietness, doing nothing-
ness, that I could not even understand myself, waiting for you to come back.
Just knowing you are there and all right makes me more restless, perhaps
because of the shortness of the distance and a desire to create something
together, but I do not think maybe a play
Time after Christmas ...
Time

and suddenly then there was no more time not because of anything tangible, immediate, human, real understandable but because we have been
tricked, cheated, foiled-fooled and the whole world is being blown up and
we didn't count on that. But how was I to know that there wasn't time to
mature but that one had to get up one morning and over the brushing of
teeth know that the foam was not madness but that one had to be different
today and from now on, that this is not life, but the end and I must be ready
and face what is not to come, and understand how to fall on my face in the
basement and not breathe the fumes, but why not? when I come upstairs
there is nothing here....

But you were really with me all the time, closer probably than when we
[were] actually together, for it stayed with me, Light in August, and is even
now, for I hate to ever finish one because I hate for it ever to be over and
the terrible horrible wonderful feeling of reading it for the first time can
never be again, and although then I feel old and wise because I have read
it and cannot go back to the time when I hadn't read it, and anciently would
like to take one by the hand and say prepare, read, feel, revel, and I would
be the teacher

And I would say this is the second greatest book in the world, after The
S and the F ...

And you come across a word and go back and say to yourself it was so
much a part of the context I almost didn't see this astounding thing, hear
the sound of the word, and yet it jumped out and was itself and you think
thank god for letting me see it

It doesn't seem like Christmas does it?

I once knew a hundred things to say to you when you got back and now
there is nothing, but that is peace I guess.

I am sorry about your not seeing the story but after awhile I didn't know
anymore what it said or whether it was terrible good fair or what but then
it is probably better because it is mine now anyway except that I am afraid
that you are probably too much there, unavoidably, being simultaneously
saturated with Light and the memory of you yourself, but then that is natural anyway to "new" writers isn't it, that's me.

You are returned.

Faulkner's concise response addresses the issues at hand. He has found
her story among other papers. It is not quite right. They must meet to talk
about the story and to rekindle what is between them. He will come to Memphis under the guise of going hunting. Like Joan, he longs to recapture the
solitude and anonymity of New York. He wishes he knew of an apartment
they could borrow, but knows only a hotel. Then he writes that with the
recent hurrah (the Nobel) there would be a risk to Joan that he might be
recognized.[227]

A 27 December telegram to Joan's East Parkway home assures her that
he will be in Memphis by bus on Thursday. Such a message highlights the

inherent difficulty of communicating. While Faulkner was partial to sending Joan telegrams, they also served as a quick form of correspondence and were safer than phone calls. When Joan remembers calling Faulkner's home he usually answered and "his phone number was in the phone book. And that's why I've always been so annoyed about writers who don't put their number in the phone book." She did not call often, not wanting Mrs. Faulkner or Jill to answer. Sometimes she wrote him letters confirming or canceling meetings.[228]

The coy nature of Faulkner's 30 December letter suggests they were able to keep their engagement. Gone is his businesslike tone. This is a love letter that she doesn't need to read. He invites her to throw it away before reading it, or better, put a match to it. Then the letter assumes a fairy-tale quality. Should she decide to read on the story goes as such: One day when Joan gets to be a big girl they will go away together, sleep one sleep as they love one love, and... The story ends there. Joan is to write him if she wants to know the rest of it.

The year closes then on a note of incompleteness. Little has happened to advance this relationship, and the affair he envisions is, like his letter, very much a fairy tale.

III

1951—Other Loves

Without abandoning the themes conceived and sustained by their letters, for Joan and Faulkner, 1951 was anything but a consistent year. There was a great restlessness in Joan and to some extent in Faulkner as well. Joan left Memphis for a temporary position in admissions at Bard College during the spring. Her June 1950 graduation from Bard with a B.A. in English was followed by a series of jobs and volunteer work in Memphis, none of which captured her interest or advanced her foremost goal—to be a writer, a "literary" writer. Feeling adrift and unproductive, the phone call from Bard with a temporary position gave Joan a welcome respite. She returned home in the summer when other options were not readily apparent. Faulkner's script-writing career took him to Hollywood. Then, attempting to adapt *Requiem* to the stage, he spent time in New York and Cambridge.

The honors the year would hold for Faulkner again seemed inadequate to dispel his inherent unhappiness. *Notes on a Horsethief*, later to become part of *A Fable*, was published in February by Levee Press. In March, Saxe Commins accepted on Faulkner's behalf The National Book Award for *The Collected Stories*. That May, the French bestowed upon Faulkner the award of Legion of Honor. This he chose personally to accept from the French Consul, traveling to New Orleans in October 1951.

What might have been a low-key semester for Joan at Bard was enhanced by a bit of celebrityism. Her friendship with Faulkner made an impromptu appearance by the author possible. Dr. Theodore Weiss, a former Bard student and a professor there for twenty years, recalled Faulkner's appearance as spontaneous and entirely Joan's doing. "She said, 'Mr. Weiss, Faulkner is in New York. I could get him to come here. If you give me your car, I'll go get him.'" Once the transportation was arranged, and Faulkner was on campus, addressing the Bard community the evening of 2 May, Dr. Weiss recounted being "startled and amazed by the short, delicate, dapper man." He thought he would be big and burly.[1] The Bard visit resulted in a 15 May 1951 article without byline appearing in *The Bardian*—"Faulkner Honors Bard with Sudden Visit"—and a personal sketch of Faulkner written by Joan for the occasion.

———

The year 1951 commenced with Faulkner pressing established themes: Joan's inability to thaw and how her frozenness impedes her artistic development. On 9 January 1951 he sends an encouraging note about a short story Joan sent him. Though too long and a little obscure, it will not need a lot of work to succeed. He writes that if it is unclear to him, it will be to many others. Instead of returning a draft he simply tells her to write it again (for him if that will help).[2]

A long letter followed just six days later. Faulkner writes that he wants no duty letters from her, only letters that will make her happy to write—news she doesn't want to share with anyone else. Domestically, there has been trouble as Mrs. Faulkner answered Joan's phone call, and, still on a Christmas bender, she began threatening Faulkner with calls she planned to make to the Williams home. His response was to put the phone out of commission.[3] He didn't know how seriously to take her threat and did believe that she might have behaved even if she had called Joan's home. Even drunk, he writes, Estelle has the instincts of a lady in her somewhere.

Finally, he hopes that by writing Joan on a day he was happy, he might send her some happiness. His believes his happiness will break down her emotional block, what is frozen inside her. He doesn't believe that she is frigid but perhaps that she was damaged by her childhood. His intention is to be the one to cure her—to help her lose her restraint and self-consciousness—because once she stops resisting he believes she will write.[4] The sheer number of letters Joan received of this nature is remarkable. All of which she characterized as "pressures. And might be true too."[5]

———

Just as Joan was gearing up for her return to Bard College, Faulkner received a lucrative script-writing offer from Howard Hawks. The job, he writes, will take him to Hollywood for about two months and he implores Joan to consider meeting him there. Once there, they will be discreet. This may be the catharsis she needs, but her heart must consent as well. That is the only way it will be right for them.[6]

About the proposed Hollywood trip, Joan said, "I didn't know how to do anything like that. If it had been Jean Stein she would have gone. I didn't know what to do. One time he said get your passport and come to Egypt. I didn't know how to get a passport. If he had gotten it for me and said go down now and get one, or I'll get your ticket to Hollywood and we'll go. I didn't know what to do. But wouldn't it have been fantastic if I had gone? I don't know [what] I would have said to my parents. 'Guess where I am, I'm in Hollywood with William Faulkner.' I couldn't see myself doing that either. I could have made up some excuse about how I got there I guess as long as I wasn't asking them for money. There again he never offered to pay my way or anything like that, but I don't think at the time I thought of it in terms of money, but you would think that would be something somebody in his position would do. There was no way I could have walked out of Parkway[7] [for] Hollywood. I wanted to be a movie star, but I didn't even know how to do that on my own, much less say I'm going to meet William Faulkner. If I had been a different type of person, but somebody from my background ... I don't imagine that once you got there you would have to be discreet either."[8] "I never would have had the aplomb to do that kind of thing."[9]

Prior to his 1 February departure for Hollywood, where he would work on the script *The Left Hand of God*, based on a novel by William E. Barrett, Faulkner writes Joan a letter that sounds as if he has given up on their future. Even though he thinks she is wonderful and he loves her, he believes he is the wrong one to help her. It is a little sad, a little grief, a little death. Perhaps someone else will succeed in removing the block. She will, he assures her, write someday[10]: "Maybe now you haven't anything to say. You have to have something burning your very entrails to be said; you dont have that yet but dont worry about it; it is not important whether you write or not; writing is important only when you want to do it, and nothing nothing nothing else but writing will suffice, give you peace."[11]

This letter also includes as congratulation to Joan securing a job as a stewardess with Chicago and Southern Airlines.[12] Faulkner thought it would be good as it would get her out of her situation (family presumably). She chose not to accept the job, returning instead to Bard.

The two letters that follow on Beverly-Carlton stationery demonstrate Faulkner's wildly shifting mood: "Here I am until about March 1st. Fantastic place, fantastic work, almost worth the 2000 a week they pay me. Send the 3rd act to me here. I wish I could see you. Talked with your mother when I passed through Memphis that day. Tell me about the job.[13] Bill."[14]

In Joan's opinion, this letter was "surprising because he was always very derogatory about Hollywood. 'A bunch of ants living on a celluloid hill.' ... He wrote so much that would have been novels of fiction that went into trying to write scripts. And they found these scripts that nobody could ever use because he wasn't a good scriptwriter. But there would be ideas in there for things that eventually he would write." Two thousand dollars a week was "a tremendous amount of money for the time. And once he got there they kept having him back and back. Lauren Bacall said he wrote fifteen pages of dialogue for the actor to speak. Well, an actor can't speak fifteen pages and that it was just awful."[15]

His next letter to Joan is more in keeping with her impressions of Faulkner and Hollywood: "This one is very belated. I have been very busy, I was to get a bonus by writing the script within 4 weeks which I successfully accomplished this morning, with one day to spare.[16] ... This is a nice town full of very rich middle class people who have not yet discovered the cerebrum, or at best the soul. Beautiful damned monotonous weather, and I am getting quite tired of it, will be glad to farm again.[17] Bill."

Included in this letter is a personal note. He asks Joan to write him, to tell him about her job, if it has made her happier, and to tell him she loves him, as that can do no harm.[18]

———

Love or at least romance was very much on Faulkner's mind during this stint in Hollywood. He also resumed writing Meta Carpenter Rebner,[19] now remarried to her first husband, Wolfgang Rebner, an Austrian pianist. Meta confided in Faulkner: her marriage continued to be difficult and unhappy. They arranged to meet in Hollywood and she was waiting for Faulkner at the Beverly-Carlton where they rekindled their love affair. As a farewell token on their first night together in California, Faulkner gave Meta a copy of Notes on a Horsethief,[20] with a tender inscription, "This is for my beloved."[21] Besides being young and attractive Southerners—Meta from outside Tupelo, Mississippi, and Joan from Memphis—the two women had little in common. Joan was well educated and determined on a life as a writer. Meta harbored no such goals and admitted to being "painfully aware of [her] intellectual limitations."[22] And while Joan fretted the emotional and moral complications of an affair, Meta quickly and willingly met Faulkner's needs.

"I didn't have sense enough to realize how involved he was in Hollywood," Joan said, "and to ask him any questions. And I was so star struck it is a wonder I didn't. But he had been out there so many years earlier. And it is funny that Mrs. Faulkner didn't ever seem to have written about

Meta Carpenter. She did know all about that because she came to some-body's party in Hollywood and they had her [Meta] there as if [she] were Ben Wasson's friend. And she wrote someplace after, and said 'I wasn't fooled. I knew who she was.' And that kind of stuff is hard I think. She said in one letter she was sick of being the woman in the background who sup-posedly didn't know about all of these affairs and relationships."[23]

Biographers have noted Faulkner's dissatisfaction with Hollywood. How that may have contributed to his depression and subsequent drinking episodes was not something he chose to discuss with Dr. Adler or Dr. McCool, even though he was under their care during some of these sojourns to Hollywood. He never mentioned to either doctor his work or time in Hollywood. Still, that Hollywood caused distress and that distress often led to drinking was part of his cycle. Adler emphasized the depression and stressed that it is difficult to discern if depression proceeded the drinking or vice versa: "What comes first—the chicken or the egg? People frequently start drinking because they are unhappy about one thing or another. Then they feel bad because they drink too much. Alcoholism and depression go together. Especially chronic alcoholism. Like all alcoholics, Faulkner was in a state of chronic depression and drugs and alcohol gave him symptomatic relief."

Adler attributes deep periods of depression to the drinking cycle. "When a man is an alcoholic and drinks as much as he did, he has many times, low points, terrible periods of depression because they don't think much of themselves and the world and are ready to commit suicide. Chronic alcoholism is chronic suicide—identical, practically—because it is a form of self-destruction."[24]

To Joan, Faulkner never mentioned needing or wanting to quit drink-ing, although he frequently wrote her about feeling depressed. "...in those letters, he talks about ... he was depressed about me because I wouldn't do what he wanted me to do and various things. And at one point he wrote a letter to Saxe Commins and to me and said I [Faulkner] used to be the cat who walked alone but I am no longer. I think that was part of getting older and he knew his greatest work was behind him and he said 'I wish writing could be fun again like it used to be.' I think that just comes with age and he had a lot of physical pain—his back. I don't know, maybe he was unhappy because he couldn't get some young girl to marry him. I don't know. I'm sure there must have been plenty who would."[25]

Despite the fluidity with which the word binge enters contemporary vernacular when discussing alcoholism, Adler bristled at the notion: "I don't like that word, binge, because it's not a binge, it's a sickness. The man drank for a period until he went to a hospital, got sobered up, goes home and decides he won't drink anymore. Then something happens, some argument of some kind, some difficulty, and he starts drinking again. Of course at that time, if I'm not mistaken, his family wasn't too happy with his association with this Williams [Joan]. His wife didn't like it too much."

Contrarily, Joan did consider Faulkner a binge drinker. "Why everyone today seems to have this idea that he stayed drunk all the time, that he was a shambling drunk. He wasn't, and he couldn't have written what he did if he had been. He was basically a binge drinker. He did not get up every morning at 6 o'clock and have a drink with vodka in his orange juice. He could go for long periods without drinking, and he could drink socially without having a problem."[26] "But when he drank and ended up in a sanitarium, he would always have started before I saw him. But he told me he took Seconal and that would last a week. Well, my father did that too and I just thought that was what Southern men did."[27]

Robert Coughlan in his *Life* magazine piece, "The Private World of William Faulkner," wrote perhaps the most telling and expressive description of Faulkner's personality and his drinking, labeling Faulkner an "alcoholic refugee":

> He prefers to be an enigma and one can believe that he will always remain one, even to himself, for his inconsistencies go beyond artistic license or mere eccentricity. His is not a split personality but rather a fragmented one, loosely held together by some strong inner force, the pieces often askew and sometimes painfully in friction. It is to ease these pains, one can guess, that he escapes periodically and sometimes for periods of weeks into alcoholism, until his drinking has become legendary in the town and in his profession, and hospitalizations and injections have on occasion been necessary to save his life. After one of these episodes he returns for a relatively long period to an existence of calm sobriety; he is not an alcoholic but perhaps more accurately an alcoholic refugee, self-pursued.[28]

According to Adler, understanding Faulkner's bouts with depression would require an in-depth look at his entire life. "If you studied his life, you would probably find that even in his developmental years, probably later teens, he must have shown signs of emotional instability. It's a funny thing how people who are emotionally unstable have certain talents, are geniuses in certain ways."[29]

The family's proclivity for alcoholism also may have been a factor in Faulkner's case. Jimmy Faulkner, Faulkner's nephew, who died December 2001 in Oxford, was among the last family members to see Faulkner alive. Jimmy said both his great-grandfather and grandfather underwent the Keeley

Cure at the Keeley Institute that was located fifteen miles from Memphis. Developed by Leslie E. Keeley in 1896, the cure treated sufferers with an injection of double chloride of gold. While Keeley believed it made those he treated disinterested in alcohol, most doctors were skeptical of its long-term success.[30] Even though Jimmy accompanied Estelle on 5 July 1962 and helped see to Faulkner's admission to the Wright Sanitarium for excessive drinking, he believed that his uncle's drinking has received inordinate attention.

————

Following a two-week trip to Paris where he absorbed background for *A Fable* or the "big book" as he referred to it in letters to Joan, and where he also spent time with Else Jonsson, Faulkner stopped over in New York. The years of Joan and Faulkner's involvement parallel Faulkner's most intense work on *A Fable*. A complex and unwieldy book, outlined on the walls of Faulkner's Rowan Oak study, *A Fable* was more task than pleasure. Considering Faulkner's frequent bouts with "acute intoxication" during these years, and given the opinions of his treating psychiatrists in Memphis, it is evident that much of the agony Faulkner associated with writing *A Fable* resulted from his state of chronic depression. And Faulkner's depression most certainly had several sources: an unhappy marriage; a difficult and unwilling lover; a falling away of the joy he had once taken in his writing; and dark moods that perhaps were an innate part of his personality.

Joan's role in *A Fable*'s composition took many forms. She would serve as muse, someone for Faulkner to write not *to* but *for*.[31] She would carry a draft from Mississippi to Faulkner's New York editors. And in the final stage of the novel's gestation, she would help Faulkner sort the pages into a proper order. More so than the technical aspects, the emotional highs and lows of *A Fable*'s composition mirror those of their affair.

Surely at twenty-two years, Joan would hardly have classified herself as a "muse," yet the way she managed Faulkner fit the appellation, almost textbook if one considers the definition provided in Francine Prose's book *The Lives of the Muses*. "She [the muse] was smart enough to leave them wanting more, behavior that illuminates two central tenets of musedome: sex has relatively little to do with it; longing, on the other hand, is key.... Certainly, domestic life has little to do with artistic inspiration.... The 'art wife' is the long-suffering soul who brings up the rear in the author's acknowledgements. The muse reclines in splendor on the title page."[32]

Faulkner's letters clearly cast Joan in the role of muse and Estelle as "art wife." His ideas for recognizing Joan's musedome vacillate from telling her he would like to dedicate *Requiem for a Nun* to her, but cannot, fearing domestic upheaval; to suggesting they make love through the title page before *Requiem* goes to the binder;[33] to telling her that if she had not been working hard at her own writing he never would have finished *A Fable.*

———

At the time of his stopover in New York, longing was still quite central to Faulkner's response to Joan, and it was as a favor to Joan that he agreed to the Bard College appearance. According to the school newspaper, *The Bardian,* Joan made it clear that this was highly unusual and explained that "the author did not usually participate in literary discussions or make public statements concerning his work; he would therefore initiate no artistic discourse on his own but would instead answer questions from the audience."[34]

Joan recalled Faulkner's presence at Bard as spontaneous. He was in New York on business and agreed to a question and answer session. Faulkner, with no prepared remarks, spoke with students and faculty for about one hour. Joan followed up Faulkner's appearance with an article entitled "Personal Sketch," which appeared in the college's 15 May 1951 newspaper. Along with Joan's sketch, *The Bardian* ran a short article detailing the nature of his discussion:

> On May 2, Tuesday evening, the Bard community was honored with an unscheduled talk by William Faulkner, winner of the Nobel Prize for Literature and author of Light in August, As I Lay Dying, Sanctuary and several more novels and collections of short stories which have sold exceptionally well in the last twenty years.
>
> Mr. Faulkner, an unexceptional-looking man, was introduced by Miss Joan Williams.... He spoke for one hour answering questions on his taste in reading, his attitude toward his works, his attitude toward present-day life and narrating stories connected with his early life in relation to his writing.
>
> One point that he brought up repeatedly was the apathy that had come over him as he had grown older, making him less anxious to set words down on paper. He connected it with greater difficulty writers of this decade had in finding an audience, but toward the end of the discussion, when he became elated over the optimistic outlook of one member of the gathering, he showed that any disillusionments he might feel were individual ones and had no relation with any spirit of the times.
>
> I got the impression from Mr. Faulkner that he was not a deliberate artist and that after he had fixed the outline of a story he worked much more by feeling than by science. The discussion contained no clue as to what made Mr. Faulkner the inventor that he is of vivid characters, and exciting scenes nor did it explain his many experiments in story forms. Also missing from his talk was the stream of lively imagery which is typical of his writing. He

appeared instead as a man who, had he not known the wife of an established author who got Faulkner's first novel published, would have told his stories on the railing of the porch overlooking a Southern village square which is frequently the starting point of a Faulkner story.[35]

This distilled version of Faulkner's publication history overstates his book sales during the last twenty years—in 1945 Faulkner was effectively out of print and rarely had sold well—and oversimplifies Faulkner's publishing history. Faulkner was indebted to his Oxford friend, Phil Stone, for his tireless efforts in seeing his first book, *The Marble Faun*, a 51-page book of poetry, published. And his first novel, *Soldiers' Pay*, arrived at the publisher's desk with a letter of recommendation from Sherwood Anderson. Faulkner met Anderson's future wife, Elizabeth Prall, in 1921, when he worked for her in a New York bookstore. They kept track of each other through their mutual friend, author Stark Young. In 1925 their friendship revived when Faulkner lived for a time in New Orleans, where Prall, now Mrs. Sherwood Anderson, resided. Certainly there was a friendship, but it is doubtful that a letter from Sherwood Anderson guaranteed publication of *Soldiers' Pay*.

Ironically, while Anderson encouraged Faulkner and even promised a favor, Faulkner's finished manuscript coincided with Anderson's immersion in his own book, *Tar: A Midwestern Childhood*. Faulkner biographer Joseph Blotner quotes the message from Anderson regarding his letter to publishers Boni and Liveright: "I'll do anything for him [Faulkner] so long as I don't have to read his damn manuscript."[36]

The *Bardian* journalist was disappointed that Faulkner failed to "reenact" his stories, to create verbally the same "stream of lively imagery." The student was relieved, however, to note that Faulkner's was a personal depression and not symptomatic of the times. Such an article probably confirmed Faulkner's expectations about personal appearances, and sustained his desire to keep them at a minimum.

Maybe the school newspaper's account would have been different if Joan's sketch had preceded his appearance. In it, Joan attempts to foreground the Southern author for his Eastern audience. Joan places Faulkner within his hometown, shows his simple lifestyle, and mainstream interests— "hunting, fishing, and farming." Her purpose is not to reveal quaintness, but to position Faulkner in his own world, peopled with folks of his own doing, and to recognize his astounding independence. If her audience should also understand Faulkner's drive and artistic vision, so much the better:

"Personal Sketch"
If you could see the town and the roads leading in from the town where they lead from, you might understand him better. A sleepy town in a sleepy state where everyone for fifty miles or so around not only knows everyone

else but also knows their kinfolks, their personal history, past and present, and are pretty willing to predict their future. Colonel Faulkner of Oxford, Mississippi was just like everybody else. He was a prominent man in the town, and therefore, had a certain pattern to follow and certain obligations to fulfill: take part in the local elections, hang around the stores on Saturday afternoons to talk, usher in the church on Sunday mornings, and speak when met on the street. And those who carry his name have carried on the tradition pretty well, except for one of his sons, the one named Bill. He always stuck pretty much to himself.

He went to the University for a few months, in the tradition, but then one day he left, taking nothing with him but a raincoat and in its pockets a change of underwear, a volume of The Complete Works of Shakespeare, a toothbrush and a bottle of bourbon. He worked in New York City for awhile, and then in New Orleans, London, Paris, a lot of places and then came back. He's been in Oxford ever since. You might see him come into the post office there any morning. If someone he knows says, "Hidy Mr. Bill," he would nod in return. Otherwise he doesn't look around much, just comes and goes; nobody pays any attention to him; they've seen him there for years. Or he might go into the Doctor's office, they're good friends, and talk for hours about hunting and fishing and farming. He did perk up once not long ago, however, when all the preachers in town got together and tried to stop beer from being sold; he wrote an article and told them to attend to things in the Church. The paper wouldn't publish the article so he had it printed privately and distributed it. When he wants to do something, he doesn't care what other people say or think about what he does or the way in which he does it.

Nobody knows exactly what goes on out at that house of his. When he's not hunting or farming he's sitting in a room out there writing books. People used to be always coming to see him, but after a while not many got far down that mud rut he calls a driveway, or passed under the white columns of the portico to enter the front door. A "No Trespassing" sign had been put up which, in Oxford, Mississippi, is an act itself worthy of arousing suspicion against Bill Faulkner. But it was because too many came who said, "Tell me how to write and I will do it, but just tell me how so it will be easier." Or mostly they said, "Here, read this, and get it published for me." He had a world of his own, which he created, and he had his own people with whom to talk, who wanted nothing from him, so that he did not need anything or anyone else really, not Oxford, or New York, or critics. They could give him nothing like what the people in the private world gave him. Sometimes these people did absurd things, and the more absurd the more he liked them, for he is full of humor, almost childlike in his love of the ridiculous and the ironical. He just likes to tell stories, unwind them to see where they are going. He does not hesitate to admit that it is nice if someone else reads them, but if they don't that's all right too. And if his people ramble down a road for pages or so, talk without stopping, except where one must pause naturally for a breath, for many lines, then that's the way it should be written down. And that's the way he wrote it. The important thing is just to try to make something that's a little better, something that is true and moving, passionate and real. Something out of courage. He has that.

And now his people are growing a little quieter. They no longer move about as fiercely, passionately, compellingly often as before. And to fill the new sudden loneliness, he takes at last the homage he had not time for before when the force that was inside driving him was enough. He is only human.

The writer does not matter. It is the man. The man who, after fifty years, knows finally that there are no answers and says still:

'The kindest things the gods can give to people at twenty is a capacity to ask why,

a passion for something better than

vegetation,

even if what they get by it is grief

and pain.'

It's that man.[37]

———

Though the campus appearance went smoothly, Faulkner became angry when he left Bard. Instead of some time alone with Joan on the way to his train, Joan and a friend of hers, Hardy Koch, son of *Casablanca* scriptwriter Howard Koch, drove him. They got lost on the way and Faulkner felt that there was some sort of trickery involved: "We drove Faulkner back to New York when we left Bard. And for some reason we got lost ... and it is still murky to me now and [was] murky at the time ... what kind of trick he thought I was using. He kept insisting that he could take the train and I thought it was nice that we could drive him back. I know it was nighttime. I don't remember dropping him off in New York. Maybe we dropped him in Poughkeepsie at the train. I just remember Hardy and I driving him and him afterward thinking that there was something shady about the whole deal. I don't remember driving him all the way to New York. Maybe we just took him to Poughkeepsie because there weren't many trains out to Bard."[38] "I know that he got very upset ... and thought that—I think that is all in the letters—that we were aiming to try to be alone together. And my real thing was to save Faulkner from having to take the train back at night."[39]

Faulkner's letter to Joan following the visit complained of his bad luck in being alone with her: she was either driving a car too fast or there were too many people around. The visit to Bard he had of course done for her, as he would probably do most anything else she chose to ask of him. He mentions receiving a nice letter from Mr. Weiss so he assumed the appearance went well. His third paragraph takes a dramatic turn. He is thinking of writing something very beautiful for Joan soon as she may finally be growing up.

The kiss she gave him that night he believes was not entirely one of gratitude. Admittedly, he is having a lot more trouble getting her out of his system than he boasted of.[40]

Along with her personal sketch appearing in *The Bardian*, Joan sent
Faulkner the following letter. In her fashion, she doesn't refer to the issues,
especially those that are unpleasant, in his 15 May letter:

> May 21, 1951
>
> Enclosed please find something I hope you won't mind, might even like,
> realizing the understanding and love from which it came. This is merely from
> the college newspaper which won't reach anyone except here on campus.
> however, the vice-president of the college asked my permission to use the
> article in what we call our Newsletter, which is sent out to alumni and to
> some other schools, wants to reprint it in that and I said I would have to
> ask you first. I have finished the story and when I get it typed will send it
> to you W. F. which will be in a few days. the ending if [sic] not right yet and
> I will send it anyway with the now weak one because I am anxious to have
> you see it as soon as possible.
>
> Am still planning to try to go to Cal. this summer,[41] and will have to come
> to Memphis sometime I know, but simply can't right away, and then will
> come back here in the Fall I think to do something. My father said I could
> go to France if I wanted to (he said I was making my own decisions now
> which adds up to the same thing, although it isn't the nicest way to be told.)
> I don't know whether to do that or not.
>
> How are things there? nothing really to write about. just anxious to hear
> from you about things and about the story when you get it and also need
> to know soon about letting them use the article. If you don't like it will you
> tell me?

A simple postcard with three words on it (a signature Faulkner expres-
sion—*All Right. Bill*) was the only response she received. Later, when Faulkner
reviewed Ernest Hemingway's novel *The Old Man and the Sea*, and determined that it was "all right," Joan recognized this as his highest praise. Yet
at this time Joan probably hoped for a more expansive letter, some indica-
tion of his feelings regarding her sketch.

———

He writes again on 7 June 1951. The Faulkner piece was all right and
he hopes she understood that his postcard represented his copyright per-
mission. He would like to dedicate *Requiem for a Nun* to Joan but fears the
family outrage. Instead, he has an idea, something they would have to do
together before the book goes to the binder. His idea—to make love through
the title page—is revealed in *The Wintering* where it receives a bemused reception: "Writing the letter, with Jeff's newly read book beside her, Amy saw

suddenly whether or not love could have been made through the title page was not the point, at all: joy was: exultation at the book's being done: after so much work, the book was simply an extension of himself. They could have tried love that way, if only to laugh."[42]

What genuinely concerns Faulkner in this letter, more than copyright issues or the new novel, is the safety of his personal mail. Mrs. Faulkner had made a remark about Joan out of the blue and he began to wonder, did his wife have the short story manuscript Joan had promised to send? Should he, Faulkner asks Joan, go ahead and rent a mailbox in Oxford for A. E., thus advancing their correspondence from general delivery to a private P.O. box?[43] Their earlier exchange of letters involved Joan sending letters to arrive on Wednesdays to A.E. Holston, general delivery "...and now he want[ed] to get the P.O. Box," Joan said. "I don't know why he is asking me. That was something for him to decide."[44]

The whole idea of the P.O. box has him a little unnerved, he writes, as it seemed akin to renting an apartment for them, and that would be a leap. In longhand at the bottom of the letter, he asks Joan if she has the carbon copy of Act I of the manuscript.[45] Joan responds with her usual equanimity, expressing only mild interest in his "dedication" idea:

> June 11, 1951
> I understand that the post card meant all right to use the article, but it was so alone written there that I thought somehow that something was wrong. No, I haven't mailed the story before because I knew that the ending was wrong that it could stand going over some more so I thought to put it away for awhile, but I think that now I will mail it anyway with its faults but I am unable to look at it any longer. I will mail it on Wednesday and to A.E. since now I think nothing better arrive at house. The box is up to you. We will probably want to write this summer from Cal. or wherever but you will know what is best to try. Perhaps, it would be better not to write so often? Cold ugly days here. Just finished Soldiers' Pay. I can understand how you cannot very well dedicate it [Requiem for a Nun] to me, but I thank you very much for even thinking of it as it would be a very wonderful thing to have done for me. I did not quite understand what you were saying about another idea? As usual, nothing to say after we have been away for a while. But at least the something of this piece of paper arriving.
> j—

As a means of courtship, Requiem for a Nun served two purposes: collaboration with Joan and a play written for actress Ruth Ford. During 1951, Faulkner was writing to four women. Besides reuniting with Meta, he was actively corresponding with Joan, Else Jonsson, with whom he was linked romantically, according to Joan,[46] and Ruth Ford. Suddenly, the dynamics of Requiem took an optimistic turn when Ruth Ford showed the manuscript to Lemuel Ayers who wanted to produce the play on Broadway.[47] Faulkner reacts quickly to this spark of interest in a letter to Ford: "Tell your man (I was so excited that I didn't remember his name) not to bother about sending me a contract, the play, part, was written for you, so no contract is needed until we have talked and decided if anything can come of the matter."[48] The play's promise, Faulkner writes, bodes well for Ford: "It will be pretty fine if we can make a good vehicle for you. I would like to see that title in lights, myself. It's one of my best, I think: Requiem For A Nun."[49]

Very possibly on the same day, Faulkner writes to share this exciting news with Joan and to tell her he'll be coming to New York for a few days. He describes Ayers as the man who produced Kiss Me Kate and who may produce what he still considers their play, "even though you have repudiated it."[50] He hopes to arrange a meeting with her and asks her to write to A.E. in Oxford and to Random House to be held in the care of Mr. Commins. He concludes the letter by asking her why she didn't stick with him and the play.[51]

Faulkner never verbally asked Joan the same question. "And even if he had, could we, really have collaborated on a play? Is that going to fool his wife or anything? I don't think it ever would have worked."[52]

The emphasis placed on Joan's role in Faulkner's final push to finish A Fable has lessened explorations of Joan and Faulkner's evolving relationship as revealed in Requiem, Faulkner's "sequel" to his 1931 novel Sanctuary. Sanctuary's theme of a coed corrupted by a host of evil forces (most specifically the bootlegger, Vitelli, known as Popeye), working in concert with her inherent tendency to sin, is revisited in Requiem. Temple Drake's "promissory note" comes due and she must face her past and her role in the destruction of several lives. While Faulkner would not have characterized his commitment to awakening Joan's artistic and sexual sensibility as a form of corruption, it loosely might be construed as such.

Requiem's plot involves Temple Drake's love letters to Alabama Red. The letters are used by Red's brother to blackmail Temple. At the very time he was drafting the play, Faulkner was quite regularly writing Joan love letters and attempting to conceal the exchange of letters from his wife. Temple explains her letter writing as a way to fill the time between sexual interludes with Red—accompanied by Popeye—in her bedroom in a Memphis brothel where she is held captive (though Temple will say she could have escaped):

So I wrote the letters. I would write one each time ... afterward, after they--he left, and sometimes I would write two or three when it would be two or three days between, when they--he wouldn't--... you know: something to do, be doing, filling the time, better than the fashion parades in front of the two-foot glass with nobody to be disturbed even by the ... pants, or even no pants. Good letters--... the kind of letters that if you had written them to a man, even eight years ago, you wouldn't--would--rather your husband didn't see them....

The letters themselves Temple describes as

Better than you would expect from a seventeen-year-old amateur. I mean, you would have wondered how anybody just seventeen and not even through freshman in college, could have learned the--right words. Though all you would have needed probably would be an old dictionary from back in Shakespeare's time when, so they say, people hadn't learned to blush at words.[53]

Faulkner's letters to Joan filled the gaps in their visits and there may be a bit of wish fulfillment in Faulkner's depiction of Temple Drake's letters. Joan's letters generally were a far cry from impassioned or inspired by sexual engagement. They were by contrast almost tepid at this point in time.

Truthfulness in Faulkner's play receives prominence. Temple assures Stevens she also is committed to saving the life of Nancy, her children's nurse who has been convicted of murdering Temple's infant daughter:

TEMPLE: Cant you get it through your head that I will do anything, anything?

STEVENS: Except one. Which is all.... What we are trying to deal with now is injustice. Only truth can cope with that. Or love.[54]

An insistence on truth makes its way into countless letters from Faulkner to Joan. And for the most part, Joan was quite frank with him, even about dating other men. When he thinks she is running or hiding from her "true" feelings, he inevitably rebukes her. In one of his late letters to Joan while they were still involved, he writes: "I love you. Don't lie to me. I don't know which breaks my heart the most: for you to believe that you need to lie to me, or to think that you can."[55] It is terrifically ironic that all the untruths and misrepresentations involved in conducting an affair somehow escaped self-censorship by both Faulkner and Joan.

One of the most interesting and compelling, though completely unintentional comparisons of *Requiem* to Joan and Faulkner's relationship surfaced in the years subsequent to the end of their affair. In *Requiem*, Temple's lawyer, Gavin Stevens, and even the governor of Mississippi, continually try to highjack Temple's story. They talk over her, interrupt her, and spin their own versions.

Joan's "story," her perspective on Faulkner, likewise has been highjacked or interpreted by writers primarily concerned with Faulkner's life and work. Conversely, Joan did not make many attempts in her own writing to fully tell her story, preferring that it come instead from another writer. In *The Correspondence of Shelby Foote and Walker Percy*, Percy comments on Blotner's Faulkner biography in a 23 May 1974 letter to Foote, noting especially its absences:

> Reading Blotner's Faulkner with interest [two-volume edition]. Don't mind the details the reviewers deplored. Pity is, he has to leave out the most interesting stuff: F's relation to Estelle, how come Jill hated life at home, sexual relations with Joan and Jean [Stein], etc. Necessary reticence of course but pity anyhow. Part on Phil Stone amazing.~
> W~[56]

———

The truthfulness Faulkner wanted from Joan was necessary if he was to have any type of realistic expectation of their future. Joan was back from Bard, her temporary position over, and she returned to her Memphis home and a busy social life. There were her friends, peers; and then there was Faulkner. She does not remember talking to any of them about Faulkner, and said it was not hard to keep her secret. "No, I'm sneaky like a cat. No, it wasn't hard. Louise [Fitzhugh] met him [Faulkner]. I don't know how much she knew I saw Faulkner."[57]

At one point Faulkner wrote Joan an angry letter, telling her that everyone is a mix of animals. He then conferred animal traits upon her: "you are a mixture of cat and mule and possum—the cat's secretiveness and self-centeredness, the mule's stubbornness to get what it wants no matter who or what suffers, the possum's nature of playing dead—running into sleep or its pretence—whenever faced with a situation which it thinks it is not going to like."[58] Upon receiving that irate letter, Joan said, "It's hard to think what I thought at the time. I knew what he was talking about, but he expected more of me than I was capable of doing, giving. That was just my personality."[59]

Though she kept at her writing, nothing had happened to rival the exhilaration and sense of accomplishment she felt with "Rain Later." Faulkner, over the summer, continued to read her work and send story ideas. Faulkner's story ideas for Joan never came to fruition and the stories she gave him "probably weren't helpable, nothing ever happened." The stories she eventually published, "they just came out and they were all right to start with."[60]

———

This also was the summer *Life* sent Robert Coughlan to Oxford for an in-depth feature on Faulkner. While the preliminary news of the article angered Faulkner, his publishers at Random House thought the publicity (Coughlan's article was scheduled to appear just prior to publication of *Requiem*) would be advantageous. Faulkner was obstinate and unwilling, writing Robert Haas, "I have deliberately buried myself in this little lost almost illiterate town, to keep out of the way so that news people wont notice and remember me. If in spite of that, this sort of thing comes down here, I not only wont co-operate, I will probably do whatever I can to impede and frustrate it."

Coughlan, who was a friend of Harrison Smith, persisted. When he showed up on the porch of Rowan Oak and introduced himself, Estelle looked "startled and horrified." Faulkner himself asked him to leave, but then allowed a brief conversation. Coughlan stayed nine days in Oxford, conducting numerous interviews, many involving personal questions about Faulkner. This was exactly what Faulkner hoped to avoid, and when he passed Coughlan one day on the street in Oxford, he did not speak.[61]

When the two-part series appeared (28 September and 2 October 1953), there was very little in it one would construe as inflammatory—certainly no mention of infidelities. It is a full, engaging look at the Faulkner family, Oxford, and the Southern milieu's influence in dictating and determining the themes of Faulkner's work. Joseph Blotner pays it a high compliment: "...as for the writing, his [Coughlan's] description of the man himself was the best ever written."[62] Faulkner's uncle, J. W. T. II, supplied Coughlan with some wonderful quotations: about his nephew's storytelling, "He never *was* nothin' but a writer";[63] and about his work ethic, "He just *wouldn't* work."[64] Oxford's prevailing explanation for the peculiar young man was "It's the Faulkner in him." "The town," Coughlan writes, "was used to expecting the unexpected from the Faulkner family, who were famous for a self-assurance that made them oblivious to the opinions of others.... On the other hand, the Faulkners were proud, aristocratic and considered snobbish."[65]

———

In the fall, Joan traveled to California to visit Hardy Koch, her friend from Bard. She did not know if Faulkner was jealous of Hardy or not. Faulkner's letter reveals a certain curiosity about California, and he asks her to write him her impressions. He believes she will like some of it and hopes she will not take much of it very seriously. It is a busy time for him. He is taking his daughter to Pine Manor Junior College in Wellesley, Massachusetts,[66] and will stay in the East to rewrite the play (*Requiem*) for rehearsals. He has a book for her and asks her where he should send it.[67]

A brief note from Joan, interpreted by Faulkner as sad, gives him some alarm. He asks her if something is wrong, something she'd like to share with him? If so, send it in a letter care of Random House. Then he writes of his farming and beef cattle and the tasks that lay ahead. He sounds as if he genuinely enjoys the concrete sense of accomplishment farming and ranching offer. The second half of the letter displays a strong tonal shift. It is a bad letter, damn it, and it all needs to be said simpler. He wishes to never forget her first letter that he describes very much like her short story—passionate, tender and true—that he tore up and threw out the car window. "Dont be unhappy, damn it. Let me be the unhappy one; sometimes I think I have enough for all the world, I mean, the capacity for it."[68]

He then imagines Joan as a small brig with a fine copper bottom running free, and he is the ocean upon which she sails. This ocean contains no shores, worries, grief, or anguish, just dark and day, sky and wind. In closing, he asks what she would like for her birthday and he expresses anger at missing her.[69] "I dont like that. I am too old to have to miss a girl twenty-three years old.... By now, I should have earned the right to be free of that."[70]

"Well, frankly," Joan said, "you can say, when he wrote all that it is almost as if those are words that just sound good. But to me it doesn't mean anything. It is like the letters of the writer."[71]

Returning to this letter, Joan acknowledged Faulkner's unhappy nature: "That may have been just an old Southern-type moroseness. Or maybe he just wanted to be unhappy." And he was never very animated. "...but that wasn't his style. There were times that his eyes were happy and he never was sitting around glumly or anything."[72] She did not believe that drinking made him feel better or happier, but her understanding of drinking, relating it as she did to her own father's, gave them a powerful connection and made Joan unique among the women in his life.

———

Wednesday Sept. 12, 1951

Well, I do not know about the sadness of the line. I was hoping that you would not misinterpret its briefness as I was afraid to write down anymore, not ever feeling absolutely safe when they come from Memphis. I was hoping you would be able to call me before you left for New York and waited to write. California was, as I knew it would be, disappointing. I do not like the weather there either, would not like to live where there is no autumn or spring. It is relaxed, not socially family minded etc. I can see the insecurity of those working in the industry, learned something of the intrigues behind the star system, producer, director, the whole ridiculousness. The ocean in some parts was beautiful, mostly too commercial, the lighted Los Angeles from the Hollywood Hills was beautiful, things like this were right, mountains—things away from the city— Palm Springs, just the country, saw nothing of the party set there, being there in the summer— but the one thing that held nothing of disappointment, perhaps because I did not know what to expect, was the drive to Mexico, Ensenada— the mountains and the ocean at once, together, apart, hills, gullies, valleys, roads, people, water waves, dirt, cafes, the most captivating place I've ever been. I did not see enough of the things you dislike about Hollywood to really comment— the movie people etc. Just the outward physical appearance of the city is of course nothing. But I am glad of it and what was good was good enough to make it worthwhile.

As for me there is nothing much to say. I am still working on the story as I know it is not yet ready although I can not get exactly what it needs.[73] Did you ever have a chance to read it? I will be here for the winter, think I might take a couple of courses at Southwestern, try to write, perhaps a part time job. This is the time, I know, if I am ever to do anything. I have not, will not give up writing, but hope of and belief in any talent is gathering doubts, no ability, can think of only fragmentary ideas with no where to go. And life for you holds excitement still. I am glad. And you answered something for me in your last letter. If it is being born with a capacity for suffering that signifies a writer, then perhaps I am signaled out for something (I don't mean without work). For suffering for what is not even your own, for things people you will, never have known, conditions which I cannot change am not even remotely connected with except by existing in the same world. Why and what does it mean. The ever present lump of deep down sadness, that does not go away even at times like the day in the New Weston bar when you said I was too happy to write. I do believe it was born inside and sometimes I wish that you could (Not you who have enough but you someone) have it for me and I would sail without thinking, and yet most of the time I know I would not trade it even though I do not see its purpose for those who do not have the capacity for it. Or maybe I don't have the capacity for it— maybe just have a sadness that will never be any good for anything except to make me unhappy. There is the cool breeze coming in now of the first rains hinting fall and for that I would not want eternal sunshine. I am looking forward to what the book will be. The birthday is for you to decide. And yours too, I remembered that the other day, so both of us soon to put away something that will not come again but not feeling any different. Until I hear from you again about where you will be and when and arranging about the writing when you are here. my love,

Joan

The story Joan sent is quite good, Faulkner writes, better than most can write today, but not nearly as good as Joan will be one day if she keeps after it. He is just home from New Orleans where he received the Legion of Honor from the French Consul. Only two sentences into this letter, his typewriter breaks, and Faulkner promises more when it is repaired. The letter he received from her this morning makes him happy and relieved. She has not, he surmises, changed as much as he had feared. He encourages Joan to continue sending her letters in professional, business-like envelopes, like the one from the Biltmore, and to mix them up when possible. These letters are safe, but if she prefers Holston, she should let him know.[74] A brief, handwritten note on presumably borrowed stationery from a Standard Service Station alerts Joan to his upcoming trip to Cambridge and contains an address for the Brattle Square Theatre where he will be working on *Requiem*'s stage adaptation.[75]

Somewhat like the difficulties Faulkner faced throughout the composition of *A Fable*, the play's evolution for the stage proved daunting and unsatisfying. Ruth Ford alone seemed able to maintain a positive outlook. The play's director, Albert Marre, sensed that "Faulkner felt the play was no good and was doing it only for Ruth.... Marre felt he [Faulkner] was beginning to despair of ever making it work. Faulkner wrote Meta Rebner that he would like to come to Hollywood and spend two or three nights in bed with her, but he could not, because of the play." Before long it was evident that the beleaguered play would not come off as easily as previously anticipated. Finances were required and Faulkner thought briefly of committing a fifteen thousand dollar advance he had received from Random House toward the play's Paris opening in the upcoming spring. Saxe Commins intervened, advising no such action on Faulkner's part.[76]

———

As for Joan and Faulkner, 1951 closed with a flurry of letters from Faulkner dedicated to Joan's short-story drafts, story ideas, and attempted meetings. Feeling he has failed to inspire her with "their" play (*Requiem*), Faulkner entices her with a new project that is best shared in person: "It's not a short story anyway but a short novel really; you will have to work at it. Do you want to? Dont decide now; I will have to see you and tell you first.... This is a reversal, isn't it? I failed to persuade you to help me write a play; now I seem determined to help you write a novel whether you want to or not."[77] The meeting he hopes for may come off if there is no mess at home. He realized after talking with Joan, hearing her voice, just how much he had missed her.[78]

In a long letter, of which only a short portion appears in Joseph Blotner's *Selected Letters of William Faulkner*,[79] Faulkner proposes various meeting sites (he even asks Joan to follow him East after the holiday). The letter, in its entirety, portrays Faulkner as besieged in his own home and quite desperate to see Joan, if only for an hour.[80] Out of this personal disarry, Faulkner offers Joan what is unusually concrete advice on writing. His initial reaction to Joan's story—what would eventually become the television script "Graduation Dress"—was its lack of energy:

"...it doesn't move. It's static. You can write about a lazy, inner character, but the character must be told in motion.... show all this in action, dialogue which carries action, tell the story from the OUTSIDE instead of
INSIDE. This is not an essay, remember. Start off by seeing if you can tell
the story orally to me, for instance, in one sentence. Any good story can be
told in one sentence, I mean, the line, the why of it."[81] He then shifts attention to one of his "other" projects for Joan. An epistolary novel he envisioned about their relationship with Faulkner portrayed as a poet: "Rewrite
that first letter you sent me, a young woman, girl, writing to a famous poet
say, whom she called on against his will probably, and wrote to apologize:
'I didn't intend to bother you, interfere, I just wanted, hoped, you would
tell me why life is, because you are wise and you know the answers.' You
wrote that once, more or less; write it again, send it to me, I will answer it
and outline your next letter. This story will be a series of letters.[82]

Joan did try to recreate her first letter to Faulkner, and what she sent
did not please Faulkner. Writing her on New Year's Eve, he told her that
was the letter, but that it must have more to it. "All I remember is trying to
recapture the first letter I wrote him. When he says, 'it must have more in
it,' then what more in it?"[83] "See what that book became was *The Wintering*,
but he always wanted me to write a book about us ... I didn't have any objec-
tion to his telling me that, it is just that I never could think of a book. I
couldn't see that as a book. I didn't know how to do it."[84]

In the same letter, Faulkner reacts to a short story Joan sent him. Unlike
the Rain story ["Rain Later"], where the people also were quiet, it doesn't
move. "Rain Later" had a continued momentum. He hopes she can understand what he means. Also, he has decided that his proposed novel, the epistolary novel of their relationship, will win Joan a ten-thousand-dollar prize
for a first novel (from *Harper's* he believes). That money, he writes, will guar-
antee her freedom.

Freedom had so far eluded both Joan and Faulkner: Joan was still financially and emotionally under her family's protection; Faulkner was free to
see her only when clear of Oxford's entanglements. Despite other, more easily attainable women, like Meta, a young woman who did not struggle with
the maidenly scruples that plagued Joan, he persisted. "One time I said,
'why do you like me?' And he said, 'because you are my countryman.'"[85] But
then, so was Meta.

What was driving Faulkner was much more than their kindred Southernness. He must have understood by now, from the tenor of her letters, if
not their conversations, that they shared a sense of loneliness and sadness.
Such similar dispositions, coupled with Joan's resistance, ensured Faulkner's
pursuit.

IV

1952—Jacob Labored
Seven Years for Rachel

Faulkner's literary influence assumed new dimensions in Joan's personal decisions and efforts, though he could not yet claim the romantic hold on her life he so desired. Restless and seeking, Joan moved from Memphis twice in 1952. In the spring, she settled in New Orleans, looking for a rich, creative environment for her fiction; and by the fall, with a job at *Look* magazine, she was lodged in a small, Greenwich Village apartment. That both environments once housed a much younger Faulkner seemed almost inadvertent to Joan until years later.

"He [Faulkner] was always trying to get me to move out of Greenwich Village. What I was really doing was following his footsteps. I went to New Orleans, then I went to Greenwich Village. Matt, my son, picked that up years later. He said, 'You did everything Faulkner did.' And I thought, I did. He [Faulkner] had been through all of that. He said, 'Are people in Greenwich Village really doing anything or just talking about it?' And that kind of thing. And then he was always trying to save me from the middle class."

Part of the young Faulkner's wandering that Joan did not replicate was an almost six-month trip to Europe in 1925. Joan remembers Faulkner telling her "that when he was in Paris he used to sit in a cafe where James Joyce would be sitting just to stare at him and he never had the courage to go over and speak to him. Well, he had to have read him or why would he admire him so much?

"Sometimes Faulkner said he had not read Joyce or Freud, yet his books show he had ... You can see the influence. He would have been influenced by Virginia Woolf and Dorothy Richardson and all those people. I think he was influenced by Joyce."[1]

Dr. Adler concurred that Faulkner would indeed have knowledge of Freud:

> People make a mistake of thinking in terms of today; that was 40 years ago. A man of his knowledge, his literary knowledge, undoubtedly knew about Freud. But you must remember that in 1949 the knowledge of psychoanalysis existed in centers like New York, Chicago, Los Angeles. Memphis was far behind. So for him to say, imply that somebody's cousin had an inferiority complex, a father complex, a mother complex, that was looked upon with great disdain; that was insane, some crazy psychiatrist talks like that....

While Adler believes Faulkner would have read Freud, he insists, "Reading Freud and reading articles about Freud are two different things. Everybody at that time read something about Freud, but you had to have the basic psychological knowledge in order to make heads or tails out of it."

This observation could be applied to Faulkner's work as well. Adler says: "Faulkner's work was considered scandalous by people who had no understanding, who didn't know anything about it. People who don't know don't know they don't know!"[2]

———

Finding little to encourage him as a lover, Faulkner embraced the role of mentor with gusto in 1952. He sent Joan's short story "The Morning and the Evening" to *Harper's* and included a short note. His first sentence read: "As is probably obvious, the enclosed was written by a student of Faulkner."[3] He asked the editor to "look at this twice, if necessary." After rejection from *Harper's* and a second reading, Faulkner still declared the story "all right."[4]

Faulkner astutely anticipated that the editor might interpret Joan's story as Faulknerian. Joan's central character, Jake, has an emotional attachment to a cow. All along Joan had aligned Jake with Faulkner's Benjy from *The Sound and the Fury* as both characters are mentally challenged. It wasn't until 1953 when Joan was re-reading *The Hamlet* that she surprised herself by discovering Ike Snopes' likeness to Jake: "...am half way through The Hamlet and Bill, Jake is not Benjy's soul mate—my god—it's Ike Snopes—my god! It was so amazing to come across it, the cow etc. I read the Hamlet about 4 yrs. ago and I honestly did not remember any of it, there was no even hidden idea of remembrance when I did Jake I'm positive. I remember the Flem part, but it seems I read it somewhere else? I have the most amazing capacity for forgetting what I read! ..."[5]

When *Harper's* rejected the story, Faulkner sent it to his agent on 20 August, writing Ober that the story "was truly conceived, with imagination

Joan Williams and William Faulkner photographed in her New York apartment. Faulkner reminded Joan that he was once a housepainter and on a whim painted her apartment one day. Joan is working at *Look* magazine and writing (courtesy Joan Williams).

and compassion, though perhaps the fire did not quite come through onto the pages. I can be wrong about this. I felt the heat myself, though this might have been because I was biased to the extent of knowing what she was trying to do. I think she will do it, maybe next time, if she keeps trying."[6] Less than a month later, the *Atlantic* accepted Joan's story and Faulkner sent Ober a note of thanks, describing Joan as "my pupil for 3 years now, when nobody else, her people, believed in her. I am happy to know my judgment was right."[7]

———

While "pupil" misrepresented the dynamics of their alliance, Faulkner tried at the outset of the year to be more specific with his writing advice. His first letter of the year addresses the complication of helping Joan without actually rewriting her material: "The story is better now. It doesn't quite suit me, but I see now that the only way for it to seem exactly right to me, is for me to rewrite it, which I think you dont want.... The piece is better now. You have got to write the first sentence of a story so that whoever reads it will want to read the second one. That is a good rule."[8] The body of this letter, however, deals far more with personal issues. Faulkner tries to persuade Joan to take a trip with him for possibly three weeks, destination unknown. He will be in Memphis but whether or not he will be alone remains in question. He is back at work on the big book (*A Fable*) at least until Joan sends him some of her material to consider.[9]

Suddenly, happily for Faulkner, Estelle decides to visit Jill at college.[10] His house will be empty and he will be free. He asks Joan to save Thursday for him, the day he will take Estelle to the airport in Memphis. He suggests also that she come and stay with him at Rowan Oak.[11] As Faulkner probably expected, Joan did not make the trip to Oxford. Once again, an opportunity to advance the affair was thwarted by Joan's reticence. One can only assume that time alone in Faulkner's home was far from Joan's imagination (although a year and a half later she did stay at Rowan Oak when Estelle and Jill were in Mexico). Instead of dwelling on Faulkner and carving out some time for him, Joan's attention was fixed on her move to New Orleans:

> Tuesday
>
> If your letter hadn't come yesterday! I did need you so last week~the depression etc. has lifted~one reason~the New Orleans thing is shaping up~my mother and I are leaving for Mobile Fri.~will be at the Battle Hotel that night~then on to N.O. either late Sat. or Sun.~and will be at the Roosevelt~or the St. Charles, second choice~will leave there probably Tue.~and come back via Natchez. I plan to find a place to stay while there and then go back. I just have to get out of Memphis~true that you would write anywhere if need be~but I just don't have whatever it takes to get it or *anything* else done here. Keep the pages I sent you until I get settled in N.O.... That does not belong in the book. I don't think. I do not like it~the embryo which I sent, not the whole book. So I will be back here next Thur. or Fri. Meanwhile you know where I am~good about the play.[12]
>
> Love,
>
> J~

At this point, Joan was sending Faulkner short stories to which he was responding in detail. The story critique he provides below involves a little girl at her parents' drunken New Year's Eve party. She is the only child there and is trying to write her name on the night air with a sparkler. Despite his generosity (as in the following letter composed over two days) with his time and fairly thorough critiques, this particular short story and others from this same time period were never published. Soon she would turn her attention to the novel Faulkner encouraged about a young girl (Joan) meeting a famous poet (Faulkner):

You are learning. All you need is to agonise and sweat over it, never be quite satisfied even when you know it is about as right as it can be humanly made, never to linger over it when done because you dont have time, you must hurry to write it again and better, the best this time. Not the same story over again, but Joan Williams, who has the capacity to suffer and anguish and would trade it for nothing under heaven....

You know: something new, so that it was worth living through yesterday in order to reach today; and since you know you can, will, find something new still, it will be worth living through today in order to reach tomorrow.

A child's loneliness is not enough for a subject. The loneliness should be a catalyst, which does something to the rage of the universal passions of the human heart, the adult world, of which it~the child~is only an observer yet. You dont want to write just "charming" things. Or at least I dont seem to intend to let you.[13]

Believing he had been insensitive to the gift Joan offered him—something both beautiful and priceless—Faulkner sent her a note castigating himself for his denseness and likening himself to a dull ox. Joan's gift at this point would be her friendship and involvement in his life, her gender, youth, and appearance a predictably motivating force. Joan once had asked him to write her a poem and the following is his offering:

> *From an Old Man to Himself*
> You have seen music, heard
> Grave and windless bells? Your air
> Has verities of vernal leaf and bird?
> Well, let this fade; it will, and must, nor grieve:
> You can always dream, and she'll be fair.

In conversation, Albert Erskine told Joan he did not believe Faulkner wrote the poem,[14] even though Faulkner made a point of taking credit for the poem. "It was signed 'Bill he wrote it.'"[15]

During the middle of the month, Faulkner sends a letter reminiscent of earlier schemes and flights of fancy. He had phoned Joan several times from the Memphis airport without reaching her and had hoped she might be thinking as he was—that they would meet, almost coincidentally, at the airport. It is revelatory how overwhelmed and fixated he appears for any opportunity to see her and for them to share time.[16] It is not difficult to surmise that his intensity in this regard dwarfs whatever interest Joan would have had in a spurious meeting. This letter, like so many of it in nature, Joan simply disregarded.

On 29 February he comments on Joan's last letter as being "so down and depressed" that he believes his best response is to snatch her from her father's dynamite salon and rescue her on a white horse.[17] About her writing, she should not worry. She will or she won't. He believes if she would

let herself go in their relationship the work would get done easily and happily.[18] Besides a return to his "pressures," as Joan referred to it, the letter
echoes Faulkner's appropriation of old ways and chivalry. Joan felt the idea
of rescuing her, taking care of her, spoke to some fatherly need in Faulkner.
"There seems to be something in him that made him want a child or something."[19]

Following the poem and the imaginary "rescue" attempt, Faulkner's
next letter ruminates on the fate of the Paris opening for *Requiem* (the play's
production was plagued by financial shortcomings), and an invitation he
received to attend a Paris literary festival which, with "his Légion d'honneur
and the Nobel and all the hurrah,"[20] he feels obliged to attend. A different
endearment closes the letter as he remembers her mouth, tells her he loves
her, calls her a pretty maid, maiden, and, peculiarly, his sweet infant. He
wonders if she received his letter at the Roosevelt in New Orleans? There
was nothing much in it but what is in all his letters that he hopes will not
make her recoil as she often does.[21]

> Thank you for the letter. I did not get the one at the Roosevelt as we couldn't
> get reservations there. I am not sure when I am going back. So will you send
> the manuscript I sent you back. I do not know what you thought of its pos-
> sibilities, but for the first time I think it has some and I want to work at it.
> I am not at all sure that I can ever write. But I want to try this. I have thought
> it out so that I see a story plot to it and know how to begin. What do you
> think of this. What I sent you, rewritten of course, is the first part-this is
> the childhood and sets up the background-the why for what Laurel [pro-
> posed protagonist's name] is and what happens subsequently-so that one
> can understand what she is looking for when she meets the poet-why she
> turns to him so-. Then the second part begins with her at the time she meets
> him-explains something of what has happened to her in the intervening
> years. I see her on a train coming from seeing her father-as her mother and
> father are by now divorced-and on her way to see her mother before going
> back to college-something of the futility of these meetings-on the train she
> meets someone who gives her the poet's name and she takes the train to
> meet him. The meeting as we know it-then the letters etc. begin-the rest as
> we have talked it out. What do you think? What do you think of what I sent
> you? Did it seem childish, hopeless? One thing-you realize the only writing
> I have done is that printed story-and the other one-so that now I am
> floundering not only with the idea of the plot, but the actual principles of
> writing. Furthermore, my mind, I think, is so uncomplex, that the writing,
> the ideas too come out uncomplex and simple. They appear and sound so
> to me and therefore certainly must to you and even lesser beings. This wor-
> ries me. Also, what I am to do, where [I am to] go.

In a three-paragraph response, Faulkner assures Joan that her manuscript is going well and he will not bother her with comments. He mentions

again his upcoming trip to Paris for the literary jubilee, and whether or not *Requiem*'s production comes off, he is planning to attend. He asks Joan to send another flower or anything.[22] "Joan, Joan, Joan, you sweet pretty I think easily of all the things to say to you, that perhaps no man ever said to a girl before, but when I try to say them this way, the damned machine the paper the postage the distance, the 80 miles, get in the way of it. My pretty love my sweet love my sweet. Here is a violet with a little star in it."[23]

———

Joan, now living at 621 Royal in the French Quarter, spent her time working in a Doubleday bookstore and exploring the Quarter. On 6 April Faulkner returned some manuscript pages to her, though during Joan's three months in New Orleans her writing stalled. Faulkner seemed intent on his May trip to Paris for the Oeuvres du XX Siècle festival and wrote Else Jonsson that he "would not be too involved in Paris. I decline to be a delegate to anything; the words 'delegate' and 'freedom' in the same sentence are, to me, not only incongruous but terrifying too. I will not accept any commitment ... That is, I will be a free agent in Paris, as far as I believe now."[24]

Meanwhile, sensing that Faulkner was distracted, perhaps losing interest, Joan writes him an impassioned note—"And is the violet finally wilted— is there no need in you any more? ... great man whom I do love, in the depths which noone else has touched"—on stationery with a sophisticated-looking dog seated at a desk, feather pen in hand.

New Orleans
May 1, 1952

Dear Bill—

This picture of the happy looking animal writing is not very true. It's a poor attempt to be gay. And while I am speaking of being gay—are you off to Paris soon? Then to return to not being gay—are you gone any way in your thoughts—in your hopes, beliefs, in and for me? In the futility which life seems to be for me, which it seems to me to be around me (what is the struggle for? and tho [sic] we have talked of the grief, the pain, and agree on the goodness of the basic gift, accept and are glad of the capacity for suffering (where is the one for happiness?), what is the use (for me) when I can make nothing of it? I have tried. Is just to love you enough? And should I be glad of the regret that our lives crossed either too soon or too late, that one of us was born too soon or the other not soon enough—you, who out of all the world I could find a peace, a belief, a hope, something good with. Regret that we could not have been callous and selfish enough to take what my walking in that day could have meant—to me anyway. And is the violet finally wilted—is there no need in you any more? Tell me—for we have agreed on the honesty, too, great man whom I do still love, in the depths that no one else has touched.

Sometime later Joan typed a copy of what was originally a handwritten letter with the following note on the bottom: "The original was returned by
W. F. as one of those Mrs. F. had taken."

The violet, he writes, has not wilted though if he wanted peace, he
would wish it faded and gone. In Paris he will see another pretty woman[25]
who has everything but she is not Joan Williams; she does not have Joan
Williams' face. He imagines there is something a little shabby about taking
the image of one woman to another, to have another face between the one
he should be observing.[26]

"I'm leading a dull, busy purely physical life these days, farming and
training a colt and working every day with a jumping horse over hurdles, a
long time now since I have anguished over putting words together, as though
I had forgotten that form of anguishment. Which probably means that I am
getting ready, storing up energy or whatever you want to call it, to start
again."[27] Which, I believe, is what is happening to you. To have written
something once which you dont need to hate afterward is like having can-
cer; you dont really ever get over it...."[28]

From a stopover in New York en route to Paris, Faulkner wrote Joan
on Hotel New Weston stationery.[29] Her last two letters were nice; he saved
them, has them with him even. He is still planning to meet her wherever
and whenever she sends for him.[30] By June, Joan was back in Memphis. Her
return was precipitated by a chance encounter in New Orleans with a friend
from Memphis, Douglas Varderman. She abruptly and spontaneously
decided to ride home with him.[31] Something did come out of Joan's wandering and work with Faulkner on various short stories, because she would
soon write effortlessly a beautiful short story about a "loony" she remembered from her visits to her mother's family in Arkabutla, Mississippi. The
retarded man would be taunted by some in the small community, asked if
he was crazy. "Naw," he would respond, "but me ain't far from it."[32] Joan
remembered thinking that the people were cruel and insensitive. "The Morning and the Evening" drew on her feelings of compassion for the man and,
true to her style and writerly instincts, she felt and described her character,
Jake, from the "inside." In her story, Jake is mute and assumed by most people in his town to be slow:

> People, sometimes even his mother, always spoke to him too fast ... If
> there was time, he felt he could know what was said; he was sure. Often he
> felt that if only he had time, he could even answer.
> For he felt words inside him the way he felt music. The words came to
> him, starting in his stomach, and he listened to them carefully while they
> moved on up to his chest, began to hurt him; then in a rush the words
> would be in his mouth, and he would open it. He would hear the words

clearly, and he would smile proudly; but he knew he had not when they looked away and said, "Wipe off your mouth, Jake."[33]

———

Faulkner's return to the "anguish" of writing was delayed by travel. What was a happily anticipated trip abroad became arduous when Faulkner's chronic back pain intensified. A series of X-rays in a Paris hospital on 27 May revealed a broken back, possibly from a fall from a horse a few months earlier in Oxford, or a tumble down the stairs of Rowan Oak some six years earlier. Despite his discomfort he managed the "business" of the trip—a brief speech at the Salle Gaveau in Paris where André Malraux was also a featured speaker. Over drinks with Marre, who had flown to Paris to see him, Faulkner conceded he had given up on *Requiem*, telling the would-be director "I'm relieved we don't have to do the play. I don't think it's [the play] any good."[34] From Paris he somehow traveled to England and then to Oslo. Once there, Else Jonsson arranged for daily treatments with a masseur that offered Faulkner genuine relief from his back pain.

Returning to one of his favorite means of communication, Faulkner sent Joan a telegram from New York asking her to meet him at the Memphis airport on 17 June. It had been over three months since they last saw each other and this night signaled change—the sexual liaison Faulkner coveted for so long was fulfilled. After dinner in Memphis near the airport Joan turned to him quite spontaneously and they made love in her car. This took him by complete surprise. He believed Joan's block had melted. Even with this breakthrough, though, he is disappointed that her passion and abandonment did not match his.[35]

The significance for Faulkner of finally consummating their affair surfaces repeatedly in letters, but it is most remarkable when he asks Joan if she ever thought of the connection between the author and the country man she knew as Bill Faulkner. He ponders that perhaps there is little connection between the two identities. He asserts, however, that his entire body of work up to this point in his life—all the years of creating—was in anticipation of that night in Memphis when they found each other at last.[36]

———

Joan's astonishing welcome home that June night was for Faulkner almost operatic. His joy in their newfound intimacy; his amusing trip home; and his subsequent letdown with her failure to match his sensual and emotional pitch occurred at one fell swoop.

Faulkner's journey home was a comic epic. The details, as chronicled

in a subsequent letter to Joan, are rendered in an understated tone that
evokes the flavor of his humorous fiction. The cab he hired would only take
him fifty miles, leaving him in Holly Springs. Then he met up with a man
en route to Oxford. His car was old and overheated so badly they had to
stop on the outskirts of town. From there he met a friend who drove a milk
truck. He picked up Faulkner, took him to the stalled car to gather his lug-
gage, and then to Rowan Oak. Certainly the irony that a trip to Paris,
England, and Norway, with two stopovers in New York, should end with
Faulkner in a milk truck was not lost on the author.

That night also brought Faulkner both promise and frustration. A part
of love, he writes, is humility, as well as pride and exultation. And even
though he too squirms at humility, Joan must accept it. She is a young,
pretty woman regardless of his age.[37] "Old eighty-year-old Goethe's pride and
exultation at having conquered (I mean half-conquered anyway) a young
and pretty woman. Only, in this case, there is a rather terrible amount of
no-peace too. If we could meet whenever we like, it might be different with
me, though probably not. But as it is, I wont get any peace until we have
finished the beginning of it. Maybe I can do even more for you then, after
there is no more barrier, no more mystery, nothing to remain between."[38]

An August letter clarifies what Faulkner meant by "half-conquered."
Joan's vacillation since their night in Memphis when she turned to him
spontaneously has him more troubled than ever.[39] Was he misreading also,
he asks in a July letter, not only the night he returned from New York but
the time under the tree on the windy hill?[40]

The summer reintroduced an old worry. Faulkner fears their letters are
being intercepted, that Estelle has access to his private post office box.[41] The
summer brought also a rush of emotions, high and low: Joan's exhilaration
with her story and Faulkner's frustrations with her maidenly scruples. Three
years after their first meeting, Faulkner describes their relationship as
baffling, puzzling, and frustrating. It has yielded heartache from deferred
hope:[42]

> I have puzzled and anguished a good deal in trying to understand our rela-
> tionship, understand you and what must have been your reasons (not delib-
> erate reasons and motives. I do not and will never believe that you
> deliberately wanted to intended to baffle and puzzle me and make me
> unhappy and heartsick from bafflement and frustration and deferred hope;
> that was I who did that, not you) for your actions.[43]

The intensity of their relationship over these summer months reached
a new level; Faulkner's impassioned letters make this clear. The sexual relationship Faulkner wanted, though realized, occurred too seldom and usually

as lapses in Joan's resistance.[44] For Faulkner, it lacked the fervor he determined necessary to consider Joan conquered.

———

Determining that he has stumbled upon something to advance Joan's writing career, Faulkner suggests they write a television script for James Geller at Warner's: "He wants names of course now, but if you and I could invent something, let him have the first one under my name, I can and will work you into the picture...."[45] Faulkner concedes that being a television writer or rewriter is paying hack work, but at the same time, it allows Joan to continue her own writing. He hopes also that their Monday meeting will come to pass and that perhaps there will be a veiled crumb for him. What he writes next is nonsense, or Stein[46] or Joyce, the essence of which is his desire that she take things seriously again. The letter closes with a code he asks Joan to translate and a note in Scandinavian. "I don't know what that code was," Joan said. "That might have been some foolishness he wrote. The Scandinavian part. That [is] fuck in Scandinavian." While Faulkner seemingly was comfortable writing that to her, "he never would have talked that way."[47]

Their collaboration on the television script evolved into "The Graduation Dress" for which they received $500.00. Joan said she supplied the initial idea; in fact, it was based on a 1951 short-story draft of hers, but Faulkner primarily wrote the revision: "In retrospect, I think The Graduation Dress started out as a short story of mine. And he took it and made it into a script."[48] "I made one or two comments on it ... but I didn't really do anything on that, so I didn't take any credit for it."[49]

At this time Joan was far too caught up in her story of Jake to concentrate on "hack" work to support her real efforts. Jake struck a chord with Faulkner as well. He immediately appreciated the story, telling Joan, "This may be it."[50] He did suggest the title, "The Morning and the Evening," from Genesis because, Joan said, he told her Jake didn't know the difference between the morning and the evening.

In September Faulkner would turn fifty-five, yet during his summer courtship of Joan he assumed the role of a dutiful young suitor with her parents, even writing Joan's father a letter (P.H. Williams was just two years older than Faulkner). Faulkner begins by thanking Mr. Williams for some advice he gave him about a saw and getting his cedar cut. "He came to Memphis ... to see us and my grandfather was there. And he [Faulkner] started talking about getting some lumber cut. And my father said, 'Why don't you do so and so, or offer his man so and so.' And he said, 'I never would have thought of that.' Apparently he went home and did what my father had suggested and wrote and thanked him."[51] After thanking Mr. Williams for his advice, Faulkner notes that Mr. Williams' good sense in this regard confirms an idea he suspected from other personal business dealings: that a writer should concentrate on writing and leave practical matters to others. He then sends his respects to Joan's mother and grandmother and apologies for keeping Joan out late. He goes on to explain that the Italian restaurant he tried first was closed and then they looked for another.[52]

Joan said her father didn't remark on the letter or have any reaction to it. The curiosity was Faulkner's apology and his deliberate decision to act more like Joan's peer than Mr. Williams.' "It's like he's my age and not married and all that stuff. We went out and he brought me home and I remember my father opening the door, and him [Faulkner] saying something like 'I kept her out later than I meant to' or something like that."[53]

———

The end of July meant more family involvement. Faulkner's long letter—what he calls whimsy but believes Joan will call sarcasm—covers the business of their check for "The Graduation Dress." Trying to convey to Joan (the experienced writer to the novice) that boring work is necessary to fund the writing that really matters, Faulkner includes this deliberately upbeat message in what is otherwise a confrontational letter: For the nine yellow pages they sent to Mr. Geller, he writes, they earned $500. Geller is calling it "Graduation Dress" and appears to like it. Maybe, he continues, this could become a business. The stories would be under Faulkner's name to fetch a higher price, though not the really good stories like Jake.

Faulkner improbably had come to believe Joan is in touch with Mrs. Faulkner, and while he expected to deal with Joan's family, he is surprised to note that his true rival is his own wife. He compares himself to the biblical Jacob, who labored seven years for Rachel, noting that he (Faulkner) only has four years left in his pursuit of Joan. Jacob was luckier, however; he had only Rachel's family to master.

Despite the negative tone of his letter, Faulkner is intent on seeing Joan. He includes bus schedules; and, even more unlikely, he mentions that she might ride to Oxford with him and Estelle after they take Jill to the Memphis airport. Joan mentions a friend who would pick her up in Oxford. Instead, he recommends she take the bus roundtrip, and wonders why her friend would be willing to drive to Oxford unless he too is in love with her; would be willing to drive 160 miles for the privilege of hearing her say no to him for three hours.

His misgivings about Estelle's involvement—she had after all unexpectedly suggested Joan come to Rowan Oak—include his worry that she would

discover the Williams' address and find their South Parkway home conven-
ient for drop-in visits (something Joan seriously doubted[54]). Then a confes-
sion: he admits he doesn't know his wife; in fact, he is beginning to believe
he knows very little about women.[55] "I don't know, I seem to know so little about her; I seem to know—I am coming to believe—so little about all
women. Which, let us hope, is the last of the whimsy. Not bitter: just
damned sad, take the maestro's advice and never never never fall in love."[56]

———

Falling in love with Joan was indeed torment for Faulkner. Instead of
reaching a period of consistency, of a sustained and enjoyable sexual relationship that occurs for many couples, Faulkner faced frequent rejection
from Joan. This circumstance in turn propelled an emotional crisis. With
the exception of an almost euphoric letter early in the month, the August
letters spiral downward. His despairing, sometimes-angry tone, and the actual
handwriting foreshadow his crash. In September he was again hospitalized
in Memphis.

The "happy" letter curiously begins with a reference to Mrs. Faulkner.
She was hospitalized for drinking; now sober, she is ready to come home.
He may soon pick up his wife and a nurse, so that means Joan's Wednesday visit to Rowan Oak is too risky. Instead, they will meet in Holly Springs
at 11 a.m. as planned. He will be parked in his usual spot on his usual street
and will have Coke for Joan and beer for himself. Whatever Joan told him
about alcohol the afternoon she read aloud Katherine Anne Porter leads
him to believe that the beer may be a favorable augury for him: that the
afternoon holds the promise of sex.[57] This letter is striking and unusual in
that he closes by telling Joan he will have something else for her, and repeats
the time and place of their meeting.

All indications support 1952 as the summer Faulkner gave Joan the
handwritten manuscript of The Sound and the Fury. Their relationship had
evolved for three years and they were lovers. Certainly this new intimacy
would come closer to inspiring this generous and significant gift than presenting it to Joan during the summer of 1950 when they were far from lovers.
Joan remembers that he gave her the manuscript in the summer but does
not specifically recall the year.[58] Contrary to what has been noted by some
biographers, the summer of 1952 was the logical moment for Faulkner to
symbolically seal their union by giving her the manuscript of his beloved
novel. The letters and advancement of their affair confirm this chronology.
Giving Joan Caddy Compson's—"his heart's darling"—story confers an emotional investment of no small magnitude. Biographer David Minter speculates:
"Joan became several things for Faulkner—not only his heart's darling, nor

merely one he had tried through love to shape into a poet, but also the daughter of his mind."[59]

Sadly, Faulkner's gift slipped out of Joan's possession. One day after Joan moved to Greenwich Village, Faulkner was visiting her apartment—painting it, in fact—and he noticed the manuscript. He told Joan that it was quite valuable and that he should put it somewhere for safekeeping. He then sent it to Commins with a letter describing his handwritten manuscript as irrevocably Joan's property: "Her right to it is not to be challenged.... It is my request to you that her right to the manuscript be defended and protected in any situation that may ever arise."[60]

A series of events then conspired to keep Joan from regaining the manuscript. Years later she asked that it be returned: "After I was married to Ezra,[61] and had been for some time, ... it just occurred to me to write him [Faulkner] and ask him for it. And that is when he wrote and said it was at Princeton in a manuscript show and it had been taken out of Random House without his knowledge.... And then he said he would send it to me but never did. I got the feeling then, well, I was married to somebody else, [that] he didn't want to give it back.... I didn't have a copy of that letter[62] so I could never have proved that he had given it to me.... I think I saw the letter at the time, but it never occurred to me to get it, to have a copy of it.... And also, all I thought about it when he didn't send it, was just he didn't want me to have it any more."[63] "And I never did say anything about it and he never did either. What I think was amazing was that the letter was still with it.... And if Saxe Commins had thrown that away, nobody would have anything except my word."[64]

When Joan received the manuscript the first few pages were missing. When she asked for the manuscript back and mentioned the missing pages, Faulkner rewrote them for her and did send them to her.[65] She still has those rewritten pages. It was sometime later that he found the original few pages.[66]

Even when, in the late 1950s and 1960, Faulkner made repeated references to the manuscript and returning it to Joan, she doubted his sincerity. The manuscript is still hers, he assures her in a 1957 letter.[67] And on 10 August 1959 he explains that the manuscript has moved from the Princeton show to a November and December show at the University of Virginia. Once that is over, he will send it on to Joan—better he give it to her than leave it to her in his will—and that once she has it in her hands again, she should not let it go.[68] "When he was writing me those letters then about sending the manuscript on, I don't think I believed then that he would. I don't think I ever believed that he was going to send it."[69]

After his death, the manuscript along with most of his papers was sold to the University of Virginia[70] where Faulkner was the first writer in residence. In 1986, the curator of manuscripts at the university cited the Faulkner collection as the most heavily used material in the library, surpassing even the Thomas Jefferson collection, which was the second most requested. "There are 75 feet of shelves loaded with works by or about Faulkner. There are manuscripts for 10 novels, 50 short stories and numerous poems. The manuscript for *The Sound and the Fury* is the centerpiece." The university refused to comply with a letter from Joan's lawyers requesting the return of the manuscript.[71] When Joan's lawyers filed a suit in federal court, the court ruled that the statute of limitations had expired.[72] "...I had a big lawsuit with the University of Virginia about trying to get the manuscript back ... Finally, a lawyer got me $25,000 for it, which is a pittance because it's worth millions now. But they weren't going to let it go and I couldn't fight the University of Virginia."[73]

———

The remaining letters from August involve a series of misunderstandings and attempts to smooth them out. Joan's work on "The Morning and the Evening" is an integral part of the emotional mix:

> It's still all right. I cant find anything you could leave out. If you could break up the idiot [Jake] section into shorter paragraphs, even at times a single sentence to a paragraph, it would help the effect: of his simple mental processes, his mental fumbling, innocence.... I dont like the title. You are writing about a human being, true. But I think the title should refer to a *condition*, some applicable quotation, like a little child shall lead them, though that is not quite right. Some word maybe, like Twilight,[74] some tender word, or, for emphasis, some savage word or phrase out of Hollywood motion picture slogans,[75] about the educational or artistic value or the importance of motion pictures.
> ... Had a flat tire on way back yesterday, changing tires did my back no good, still painful this morning, though probably that is not the reason, but the unhappiness from yesterday, very unhappy, but after all they are your mouth and your bottom and yours the right to say no about them and anyone that dont like it should better go back where he came from and maybe stay there, hadn't he?
> ... The story is laid in Miss. and a mag. editor may find a little Faulkner in it (idiot and cow), so I think better not to enclose my letter with the story ... I think you can stop worrying, and just write. The next one may not be this good, but dont let that trouble you either.[76]

While Joan doesn't recall the exact source of her anger with him, it most likely involved the pressures Faulkner exerted, which she found burdensome. She also was at a highly creative pitch with her short story when she wrote Faulkner this short note complete with a drawing of a frantic "stick woman": "I was writing Jake OVER again. It was the deliberate antagonism I couldn't stand. But anyway, Monday, same time and all, if all right—if not call me Sunday and we'll decide another." Her criticism elicits a telegram with Faulkner's assurance that it is never antagonism, deliberate or otherwise.[77] About this exchange, Joan said, "A lot of the time I didn't know what he was talking about. You've got to realize he was thirty-one years older than I and he had a different perspective."[78]

Joan and Faulkner's epistolary discourse on occasion did confound both parties. In *William Faulkner: Letters and Fictions*, James G. Watson asserts "Expressions must be shared, and nowhere more than in letters where the Sender-Receiver relationship is implicitly at stake in every communication. Faulkner's love affair with Joan Williams began by her mailing him stories to critique, and often in their letters love and fiction are mutually at issue."[79]

Their next meeting involved Joan telling Faulkner that she is bored in Memphis and ready to get away. This remark threw him into a tailspin. Where one might normally find the date, these hasty letters are instead noted as: Midnight, Thursday 8 a.m., Friday, and Sunday. The letter typed at midnight includes his initial reaction to Joan's plan to move to New York. He had been home eight hours and feels sick with worry and bafflement. He understands her need to meet new people and move on, but he believes that if she wanted passionately and fiercely enough to be a writer, boredom or unhappiness would not stalk her. He surmises what she really wants is escape, physical escape, to retreat into a conventional marriage, or at least a permanent alliance, with someone young and free whom she can respect, trust, and one day love. Then a question, is he right? Is this what she has been telling him all along but he hasn't heard?[80]

Yes, he agrees, she must get away. He will write Geller and Cerf and any others who come to mind who might help. If their afternoon together that day and all of their times since she met him at the Memphis airport in June have been a form of goodbye,[81] "that's all right too; haven't I been telling you something too: that between grief and nothing, I will take grief."[82]

Joan remembers him saying, "He thought I was looking for something that doesn't exist the way he always had."[83]

The Thursday morning letter finds Faulkner calmer and less anguished. Though he always said to believe the heart, not the mind, Faulkner finds he must listen to the mind in order to quiet his heart. The block between them he had rationalized as his age, but he felt, hoped, that it would diminish in time (at her age, Joan gets older faster than he does). Their night together in Memphis in June; the afternoon in the old church near Senatobia (Mississippi); and the day Joan handed him Jake allowed him to believe the block had melted until she told him no. Even then he didn't believe it, as her "no" came from the mind, from mental reasons, rationalizations, and morality. The only reason he can accept is simply that she doesn't want him, doesn't love him that way.

Then, the next time they met, he set out to break down her mind and she cried. It was her gratitude, honesty and tenderness that finally allowed her acquiescence. More troubling was their meeting the day before when he forced her compliance, not by physical force, but by relentless insistence. Faulkner is so troubled by his own behavior that he promises not to worry her again. They will only be together if she again turns to him spontaneously as she did the first time. If there is no next time, he hopes she will one day tell or write him the truth.

She is not to believe he has changed. Whatever he has is already hers. He will help her and give her what little of him she really does want. Finally, she must know none of this has anything to do with Jake or the writing that will follow once her block disappears.[84]

The tone of the next day's letter is softer. Having spent twenty-four hours writing what he believes would be, to Joan, dreary, dull whining, he threw the letter away, regretting only that he hadn't done the same with his 7 August letter. This new letter will be better if he doesn't lapse into whimsy, which is even worse than dreariness. He asks Joan to please forget that last letter, fearing it may have disgusted or troubled her.

> I still felt so rotten yesterday morning that I had to do something, so suddenly I dug out the mss. of the big book and went to work at it; suddenly I remembered how I wrote THE WILD PALMS in order to try to stave off what I thought was heart-break too. And it didn't break then so maybe it wont now.... did a good stint on the mss. and yesterday went sailing along all afternoon, not much wind so I lashed sheets and tiller stretched out on the deck looking up at the mast.[85]

Half asleep on the deck, looking up at the mast, reminded him of the Holly Springs hill where they listened to the trees above them breathe. And he wanted Joan there with him listening. Maybe he wanted her listening to him telling her how ashamed he was of his letter. Then he is rescued by a sweet moment of escape. He is free of the stupid, hard, compulsory ground, it's like being on a cloud, like maybe being an angel, yet still he is regretting his stupid letter. There is a little ache, a little sadness, because she can't give herself to him, and he tries to give her everything she wants, needs, or will accept.[86] These emotions remind him of something he learned long ago, "that it is never the things that you did that you regret when it's too late, but the things you didn't do, didn't commit, didn't have; worse even than to have had something and lost it."

"Read Jake again," Faulkner writes. "It's still all right, but maybe I shall keep it a while and think about it again. You must learn more. Where I beat you was, I set out to learn all I could sooner in my life than you did. I mean, the reading...."[87]

Perhaps if they had been closer in age—he just ten years older—and they had met for the same time periods, he could have given it all to her and Joan would not have to read all the books he has or learn all he has learned. Will she promise to forget that letter?[88]

Instead of forgetting the letter, Joan must have communicated her unhappiness with him because Faulkner quickly backtracks. He insists that he did not mean goodbye, but meant goodbye to his bothering her for what she wasn't prepared to give. He believes he has been so blue since their Wednesday meeting because that was the first time they parted without setting a date, even tentatively, to meet again. Will she?

The letters aren't enough. He could write endlessly without telling her what he needs to. He hopes to see her next week, and he will even reschedule his deer camp job if necessary.[89]

Faulkner believes Joan's short story ("The Morning and the Evening"), which he refers to as Jake, confirms her choice of art over the middle class. He also is excited by the level of her work and says Ober has agreed to help place Jake:

> "You have to learn how to do ones like Jake from inside yourself, because JAKES are not commercial tricks, which is all anyone, Col [lege] or correspondence or anyone else, can teach from the outside. You have to feel Jake from inside, as you did. To write him properly, you must have not instruction nor criticism, but imagination, which you had to have to invent him, and observation and experience. Which you will get partly from reading the best which others have done, and from watching people, accepting everything. You have got to break your wall. You have got to be capable of anything, everything, accepting them I mean, not as experiments, clinical, to see what it does to the mind, like with drugs or dead outside things, but because the heart and body are big enough to accept all the world, all human agony and passion.[90] Am going to read Jake again now. May send it to Ober unless I can find some glaring fault which I can point out to you. But Jake is too good for that, even for me to touch....[91]

Having assured Joan of her success with Jake, he shares some satisfaction in writing that the "big book" is going well. Still there is his deep need for someone to write not to but for. Perhaps he too will go to New York. He hopes she will write him and set a date to meet.[92]

With maturity Joan came to understand this need of his: someone to write not to but for. Only after her own years of struggle with writing would she clearly envision the perfect reader Faulkner knew already: "someone near and close to read it, though not to ask what that person thought: only to have someone say, almost inattentively, 'Yes, keep on. I love you and believe in you.'"[93]

At this point, however, she was far from such moments of clarity. When eleven days passed and Faulkner hadn't received a letter from Joan, he sends her an angry note. Her letter didn't come today. She shouldn't stop working because she can throw Bill away and keep Faulkner, but if she stops working she will indeed have wasted two years. "Sent Jake to Ober yesterday.... If he [Geller] would take one [television script] from just you alone, and Ober places JAKE, then you could throw F. away too."[94] He hopes she is happier than he is. He is not completely selfish and only unhappy because he had her and lost her. He is unhappy for her because she is a poor love, poor frozen heart, poor child, poor baby.[95] Faulkner's anger revealed itself "mostly in the letters."[96]

Joan receives just one more short letter before Faulkner's collapse and September stay at the Gartly-Ramsay in Memphis. Written at 11 p.m., it is a very strange letter, typed but with less precision than most, in which Faulkner recreates dialogue with a little beast: a representative of his sexual ardor for Joan. This imaginary tormentor is a relentless reminder of Faulkner's obsession and his desire for exclusivity in Joan's life—"I will not spoil my sheath with lesser brightness."

Faulkner imagines approaching the miniature creature and telling him he doesn't need him anymore. At that point, the beast rears on his hind legs and brandishes a needle-sized rapier and a cornflower, saying I am Joan's possession now. Faulkner tells the beast he can't belong to Joan because she doesn't have a broken heart. The beast tells Faulkner the only lug to break Joan's heart is Faulkner himself but he doesn't have the nerve to break anything. When Faulkner tries to go to work, the little beast sits on his typewriter, telling him all about Joan, her heart-shaped face and azure eyes. Then the minute nuisance follows Faulkner to bed, landing on his pillow, taunting him. Faulkner responds by quoting—sometimes misquoting— or perhaps in his opinion improving, part of Ezra Pound's sonnet "A Virginal":

> No, no! Go from me. I have left her lately.
> I will not spoil my sheath with lesser brightness,
> For my surrounding air hath a new lightness;
> Slight are her arms, yet they have bound me straitly
> And left me cloaked as with a gauze of aether;
> As with sweet leaves; as with subtle clearness.
> Oh, I have picked up magic in her nearness
> To sheathe me half in half the things that sheathe her.[97]

After these attempts at originality and borrowed verse, Faulkner closes by asking how can he express his love except in the old way, the one way?[98]

———

Faulkner's emotional and physical health was in great jeopardy in the fall. There was a series of hospitalizations triggered by accelerating back pain and depression. He wrote Else Jonsson "...probably the great trouble is unhappiness here, have lost heart for everything, farming and all, have not worked in a year now, stupid existence seeing what remains of life going to support parasites who do not even have the grace to be sycophants. Am tired, I suppose."[99] By now, Joan was living in New York and Faulkner imagines, in a letter from Gartly-Ramsay, that if she hadn't moved they might have been together every day of his stay.[100]

On 18 September, Faulkner suffered a convulsive seizure and was, according to his letter to Joan, transported to Memphis by ambulance. When Dr. McCool examined him, his x-rays showed no new injuries to his back but revealed old ones. Treating his depression involved more drastic measures, however, and even though Dr. McCool ushered in the use of electroshock treatment in Memphis, he firmly maintained he did not administer such to Faulkner. Dr. Adler also said that he never prescribed electroshock therapy for the author.

Before the use of electroshock at Gartly-Ramsay, physicians there used Metrazol shock for depression. According to Dr. Adler, Metrazol was the intravenous injection of approximately 5cc of Metrazol, a preparation chemically related to Camphor. It produced within a few seconds a violent convulsion that lasted about 20 seconds, after which the patient fell into a deep sleep for two to four hours. After a short period of confusion he felt better. The treatment was used almost worldwide for possibly one to two years. "It was a rather drastic but effective treatment for depression at the time and shortened hospital stays considerably," said Dr. McCool.

In 1940, Dr. McCool visited a friend and colleague at the Institute of Pennsylvania Hospital where a doctor showed him the "new" treatment: electroshock. Dr. McCool found it preferable to Metrazol because the doctor did not have to find a vein. Before the advancement of drugs, Dr. McCool said he routinely used electroshock therapy for schizophrenia and depression until it gradually faded and began to diminish in 1959. "I think in some instances it [electroshock] is a life-saving measure. It'll clear up depressions when drugs won't. And faster."[101]

Whether or not Faulkner received electroshock during the 1950s is a point of contention among biographers and those who knew him. That it was the leading remedy for depression at the time of Faulkner's hospitalizations further calls into question how he would have avoided the treatment. Blotner writes in his two-volume biography that during a November hospitalization in New York, Faulkner received, for the first time, electroshock.[102] Joan visited Faulkner at the Westhill Sanitarium; in fact, her own doctor from New York, Eric P. Mosse, saw to his care and presumably prescribed electroshock treatments. (Dr. Mosse told his wife he had administered a series of treatments, "perhaps six in all.") Seeing Faulkner fairly often during this stay made Joan question how such extreme measures would have been possible, believing she would have sensed a more obvious change in Faulkner. "I don't think Faulkner would let anyone fool with his brain."[103]

When Blotner released his 1984 one-volume biography, he qualified the Westhill Sanitarium stay, noting that Jill Faulkner said on no occasion did she have reason to believe her father had undergone electroshock treatments and she doubted any had occurred.[104] Possibly, this issue will never be resolved with any real clarity. While Joan and Jill are certainly powerful and intimate voices to the contrary, one must consider the medical climate of that day. Electroshock treatments were widely prescribed for depression, and given Faulkner's increasingly severe bouts, if he did avoid the therapy it was nothing short of amazing.

Upon her arrival in New York, Joan sent Faulkner a handwritten letter including her new address and her "advice" on his manuscript of A Fable. (When Faulkner returned this letter to Joan, he noted on the front of the stationery that she [Estelle] had this one and presumably had read it.) Joan sends Faulkner a very important message in this letter. She writes, "If Jake is good then it can begin to be us as I have always wanted it to be." This is the clearest, most specific definition Joan provides in all her letters and her fiction of the relationship she desired:

> I can't believe the summer is over—only I think that this summer never will be over because of those days: the ones in the woods—they alone made everything else worthwhile: that is good, knowing they are something can never be taken away from us: I think I shall see them in my mind's eye for a long time—the sun, church, house, trees, woods. If Jake is good then it can begin to be us as I have always wanted it to be.
>
> I *must must must* start on the novel. I must know that the writing is good. Will you let me know how to get in touch with Mr. Ober? On the plane I read the Part I of [A Fable]— haven't had time to read more— but my verdict so far— it is good— I advise you, ... to finish: the only thing I would venture is not to complicate it. And I say, G.D. What a strange place to carry a letter!![105] Will be moved in by Wed. or Thur.—288 W. 4th N.Y.C.
>
> I love you, J—

Joan wanted Faulkner's role as mentor to be a realistic and achievable goal; that the fruition of their friendship and intimacy would foster her natural talent. Admittedly, Faulkner's many attempts to differently define their relationship show why the couple faced so many upheavals.

———

Besides receiving a letter on her birthday, Joan also received the customary telegram from Faulkner, sending his birthday wishes and love. By now Joan was settled at 288 West Fourth Street, and in accord with Faulkner's wishes, delivered three sections of *A Fable* to Saxe Commins at Random House. Joan arrived at Commins' office before Faulkner's letter. Commins, therefore, was surprised and at first skeptical of the material Joan gave him:

> I mailed you a letter on Sept. 2; have heard nothing from you and couldn't help but wonder?
> So to bring you up to date: I delivered the mss. safely to Commins, however, he had not got a letter from you saying I was going to do so and when I presented it to him he looked at it carefully and finally said, It's Bill's all right— which I took to mean he thought I must be trying to pull something over on him? But seriously he was very nice although I would estimate I spent about 3 minutes with him; he said I could use his name for reference or to call on him if I needed to. Also saw Ober and took him a half done rewritten Jake and have not heard a word from him since then; he was nice too; they are both seemingly shy men which makes me so too; I am always completely amazed when I meet such people and they are shy. So then spent a week of pounding the pavements from 9 til 6 and was offered several jobs, of which the most interesting were one with McCall's magazine, one with the Dryden Press, and one with Look magazine; the latter is in the reader's mail depart. and I really think it will be interesting, working with people at least second hand, something different, and it will require keeping up with things, etc. and etc. as they have no form letters and each is answered individually; so this was the one I thought would be fine and good enough so that I didn't think it wise to turn it down in order to look further. Then dropped in to see a girl I know who works on another magazine and she gave me all this about what a terrible rut I would get in to, that I could certainly get something better etc. and mentioned that she had been sailing with Harrison Smith, mentioned that she knew me and I knew you and he said he remembered me so she said to call him up— in sudden panic I bolted over to his office— not to ask him for a job but to ask him what he thought of the Look thing; my memory of him was certainly wrong; I must be thinking of someone else I met that night that I thought was Smith or either he has changed; he seemed so much older; in fact he seemed quite old, even shaky old. But was extremely nice and without even waiting to find out why I had appeared in his office after three years began entertaining me with tales

of you; we discussed books (I told him to revive Mosquitoes and he also gave me a long tirade on Hemingway— his thing in Life, his beer ad etc. on the stuff written by most young writers (homosexuals, he proclaims), talked about R. for a Nun as a play (he thinks it should be put on it [sic] a very very small place, maybe a circle theatre) and when I finally told him why I had come he encouraged me to take the Look thing, said mag. jobs were hard to find, that he could introduce me at Good Housekeeping etc. but that he thought the reader's thing by far more interesting than anything magazines of that sort would offer and I agree; so starting Monday Fleur Cowles[106] had better start watching her step. S. also said for you to send him some more people like me so guess you will have to pack off the rest you have— oh yes I told him you told me to go to see him if I ever needed advice; he said "3 years ago or just lately" and I said, "Lately." Mulling that over I wonder why he said that, but on second thought I think it was to find out when I had seen you last as that was the next piece in the conversation. So a lot has happened tho I have not been gone so very long, but it seems like a very long time, Bill, a very long time. My heart aches for those days in the woods, aches and hurts really— oh oh oh the lost lost lost days. It's all so quick quick- ~ and I can't fool myself any longer: there will not be anybody to fill your place in my heart, thoughts, to ever ever ever understand me as you do, to console, love, feel for me as you do; and if I would let myself stop to wonder and worry about it, I would be afraid (I said I wouldn't be anymore and I am not in the way once I would have been: I'm saying it aren't I?) of what the future is to hold in this way; probably I will go through life looking for another you. Oh Bill, Bill, the sun, the red roads, the houses, the school, the woods, the trees, the beer, the talk, the everything. I remember that I wrote you all this in the last letter but I had to say it all again; and to tell you that I love you.

I finished all of your mss. and as I said in the first letter— I like it and it is of course good; I really tho couldn't say that I could tell anyone what it is *about* (yet). Is that me off, or that I haven't read enough of it?

The morning I left my father got up and said: let me know if you need anything. I want to help someone.

Oh God, Bill.

They're going to Arizona for Oct. so that's something.

How is the book progressing; what else are you doing, thinking etc. This seems like the longest letter I've ever written you. That too is a good sign; not for things *between* us as that was always allright [sic], but of the iceberg melting. Isn't it? Please do write. I'm worried about what happened to the other letter.

On 27 September, just home from a long stay at Gartly-Ramsay Hospital (nine days according to his telegram), Faulkner writes Joan two letters and sends an evening telegram. The first letter, simply noted as Saturday, reports on his low spirits. The country is ghastly without her. His back is still painful and he hopes that the brace will help. And there is much ahead of him. The Ford Foundation is making a history of his apocryphal county and there is to be a TV piece from one of his short stories. He needs to feel better, specifically, he needs a letter from her assuring him she loves him, if only a little.[107]

Then in a second letter, again citing Saturday but adding the time, 2 p.m., he returns to his emotional illness, referring to his aching heart and not his aching back. He has been so sick, miserable, that he had not even properly read her long letter until that afternoon. They must be together; this must not end. He pleads that she not replace him and assures her that he will never let her go. "Smith is a good man for you to have seen. He will do a great deal for me that doesn't cost actual cash money. Dont hesitate to demand of him nor of anyone at Random House in my name."[108] He must hold, touch, and see her. He plans a trip to New York in October.[109]

Finally, the correspondence concludes with an evening telegram, reiterating that he has just returned from a nine-day hospital stay; has found the long letter and now remembers the 2 September letter. What's more, he put two letters in the mail to her that very night.[110]

Joan vividly remembers Faulkner's struggle with back pain. "He had a lot of problems with his back and some of the drinking he blamed on that, that his back hurt so bad ... he complained about his back hurting all the time. And of course, sitting there at a typewriter all those years didn't help it. I don't know when this was, or how it happened. I remember about his back, that we were at the Plaza Hotel[111] with a table full of people, one of whom was William Inge,[112] and Faulkner was drinking heavily because his back hurt.... and he frequently talked about taking Seconal."

Sometimes, in bursts of anger or despair, he would write Joan that his back wasn't hurt and broken, but his heart: his aching heart and aching back.[113] Those kinds of "pressures" Joan coped with by "not paying any attention to it."[114]

———

In these September letters, Faulkner's references to Joan's role in his drinking are oblique; he merely makes repeated comments about his aching heart. "I still feel rotten ... and will until I see you again. I dont think it is my back really, I think my heart broke a little."[115] Later in their relationship, Faulkner would openly accuse Joan of culpability when he required hospitalization for his drinking: her behavior hurt and disturbed him, and those emotions led to his collapse. Such an episode appears in *The Wintering*, when Amy and Jeff, having spent the night together in a New York apartment, find only disappointment. Jeff is described as impotent and Amy relieved to be released through sleep. In the morning she finds him drinking:

> Her face registered disbelief while she stared at the unshaven man, dispirit-
> edly at the kitchen table, on which a whiskey bottle sat....
> Jeff said he was sorry. Crumbs were not enough, after all. But she had
> gotten into bed with him! Amy said.
> "The whole time wishing you were not, Amy. Don't you think I could see
> that? I don't want pity."[116]

Joan's use of the word "crumbs" in this dialogue reflects Faulkner's frequent use of the word in his letters to her. Using this real-life word in her
novel is just one of many instances where factual events and actual conversations suit her fictional needs. The preceding morning scene in the novel
is followed by Amy's decision to spend another night with Almoner:

> She came to bed less reluctantly and put her head on his shoulder.
> "Amy," he said, "you're the most dear and precious thing I've ever held in
> my arms. Does that embarrass you?"
> "No."
> "Good," he said. "I don't ever want you to be embarrassed by sentiment.
> That's one thing wrong with the world today." He then whispered, "I'm
> afraid of failing you again, tonight. Poor baby. I keep trying to help free you
> of all your Sunday-school morality. On the other hand, I'm stuffing some
> back into your head, preaching. But, Amy, to give is to get back so much
> more.... I've learned something about my life recently, too." Immediately
> she was listening. "Everything I've done was for you, Amy, even when you
> were still in darkness. I know that now."
> "Before I was born, you mean?"
> "Yes," he said. "Yes, even before you were born. It was all for you. I know
> that, now."[117]

Faulkner writes in a long, undated letter, following a night they spent
together, that he doesn't like subterfuge and crumbs. That morning, before
she left for work at *Look*, he chose not to tell her of his disappointment,
not wanting to make her work day more difficult. He wants more from her
even though he admits it is his own hunger that creates the subterfuge. If
all she intends to do is sleep with him—not make love—he wants her to say
that. He would have preferred her just telling him "let's just go to sleep."
Instead she tried to avoid saying even that by escaping into sleep with her
clothes on.

Crumbs are doing things without really wanting to; crumbs result
in unhappiness, anguish and grief; crumbs are what one gives to pay
for things. If they are to create a ledger between them, then they have nothing. For Faulkner, Joan's generosity must involve truth, and without the
practice of generosity she cannot learn enough about the human heart
to write her best. She will not be able to write the truth about Almoner and
Laurel[118] without practicing truth. The gods won't have it or let her.

He hopes her soul and spirit can be as truthful, simple and beautiful as her body.[119]

———

Making good on his promise to assist her once she settled in New York, Faulkner wrote Commins a letter designed to serve as Joan's introduction. However, it literally was interrupted in the middle by his hospitalization and finally was finished on 28 September 1952.

> Dear Saxe:
> .... This letter does not make sense; you can see that I am in a bad condition.
> Please send me $5000.00.
> Miss Joan Williams, whom you will remember from two years ago, is coming to New York. She will bring to you 3 sections of the rewritten mss. which is right.
>
> 28 Sept.
> I should have got this letter off to you almost a month ago.... If there is anything she [Joan] needs that you can do, do it for me. I have made a writer out of her, showed her how to do one TV script which she sold, and a story which Ober has just sold to the Atlantic. Now I am going to make her write a novel for Random House. She is shy and independent will probably ask nothing of you. Will you write her a note and tell her to call on you at need, for my sake? ...[120]

Though belated, this letter was important for Joan, as she would soon hear from Commins.

———

Joan's letters from New York reveal high spirits that are in stark contrast to Faulkner's gloomy mood. September held much promise for her: the move to New York; a new job; and most importantly, the *Atlantic Monthly* taking her short story, "The Morning and the Evening." Ober forwarded the acceptance letter from Seymour Lawrence, then an *Atlantic* editor, to Faulkner. Faulkner thanked Ober for the letter and his assistance, telling him, as he had Commins, "she [Joan] is shy and independent, will ask no help. But for my sake, do whatever you can for her."[121]

Clearly their physical separation rattled Faulkner. He writes letters in quick succession. In one, he begins by telling Joan how proud he is of her for the *Atlantic* acceptance, that he was right in believing in her, and was in fact the only one who believed in her. He writes that those days in the woods meant more to him than to her, being able to spend time with her and touch her, her body and mouth. Once the Ford Foundation people have gone, he hopes for at the least a fortnight in New York. Feeling both proud and unhappy, he asks for letters from her, tells her she must write the novel[122] now, and that he, who never needed anyone, needs her. The fitting for his back brace is scheduled for 10 October and he is hopeful that the pain will lessen, even though now he knows, he repeats, it is his heart hurting, not his back. Their phone conversation the other day was not what it might have been. His wife was listening.[123]

On a *Look* interoffice memo, Joan dashes off a note conveying her absolute happiness at placing her story:

> Thank you for just those words: I'm so damned proud of you. That's all that had to be said to make me able, were it the rest of my life, to go to sleep saying: he's so damned proud of me.
>
> When you come when you come and there will be sun and laughter and lovely sadness in every face and every building and everything that we shall see and do.

A more in-depth letter follows this note:

> Tuesday
> Sept. 30, 1952
>
> Dear Bill,
>
> I got the telegram and special on Sunday, then two letters on Monday, I believe, anyway when I talked to you I had had none of these and so didn't say a lot that I could have otherwise. Or maybe there wouldn't have been anything else to say except what I did--tho I wouldn't have asked are you happy, but, aside from unhappiness about me are you happy; if there were no me, and you were you, would you be happy; doing anything any differently? all that I want to know, for I no longer have to ask are you happy when we are far apart, knowing the answer to that already, as you do about me.
>
> Old Jake. At Harvard![124] Ober didn't send me the check, as he wasn't sure about the address and said for me to come in and he would leave it with his receptionist--so having got it I was walking down the street and saw him sitting in Longchamps[125] so went into [sic] to see him, walked up to the table and he didn't know me! And after I had just made him a whole twenty-five dollars, too. (I still owe you same for t.v. thing, I know). I told him that I would like to suggest to the Atlantic that they, in the second part, refer to Jake as *he* instead of by name, after the first sentence, as you suggested (I didn't tell Ober you did, but I personally am acknowledging same and thank you, as it is right.) He said o.k. and to send him a marked copy of story and he would send it. Bill, I can't do that. I'm too tired to type it all over, so thought I would just write to the Atlantic myself; is that all right? I can't decide whether I like Ober or not. As an agent of course I find him unbelievable, but he scares me to death. Is he just tired? He seems so cold and remote and formidable and detached or something ... I don't know, maybe it's just because he isn't jumping up and down in excitement too, but that isn't

all, really. In fact, I myself have not really felt like jumping up and down either; I felt glad, and sad. And so encouraged, I wrote on the Laurel thing[126] all weekend. It is started now, for the first time. I mean I know that this is the way it's going, whether what I've got down right now is valid or not–I think it can be done–only now, there's so little time to try to write. But I will–if just tonight I can sleep and sleep and sleep ... Whatever I have achieved, Bill, its been you that made it possible. I am very glad that this wonderful thing happened to Jake, whom you did not touch with *pencil*, you know what I am trying to say?

I wish, since you had to be in at all, you could have come to N.Y. to be in the hospital; it would have been a good reason and given us longer. About your coming, I want to see you and anytime; I only don't like the fortnight idea. Can't you get another medal or something and stay here to work for a long time. Whatever you decide about and when coming, I'll be here.

And Bill, your back. You do not deserve physical pain too. Ever. And I do not want it to hurt you. Do something about it. Let it be well forever. Yes, I would have come everyday and we would have read.

No, there is nothing that you can do for me there; and I would demand nothing in your name from anyone. What do I want anyway, except to know your name, to have the right to speak it to myself privately. On a little silver bell hung in my heart. That's what I would like, a little silver bell with your name inside.[127] I finally thought of that you could give me. You know, just sometime, whenever we could and I could give you one, or maybe you don't need tangible things. I never can not let that bother me–to ask you for anything, tho how often I said inside me–Bill, make me able to write! In all that frustrating time. And you did, and able to live too–live unafraid, and giving of my heart, not afraid what and if anything it would get in return.

So silver-head, I saw you standing in a dark hall with the phone, with the hurt back, aching heart, sad voice, and kind–kind all over, inside and out. So now, goodnight from Jake and me, and to Caddy too, wherever she is.

Joan[128]

———

When Faulkner and Joan discussed Harold Ober, Faulkner concurred that he was a very reserved person. He related their exchanges as, "How are you, Mr. Faulkner? "How are you, Mr. Ober?" Joan found it remarkable that her mother-in-law, Catherine Drinker Bowen, also was represented by Ober and was considered one of the few individuals who could draw Ober out. She told Joan once of being in Ober's office when he was looking at a picture of F. Scott Fitzgerald and was crying. An incoherent letter from Fitzgerald to Ober revealed the author's deteriorated condition and moved Ober to tears. Even though Fitzgerald ended his business dealings with Ober in 1939 when the agent would no longer authorize advances for unsold stories, they remained friends. Ober and his wife, Anne, often cared for Fitzgerald's daughter, Scottie, and have been described as parents to the girl.

On 1 November 1952, Faulkner wrote Joan regarding Ober: "I would hate to be marooned on an island with Ober too, but he is a fine agent and a good person. I never see him, because we have nothing to talk about. We correspond, but that is all. Let that be your attitude toward him. He is all right, just horribly shy, and I mean horribly."[129]

Another important connection for Joan made through efforts on Faulkner's part was realized at the outset of October. Joan receives a highly encouraging letter from Saxe Commins. He has been unable to reach Joan by telephone and he asks her to call him, writing that he wants very much to meet her and talk about her writing.[130] Joan relates this news to Faulkner, who at this point in the month, is succumbing to another collapse:

Monday

Dearest Bill~

I got home Friday night and found a note from Mr. Commins, saying he had been frantically trying to get in touch with me and would I please get in touch with him, which I did today and when I talked to Him (sic) over the phone he sounded so desperate I was sure something really terrible had happened and was worried to death til I finally got to see him at noon. He began by saying he had received your letter etc. and then about the Jake story etc. and that I must write a novel! That since you thought I had talent that was good enough for him~ that he wanted to help me, to be my editor, and etc. And then, as I knew something was coming, he asked me about you~ how was your health when I last saw you, did I think you were unhappy~ and so we talked about you some and your situation there altho I guess I was hesitant or something because he said once~you can tell me; Bill keeps nothing from me~and I guess I could talk of you more freely then, altho I just wanted to cry and when I left and was out on the street I did and then walked on Lexington, where somehow things seem more real. But he was so damn nice~and I could tell how much he loved you and I guess he could tell how I felt and so there we were and I felt really that I or we didn't get anything settled and I wanted to say and so now I've told you what you want to know~what are you going to do? And he said you could always stay with him in Princeton and I wondered if you had considered it. It won't be nice for you to stay in a hotel and try to work. I felt~God, I'd kill myself if it would help me write a novel for Bill and Mr. C. He was so nice saying did I have enough companionship, happy in my job~and knowing it was because of you made it even nicer. And so no matter what, you have me and you have him and two people loving you so much out of all the world should make you proud and don't be unhappy, cat-who-used-to-walk-by-himself. Write me what you are *doing*. Do you go outside and look at the woods, go here and there, and what thinking too. Thank you again for everything in the world, and thank you for whatever you said to C. when you wrote him. I am so overwhelmed by people being kind (really sincerely so) that it was a wonderful experience talking to him for twenty minutes whether I ever have a book to bring him or not. write~it is a beautiful day~a day in the woods day.

Joan

Did she [Estelle] know that was me that phoned? And what did she say?[131]

———

Shortly after his meeting with Joan, Commins flew to Oxford at Estelle's behest to help with Faulkner who had fallen down the full flight of stairs at Rowan Oak. In letters to his wife, Dorothy, and to Robert Haas and Bennett Cerf at Random House, and in gothic language suited to his patient's fiction and Southern setting, Commins relates his time in Mississippi. His first night was "harrowing" and full of "strange and pathetic happenings" that will be chronicled in full in his journal. It is a "ghastly" tale he relates to his wife:

> ... I found Bill completely deteriorated in mind and body. He mumbles incoherently and is totally incapable of controlling his bodily functions. He pleads piteously for beer all the time and mumbles deliriously.... His body is bloated and bruised from his many falls and bears even worse marks.... The disintegration of a man is tragic to witness.[132]
>
> It was pitch dark when I arrived in Memphis and now I am getting my first glimpse of Southern daylight. So I have no impression whatever of the country. The house, however, has left a strong and rather distasteful impression on me. It is a rambling Southern mansion, deteriorated like its owner, built in 1838 and not much improved since. Ours is a heavenly mansion in comparison, if very much smaller. The rooms are bare and what they do contain is rickety, tasteless, ordinary....[133]

To Haas and Cerf, Commins is no less vivid, writing "My first glimpse of Bill made me realize how accurately they [Estelle and the family] had reported his condition. He was lying on the couch in the drawing room in a stupor.... He greeted me mumblingly and incoherently, saying, 'I need you. Get me beer!'"[134] Commins then, almost as if talking aloud to himself, considers his options: the local hospitals could not handle the situation and he doesn't believe they could get Faulkner to Memphis in his current shape; the one-time idea that he might bring Faulkner to New York for care is now completely out of the question. "If he regains consciousness to take care of himself I'll beat a hasty retreat to New York and the amenities of publishing."[135]

After deliberations, Commins and Estelle finally managed to get Faulkner to Gartly-Ramsay on 8 October. Despite the severe fall, there were no new injuries to his back. By 15 October, Estelle reported in a letter to Commins (now back in New York) that Faulkner was responding to treatment. Her letter highlights as well the extent of her misgivings regarding her marriage. She fears Commins may know of Faulkner's intent to leave her. (She later writes Commins that "Estelle Faulkner, without Bill & Jill, *would* be a total nonentity—"[136]):

> Dear Saxe~
>   Have just talked to Dr. Adler~He says Billy is doing wonderfully well.... Still has beer three times a day, but the doctor, being a good German gentleman~evidently things it's good for Bill, and no doubt is~I was a little startled when I saw your letter addressed to Mrs. Estelle Faulkner~Aren't you a bit premature~or has something happened that I'm in the dark about?....[137]

Upon his release from the hospital on 21 October, their marital conflicts would peak. Estelle found and read many of Joan's letters to Faulkner while he was in Gartly-Ramsay.

—————

Again on hospital letterhead stationery, Faulkner writes Joan an impassioned letter, pouring out his love, telling her he now believes he probably never really loved before, never loved anyone the way he loves her. Just as he has made her, she has made him over. Here, as in many others, the woods are remembered and romanticized just as they are in Joan's letters. He never tires of telling her how much he loves her. The only "break" from such language is his request that she give his regards to Mrs. Cowles.[138] Joan remembers Mrs. Cowles, the associate editor of LOOK and *Quick* magazines, as someone who was doing a lot of writing. While Faulkner probably knew her, Joan personally did not.[139]

During a later hospitalization in New York, Faulkner would describe the facility as that jail place. Gartly-Ramsay in Memphis escaped such a vitriolic definition. Founded in 1934, the Memphis hospital met several needs. While primarily providing obstetrical care, it was also a general hospital that had always admitted psychiatric patients. Until 1942, it operated a nursing school as well. "'From 1950 until it was closed January 1, 1973, it served as a specialized psychiatric hospital'—or as described in a 14 September 1937 Memphis *Commercial Appeal* article—'a place for the care and rest of nervous patients and those chronically ill.'"

Dr. McCool said that at the time of Faulkner's troubles, it was the only hospital in Memphis where you could admit a private psychiatric patient. According to Dr. Adler, the patients were mostly middle and upper middle class. The facility itself he described as having "spacious and well-kept lawns and comfortable airy porches. Through the years it ... had a reputation for good food and friendly personal services." Even at its peak, Gartly-Ramsay was never a large facility and most employees knew the patients. Mary Alice Crockett, who worked as an assistant administrator there, said Faulkner was "a very quiet man. Very into himself, very cordial. I can still see him now walking in the halls wearing a tweed jacket with leather elbows and leather shoulder pads. It was a beautiful jacket. It seemed well worn and well loved." She remembered seeing Mrs. Faulkner only once but she did recall a nurse, Sue Adkisson, whom Faulkner would speak with at great length. "She [Adkisson] had more to do with him than anyone. I don't know what was going on with them."

Mrs. R.G. Ramsay Jr., whose husband co-founded the hospital, remembers Adkisson as "kind of a loner. She was liked, but maybe she was a little shy." Faulkner also enjoyed talking with her husband, telling Ramsay once that until he changed his type of writing he never sold anything. Faulkner implied that until his writing contained more sexual content no one cared for it. These memories may well be the only record left of Faulkner's stays. When the hospital closed, the records were transferred to microfilm and the paper records were burned. Then the microfilm subsequently was burned. According to McCool, "There are no existing records. The hospital closed ... and as astounding as it may sound, within weeks or months after that all records were destroyed."[140] After the early 1950s Faulkner usually was hospitalized in Byhalia, Mississippi, at Wright's Sanitarium, primarily because the facility was a good deal closer to Oxford.

Just one day after returning from Gartly-Ramsay, Faulkner sends Joan a short note telling of favorable reports from both Ober and Seymour Lawrence at the *Atlantic*, the latter wanting her novel when she writes it. Such good will and pleasant feelings are short-lived, as both Faulkner and Joan must soon confront the reality of their affair. Estelle has gathered and read many of Joan's letters. At 10 p.m. on Thursday, 24 October, Faulkner alerts Joan to this development. He recounts his two hospital stays—18–26 September and 8–21 October—as the result of a nervous collapse precipitated by knowledge that Joan was going away, her actual departure, and his summer-long back pain. Those ills he believed he could self-medicate with beer and Seconal. After the first collapse and hospitalization in September, he returned home and again turned to the beer and Seconal regimen. Soon he was back in Gartly-Ramsay.

Upon his return to Rowan Oak, he asks his wife if he has accumulated mail. She said yes and he went through his desk but there was nothing from

Joan. Faulkner believes Estelle has taken Joan's letters—some he previously
had read and also one she sent him while he was in the hospital. When confronted, Estelle admitted reading the letters. Faulkner hopes Joan will
respond with anger rather than fright. He plans to threaten Estelle—if she
tries to make trouble—with his own love letters to Joan. Joan will reveal them
should the situation warrant.[141]

This domestic saga is repeated in a 25 October letter to Commins in
which Faulkner's preoccupation not only with the crisis at hand but also
the pressure of A Fable's unfinished manuscript spills over dramatically. He
would like to accept Commins' offer to visit Princeton and finish the book.
Yet, given Estelle's present condition, Faulkner is convinced his wife would
see the trip as a ruse to be near Joan:

> Dear Saxe:
>
> Hells to pay here. While I was hors de combat, E. opened and read Joan
> Williams' letters to me. Now E. is drunk, and I am trying to nurse her before
> Malcolm sends her to a hospital, which costs like fury and does no good
> unless you make an effort yourself. I cant really blame her, certainly I cant
> criticise her, I am even sorry for her, even if people who will open and read
> another's private and personal letters, do deserve exactly what they get.
>
> But this is a terrible situation; never can I remember being so unhappy
> and downhearted and despaired. I have done no work in a year, am living
> on my fat, will begin soon to worry about money, and I do not believe I can
> work here. I must get away....
>
> .... I can take the mss. and come up and finish it in peace. But I am fear-
> ful about Jill. I mean, to disrupt her in the middle of her senior year at her
> school. I am afraid that, if I came up, E. would insist on some public for-
> mal separation and so forth, so that every time Jill entered a class room or
> the dining room, she would think: *All these people know that my parents have
> separated*, and it would ruin her year, even if she herself did not do some-
> thing in desperation.... I will always believe that my first responsibility is to
> the artist, the work.... But there is a responsibility too to the female child
> whose presence in the world I am accountable for. I used to be the cat who
> walked by himself, and wanted, needed nothing from anyone. But not any
> more....[142]

Joan is unclear as to how Estelle might have obtained her letters from
the Oxford post office. "I know by that time I wouldn't have been writing
letters to his house since we'd had all this trouble." In an earlier letter,
Faulkner is concerned that Estelle has been checking his P.O. box (A.E. Holston), and writes in the 24 October letter that he is careful to reach the P.O.
box first. All of which suggests that Estelle knew what name to request. Joan
surmised that "she found his key and went there, or maybe they knew each
other well enough in Oxford that the postmaster would let her look in his
box." Estelle's discovery prompted Faulkner to return Joan's letters to her:

"That is when he sent me all those letters back that you have. He said she had this one and all of that, and that is why I have any of them."[143] Later he writes Joan that the letters he has recovered are for her to keep and use for Laurel (*The Wintering*).

––––––––

Faulkner fears the uproar over the letters has scared Joan, and on 1 November he writes Commins: "I have not heard from Joan Williams since I wrote her, which I felt I had to do, that Estelle had opened her innocent letters and misconstrued them. Joan knows E. a little too, and the poor child is probably afraid to write. Will you telephone her at LOOK and see if she is all right, if she needs anything? Tell her I asked you to, if you prefer."[144]

Relieved to get a letter from Joan, his correlating letter relates the recent compliments she has received. Ober told him that Joan is intelligent and bright, which is a lot for Ober to say, and since Faulkner has confidence in her, he does too. Saxe Commins and the *Atlantic* editor[145] share that sentiment. Tongue in cheek, he writes that she had better be a good writer after he has crawled as far as he has for her on three different limbs. The Comminses have invited him to stay with them in Princeton while he works on *A Fable*, but he hopes for weekends in New York with Joan.[146]

He returns to these issues in a longer letter where he is much more focused on Estelle's reaction. Now that she knows Joan is in New York, his wife can imagine no other reason for his trip. He has tried, he writes, to reason with her, assure her that between a 24-year-old girl and a 55-year-old man, there is only admiration and gratitude. She is drinking and he is trying to get her sober. The wasted time haunts him as well: "I have got to get to work, and I am too unhappy here now; never in my life have I ever been so unhappy and depressed." He cautions Joan not to use Look envelopes for a while.[147] And after returning to the trials of being an artist, writing her to prepare for "scorn and horror and misunderstanding," he assures Joan that she will prevail, because "there is a God that looks after the true artist because there is nothing as important as the necessity to make things new and passionate and He knows it."[148]

About this letter, Joan remarked, "Now Mrs. Faulkner.... I still think that he is not giving her credit. This woman is living daily talking about this young girl her husband is going with and is apparently serious about. That would drive any woman crazy. And she probably imagined a lot that didn't take place. And every time he went out of the house she probably thought he was meeting me.... See you have also the dependency thing between them. Alcoholics today would call it enablers. He condones her drinking, she condones his drinking. He understands he can't leave her. He doesn't seem to want to."

Joan believes there was a part of Estelle that understood her husband as an artist. "In her letters that she wrote to Saxe she wrote about trying to protect his quiet. They don't mesh at all with what he [Faulkner] said. I'm sure she understood some part of it. After all, she was an older woman when they got married. Somebody else said that to me, at that time it was difficult to be divorced. And she came back in defeat kind of to Oxford with two little children in her thirties. So all she had was to be married. There wasn't any other life."[149]

———

Early November continues with discussions of revisions on Joan's short story and Faulkner's pending trip to the East. In what is slightly out of character for him, as modesty usually prevails over egotism, he writes that when Joan came to visit him that first afternoon in the rain, she put her little star in front of a comet, whatever her intentions may have been. Jake has helped her grow up. And since he did something to create her, Joan was then able to create Jake.[150]

Still preoccupied with the "stolen" letters, Faulkner writes Joan that he retrieved them in a shabby fashion. He refused to give Estelle a drink until she turned them over to him. He thanks her for reminding him not to be afraid and he reminds her of the same, declaring again that Jake has freed her from the middle class:

> You cant be both, and being an artist is going to be hard on you as a member of the human race. You must expect scorn and horror and misunderstanding from the rest of the world who are not cursed with the necessity to make things new and passionate; no artist escapes it. You have to say to yourself: Are Jake and Bill and what Bill and I have between us, which produced Jake and, continued, will produce still more beautiful Jakes, more or less important than the conventional approval of me by the mass of people who see nothing but ugliness and even obscenity in Jake's beauty. If you choose Jake nothing can hurt you. It will not be important enough, no jealous husband nor wife nor public smear, anything.[151]

He wants to believe she thinks also of last summer, when she turned to him without caution, and Jake came from that, from when he touched her and she allowed it. If they had been only child and teacher, he could have taught her only cold mechanics. The passion in her work came from their intimacy— their flesh's, their bodies' intimacy. This, also, an artist must not fear.[152]

Prior to leaving for Princeton, Faulkner asks Joan to send a telegram to Holston letting him know if she can meet him in New York. His tirade against Estelle continues, as he reminds Joan that he was honest with his wife from the beginning; that he introduced Joan to Estelle soon after they met and that he suggested Joan come to Rowan Oak to work.

Then he envisions a future with Joan married. He believes that unless Joan should marry an artist, her husband will probably forbid her from seeing Faulkner. Still, Faulkner doubts she would cave in to such demands.

"He was always trying to save me from the middle class, from some conventional middle-class marriage where the man wouldn't want his wife to do anything.... As long as you didn't do the conventional in the South those days there was something the matter with you. You had to be very conventional. That is why I felt so much sympathy for Flannery O'Connor. I can just know what she must have suffered with those tea parties and not being pretty and not doing this or that [that] the other girls [were doing]."[153]

For this November trip, he plans to stay at the Algonquin before moving on to the Commins home, as that was where he and Joan spent their first evening alone when they barely knew each other. His kiss wasn't even really a kiss, just a slight brush against her mouth.[154]

———

Faulkner's arrival, first at the Commins house and later at the Princeton Inn, relieved some of his anxiety at his physical separation from Joan and allowed for a period of sustained focus on *A Fable*. The Comminses invited Joan and Faulkner to their home for Thanksgiving, and over the relaxed holiday, Joan did not notice Faulkner doing any actual writing on *A Fable*.

"He thought *A Fable* was going to be the greatest thing he'd ever written.... I don't remember the reviews for *A Fable* when it came out. I don't know if he ever knew in his heart that that book was not as good as he thought it was or what. And I don't remember ever reading anything like Saxe or anyone else disliking the book.... I think he could fool himself about it. He had worked on it so long; he didn't want to ever give up. I think probably it didn't need to be so long, maybe."[155]

Unfortunately, Faulkner's respite was short lived and by the end of November he was admitted to the Westhill Sanitarium in the Bronx. Joan remembers saying to "him [Dr. Mosse] that Faulkner was on this thing and I didn't know what to do and he sent him out there. I don't remember that he stayed very long. And I feel sure, but I'm not positive, that this is the time they said he had shock treatments."[156] Joan saw Dr. Mosse herself, and according to Blotner, the European-trained psychiatrist specialized in treating artists and he was especially eager to help Faulkner as he admired his work.[157]

Back in Princeton, after saying goodbye to her in New York that evening, Faulkner wrote Joan a letter at 1:30 a.m., with a closing note penned at 7 a.m. Quoting a Frenchman who said to part is to die a little, Faulkner chronicles their various partings and the devastation he felt each time. He is writing instead of phoning her, as he would prefer, like the time he woke her at 4 a.m. just to sleep beside her and breathe the same air.

He is coming to believe that he cannot work away from her and if he does the work will suffer. The work is nothing measured against her: her eyes, her mouth, her breast, her navel, and the inside of her body. Poor baby, infant, she didn't know what would come of driving by a man's house who wrote books, did she?

In just two weekends he will die again as he must return to Oxford. Maybe he'll come into New York and get a hotel room near her, but no, he realizes she has her own life. He is just thrashing in agony and will not take the pill or drink that might help him sleep. Through the suffering and the anguish perhaps God may decide to let Joan's life come into his, her physical life, her spirit and soul.

His 7 a.m. handwritten note apologizes for sending this depressing letter. It reminds him of her phone call to him at that jail place when she cried so terribly. She should not have to receive such a thing but it is an occupational hazard of being loved and beautiful, or maybe just loved.[158]

"I did phone him out there. It was a drying out place. As far as I know it may have been more.... Now I was crying and I was upset because he was in it. Particularly when he would always be telling me it was my fault.... But I remember crying when I called him up at that place. But that was because he was in it. I mean it disturbed me that he would go to these places."[159]

Having been through such episodes with her mother and father, Joan, while not surprised, was no less moved by his breakdowns. Her family history also allowed her to empathize with Jill. "...he was telling me always what a terrible childhood I had and feeling so sorry for me, and he's doing the same thing to his own daughter. But he doesn't seem to have any concept of that and said 'they never argued in front of the children and servants.' Well, you know that's not true. And his drinking must have been very upsetting to her [Jill] and her mother's would have been too."[160]

"Jill wrote him a letter when he was drying out in New York and he asked me to read the letter to him in the hospital. He didn't say anything about the letter. He was probably semi-doped up. He probably didn't take it in at the time. I just left it there. I'm sure he read it later, I guess. I don't know. I never mentioned it again."[161]

———

On 9 December, Faulkner sent the *Sound and the Fury* manuscript to Saxe Commins along with his letter declaring the manuscript irrevocably Joan Williams' property. The next day Faulkner's letter to Joan takes a story-like tone. There was an old man, gray on top, who worried his heart might be gray as well because he had used it without calculation. His heart had been used to seek pity, compassion, beauty, and truth and to ward off being shocked or afraid of anything. This use of his heart made him a better person, though he doubted at this time in his life there would be anyone to share it all with.

One day a wind brings with it a scent of apple trees. As it blew over him, he realized it was full of the same belief in tenderness, beauty and truth that constituted the only worthwhile things in life. Now he knew that his heart was far from diminished; it had only just begun to love. It was not old at all and never would be as long as he breathed.

Closing with a question, he asks Joan if this will suffice until Thursday.[162]

———

Disquietude settled over the couple with Faulkner's departure for the Christmas holiday, and an intensification of Joan's stresses and depression. When Faulkner receives this moving letter from Joan, he writes in response three days later that he will be damned if he'll destroy her beautiful letter. It is too sad. He asks that she keep it for him; that perhaps they will one day read it together when they have truly become one and the reason for her writing is no more:[163]

> This could have been dated days ago, anytime, for I know already and again the fear and the loneliness and the emptiness.
>
> I have the memories— and I have most the memory of you coming thru the door saying only without question, "I'm here, I'm here." And of the way your hair is there by your ear where I cried. And of what I threw away when it was our last night. Oh Christ and God and Mary— if only anything anybody could return it.
>
> There, the last split moment when I could have gone out that door again and said. "Yes, yes, I'll come." Because God will be God for only so long— before even he cannot be God anymore, can give no longer to such a silly and empty fool as I.
>
>   J
> Only a bell—only the faint tinkle, as memories become faint too.

If only I could say wait one day and I can't—because of the other factors you can't. If to sit thru the twilight again would be enough. Just one more, God, God, God. If only, if only.

———

As the year drew to a close, Faulkner, back in Oxford, declares in a letter he fears may stampede Joan into flight that he cannot, will not, live so far away from her. He yearns already "to talk fantasy and nonsense and good sense and truth to a beloved face, eyes, mouth, bitten-off finger-ends, to drink and eat with equals, to believe in the same things."[164] He insists that they never spend another Christmas apart. It is too agonizing, even for a hog for punishment like himself. He already is preparing a return to New York. The situation at home is ghastly. Estelle was drinking, nagging, and as it was too cold to stay away from her outside as he does in the summer, he put on his overcoat and walked up and down the gallery until midnight when she went to bed.

He remembers too much of their times in New York—the New Weston bar, sleeping in beds never big enough for two—to settle for this distance between them. In vivid prose, somewhere between erotic and pornographic, he recounts sexually fulfilling episodes—the taste of her navel, her nipples growing hard between his fingers or tongue—all too fresh and tangible to have to be remembered 1500 miles away. There also is the patina of Joan sitting beside a sunny window in Linscott's[165] apartment in a transparent shift where he could admire her body, especially her pretty legs. One can get too tired of long-legged but short-brained girls. Bougereau,[166] he believes, would have liked her thighs and legs.

Now she can have a good run, and he won't be alarmed, because the faster she runs the more rapidly the little bell he gave her will tinkle, so that running she will hear his name.

Should he write her so many letters that she stops opening them, that is all right. He asks that she wear the bell on New Year's Eve and think of him for a moment. He asks that they not spend another Christmas apart. It is too painful even for him. This is a love letter, whether she recognizes it as such or not, and he is proud to have written an entire page without using the word love until now.

Abruptly, in a scolding tone that he believes necessary if her talent is to grow, Faulkner speaks of Joan's need to face the fire; to go and meet the fire; to let it burn and sear. The artist must be braver, more truthful and more generous than anyone else in the world. She must be capable of giving more than anyone can give her in return. She makes a big mistake thinking that she can pay a psychiatrist to do it for her, to accept her responsibility for something she has done and later considers a mistake. This is all running: running from godhead, ecstasy, truth, reality and fact. If this angers her, let her make bitter retorts. That he also calls running. He loves her, and if this hurts her, she must know it comes after reflection on his part. He believes she must understand this for the sake of her talent and their relationship.[167]

"He thought I had run from my heart and my body, back into my mind. 'which is dead matter, nothing, since only the heart, the body, the nerves, are capable of feeling fire, anguish, passion, exultation, happiness, hope. No wonder your mind walled your heart and body in, once it got them, since the mind is afraid of fire.'"[168]

By now Faulkner should have known that Joan would find daily letters daunting. When Faulkner writes that she must be brave and generous for her talent to grow, what he means is that she must be sexually and emotionally generous with him. Regardless of the tone he took—needy, kindly, scolding, paternal, flattering, extracting—to Joan it all amounted to pressure. Confronted with such her inclination was detachment and flight. Thus, the very running Faulkner so criticized he did much to provoke.

———

Faulkner's anger and negativity toward psychiatrists resulted in part from his belief that they overcharged their patients. This was especially the case with Dr. Mosse in New York. Joan said that Faulkner often told her it was wrong and destructive for a writer to see a psychiatrist, that it would be giving away the pain and emotions a writer needs to work.

Tellingly, though, Faulkner himself failed to follow this tough advice. Instead of confronting the "fire" and "pain" in the forthright fashion he recommended for Joan, Faulkner usually did just the opposite. According to Dr. McCool, it was the disposition of the alcoholic, a term he firmly applied to Faulkner, to try to evade or deny pain. "A person addicted to anything, one impression, to me, I had was that an alcoholic, any drug addict, is unwilling to be uncomfortable. I'm not saying that any sensible person would choose to be uncomfortable, but you have to be willing to be uncomfortable. You touch something hot you have to be willing to be burned." Dr. McCool concluded that an alcoholic was unwilling to be uncomfortable, and those reasons could very well be mental or physical.[169] Dr. McCool's appraisal concurs with a statement made by Faulkner's stepson, Malcolm Franklin, "who said, simply, that when Faulkner was pushed he hit the bottle." Faulkner biographer Joel

Williamson notes "several people close to Faulkner agreed with his step-son."[170]

———

Separate letters to Joan mark the last two days of the year. On 30 December he mails a short note—more suited to February than December—with a large heart sketched on it and "I Love You" in cursive. He is finding the urge and desire, the beautiful ache and anguish for her, helped only by writing daily letters to her. It is a delightful discovery, this resurfacing of a need that had been gone for years. Someday he hopes that she will grow up and stop running. That she will be generous and brave enough to be worthy of Jake and Mrs. Murgatroyd.[171]

By New Year's Eve the delightfulness of the situation has abandoned him. His writing has gone "dry." "What I expected seems to have happened. I have run dry, I mean about the writing. What I put on the paper now is not right. And I cant get down what I know is right.[172] I cant work here ... I will be able to do nothing until I get away."[173]

He finds he needs Joan for his work, the way she used to need him for hers. He wonders if being needed will propel her into flight as being wanted does.

Hoping to finish Jill's holiday as peacefully as possible, he will wait until she departs to confront Estelle's drinking. Her son believes she should go to Whitfield, the state asylum, but Faulkner is against such a drastic measure. He interprets Malcolm's suggestion as meaning he doesn't want to deal with Estelle when Faulkner returns to the Northeast.

Still, he would rather think and talk about Joan, and leave these dreary and dull details behind. His work at home is impossible because there is no one giving sympathy, affection and warmth, so that he may give the same in return. All anyone there wants is money. He asks for a letter from Joan, dictates even what will suffice, what may be enough to get him writing again for his last days at home: simply Joan's assurance that she understands and will wait for him.[174]

V

1953—One Fifth Avenue

In many ways, 1953 started out as a year of wish fulfillment. Joan's short story "The Morning and the Evening" appeared as an *Atlantic* First in the January issue. She was enjoying life in New York City, working in *Look* magazine's Reader-Mail Department, and continuing her growth as a writer. The long, arduous task of *A Fable*'s composition was winding down at last and Faulkner had time even to write a few short articles and stories.

Joan's friendship with Faulkner was different this year with Faulkner in New York for months at time. The freedom the city afforded them allowed for a more settled routine and a chance to realize a new closeness. Random House, where Faulkner worked many days, was located next to the building that housed *Look* magazine, and they often met at a nearby corner. Joan remembers meeting Faulkner one day. He was leaning against the Random House building smoking a pipe and she thought to herself, "He *is* Random House."

Even though he wanted to spend as much time as possible with her, Faulkner knew that Joan saw other men and enjoyed her own social life. When intervals occurred forcing his return to Mississippi, he wrote Joan that the separations actually hurt; the relationship had assumed a heightened poignancy and urgency for him. He tells her again in a letter from Rowan Oak, as he told her four years ago by the river when she was home from Bard College and they were alone together for the first time, that he was afraid for him this was for keeps.[1]

———

Joan's first New York apartment on West Fourth Street was a one-bedroom walkup she shared with Ann Gambee, the sister of a friend from Bard.[2] The tiny apartment offered little in the way of writing space and even less in terms of privacy. Her circle of friends in New York included among

149

others Louise Fitzhugh, Brandon Grove and Faulkner. Though he was busy with graduate school at Princeton, Grove still made time for Joan, and sometimes Joan, Grove and Faulkner got together socially. Later in the year, when Joan moved to her own place on Horatio Street, she settled into a more satisfying writing routine.

Faulkner's many stays in New York involved a series of different residences and hotels: Hal Smith's apartment, the Haases' home, the Algonquin Hotel, Frank Waldo's Greenwich Village apartment, Bob Linscott's apartment, the Commins' home, and an extended stay in a suite at One Fifth Avenue. "One Fifth Avenue was a residential hotel near Greenwich Village," Joan said. "Faulkner had a bedroom and a sitting room and he stayed there quite a while."[3] As Joan recalls One Fifth Avenue in an unpublished sketch, it served comfortably as a work space and living quarters. It was at One Fifth Avenue where Faulkner one day took a picture of Joan he would not even be able to keep:

> And so back I must go, as requested, to the picture—only a snap shot, though I do not remember Faulkner having a camera and yet he must have for there I am a fairly young woman staring shyly at it: or so it seems to me for I look, to myself, uncomfortable in that photograph. It's tiny. I have no memory of it being taken and yet I remember exactly the place I am in and approximately the year.
>
> In the room, and there are two of them, the living room where the picture is taken and a bedroom beyond: Number One Fifth Avenue at the very end of that once posh street and adjoining Washington Square. Sometimes, we have walked there. I have my apartment nearby in Greenwich Village. I came over often to lend support or to have it. Faulkner is determined I am to write a novel following the two short stories I have published. It is to be a quick exchange of letters, he said, the

Joan Williams in 1953 (courtesy Ezra and Dawn Bowen).

way it really was, determined always I was to write a novel about us and our meeting~"soul mates" and some reason we met and "spun round in orbit together a while," he said. "Do not be ashamed" as if I could be of know- ing him~"an old man"~he always characterized himself that way. "A tired and battered bloke," he said in the very first letter he wrote, and he was only fifty-one.

"Call the girl Laurel, " he said about that proposed book. "Laurel Wynn," he added gazing out a car window in Memphis when we drove through Over- ton Park. The idea of the book followed hauntingly whenever we met for years, and a quick exchange of letters was not for me. I wrote The Winter- ing eventually, but he was not here to see it.

I came willingly, dutifully, to One Fifth Avenue in the mornings where he had thoughtfully provided a typewriter. I was to sit at it and write that book: and type, write, I did trying to tell that story but not in the way he prescribed, and I remember sitting there writing and feeling quite guilty. I never used any of what I wrote nor do I remember his ever reading any of it.

Faulkner himself went off those mornings to Random House, to the office of Saxe Commins, his editor, where he was writing or picking up writing after a hiatus of many years A Fable. Once, at least, he came back quite proud of himself; it was about forty blocks to Random House and he had walked all that way, keeping fit. In that suite where I sat~and I remember his worrying about the cost~Random House was not picking up the tab I don't believe. He had come to New York to spend a long while. On another table in the room~I think these long years later I was provided a card table~sat a typewriter Faulkner used, his paper in it, some laid near by. Occa- sionally he had gone over to it, his method of typing was with a finger or two. I went over and gazed at what was in it, longing to type something to have somehow hidden in Faulkner's manuscript: a word or two that was mine. But I could never bring myself to touch the keys.

I went out, came back. A lot of evenings I was there for dinner and we ordered up from room service~sitting only the two of us at a white-colored table, a waiter having hovered about setting things here, there. Faulkner liked it, I think, the civility of it all. Countryman that he liked to call him- self, he liked New York. I would walk home to my apartment afterwards, those being the days young people today do not know, when there was no fear: ride the subways at any hour, leave your doors unlocked, pass people on the streets, even loiterers in doorways without your hackles rising.

....

I do not remember Faulkner ever having a camera. And yet surely because there was never anyone else there~only a waiter who vanished. I did not own one. And I wonder that we did not roam about taking pictures, but that never happened either. And I did not have the sense to think, Why I ought to have as many pictures of Faulkner as possible. And we did not take any others. Why then that time, that day, I have no idea. I only know there I was wondering what to do about everything, an unexpected future ahead, and this great man taking a picture he could not even keep, so that even

then we must have known it was a memento for me~to keep and have surface again and again over time: never quite understanding why he wanted
to be there, the extent of an inborn loneliness that went so deep....

And there in my mind's eye sits the typewriter he insisted on and his own
in the same room, the paper in it, and how randomly he might go, as if
there were no import to it~and of course there was, every word, every
instance~to add something else to the monumental work. "Writing," he
said, "was all he ever found to alleviate the boredom of living." And perhaps with a camera which would not have been expensive to take a snap-
shot of a young woman admirer at a spot on Fifth Avenue, then lavish,
which he enjoyed.[4]

——

With Joan settled in New York and Faulkner plotting a way to join
her there, he still managed to turn his attention to A Fable. His discouragement with his progress at the end of 1952 turns optimistic, though with a
realistic bent, at the outset of the new year, writing Joan from Rowan Oak:

I was wrong. The work, the mss. is going again. Not as it should, in a fine
ecstatic rush like the orgasm we spoke of at Hal's [Harrison Smith] that
night. This is done by simple will power; I doubt if I can keep it up too long.
But it's nice to know that I still can do that: can write anything I want to,
whenever I want to, by simple will, concentration, that I can still do that.
But goddamn it, I want to do it for fun again like I used to: not just to prove
to bill f. that I still can.[5]

He then describes a long dream in great detail:

It seems I had an apartment in Princeton, we had spent the weekend and
we were giving a party Sunday afternoon, you were hostess and suddenly we
decided you had to have a new dress, then we were in New York, trying to
buy the dress in time to get back for the party; the dress was something
between gold and rust-color, it shimmered; I snapped you up into it in the
shop and then we were running, hurrying back to Penn station not to miss
the party, you holding the skirt of the dress up like an apron with three or
four bottles of champagne and tins of pate and caviar in it, and a cop trot-
ting along with us saying "If she dont put her dress down I'll have to arrest
you" and me saying we'll have to get to Princeton because they're going to
give you the Nobel prize this afternoon. The cop said, "for what?" and I said
"For her novel. Here it is. I'm trying to finish it and think of a title for it."
Then Lois, the Frenchman from the Princeton Inn ran up and took the manuscript and said, "I'll finish it. You help Miss Williams." So I gave him the
manuscript and then you and I were in a bar, you looking all flushed and
pink and tender and shimmering and beautiful and telling me something,
a blue streak, and I said, "We must get to Princeton" and you said "of course
we must. But I can make the bell stop ringing. If we come in like this, they
will all know." And I said, "Know what?" only it had begun to fade, your

face, fading, still smiling a little, and me trying to hold on to the dream, knowing by then it was a dream, still saying No, no, no, wait, wait and you saying
Yes bill yes bill I know I know it's all right it's all right and I said Joan Joan
not goodbye and you said It's all right, Bill. I know, I know. Not goodbye.[6]

Joan's response picks up the fanciful spirit of Faulkner's letter though
she bristles at the suggestion he is "going to finish her mss." even in a dream:

1/7/53

Dear Mr. Faulkner:
Sometimes, you are very funny. Running through Union Station the other
night in my shimmering gold dress (how I wish I could shimmer and shine
and join you in your halo of light) I thought how very funny you are.
Oh Bill, Bill, Bill what a heavely [sic] wonderful dream~except for the fact
that you were going to finish my mss.~that you were going to name it certainly seems true enough~and that you were going to give it to Louic [sic] to
finish~my nobel novel~is just too much. But what a wonderful dream. Please
write me all your dreams. What an awful lot I'm sure Dr. Mosse[7] would make
out of it. I sent you Jake by air mail today. Hope you did not already have
it. Have heard nothing from HO [Harold Ober] about Mrs. Murgatroid[8] or
from Smith about the key.[9] What repercussions are happening concerning
this? there is nothing else of news~I am the same~started trying to do another
story~stopped and wrtoe [sic] two pages on Laurel~stopped and went back to
the story~did six pages~terrible contrived stuff so quit because suddenly got
caught up in the fact that I was only doing character sketches~and I realized
I don't know how to write a story. In case you saw the write up about the
"first" in the Press Scimitar I had nothing to do with it. Mr. meeman[10] [sic]
saw the story and called my mother. Well, when you get hear [sic]
you can tell me how to write a story. I know how disappointed you must be
because of the letters but I hope that's all right. Also, I didn't sign
Jake because I was afraid someone else might see it. If you can avoid anyone
there seeing it, I hope you will~you can't refuse of course. I sent it straight
from the way HO sent it to me~I presume there is no bil'let doux [sic] inside.
      Many and many small golden ringings.
      I am so glad about the book[11] coming back but not surprised!
      Same also Sat. Many thanks for your note. It meant a lot.

Before Faulkner receives Joan's letter, he writes that he already has Jake
(the January *Atlantic*) and that she should keep the copy she has for him until
he gets home again—home is no longer Oxford but a reference to New York
City. He promises they will celebrate when he arrives with a thousand violets
and champagne. Joan never has lain in a bed of violets before, he imagines,
but then she never wrote Jake before either. His letter then shifts to his notions
of the short story: "A short story is a crystallised instant, arbitrarily selected,
in which character conflicts with character or environment or itself. We both
agreed long since that, next to poetry, it is the hardest art form."[12]

"Work is going damned well. Very hard to do here, and slow. Am doing new stuff now: it is all right. I still have power and fire when I need it, thank God who is good to me, lets me be able to write still and to be in love...." [13]

Faulkner reasons that Joan considers her short stories character sketches because they are still thin and lack fire and passion. This shortcoming is due to Joan's insistence on clinging to her iceberg, the frozen place inside of her.

He asks Joan to write him only when she feels an ache, a need, to tell him something. He hopes for spontaneous letters. As far as his letters are concerned, he is not surprised that she likes them. "Of course you like mine. Who wouldn't like to read the letters Faulkner wrote to the woman he loves and desires? I think some of them are pretty good literature, myself; I know what I would do if I were a woman and someone wrote them to me."[14]

He closes with a sample of his literary, love-letter technique. Joan walks in beauty much as the night walks in stars. Has he forgotten to mention her beautiful face, her soft mouth and thighs, and his hungry hands? Is he right to believe their separation has made her eager for him?[15]

———

Two letters follow dealing with details about Hal Smith's apartment[16] located at 9 East 63rd Street and Estelle's upcoming cataract surgery. Faulkner believes that she decided to have the surgery after putting it off for a year upon news that he was leaving for New York. Still, if he can get a nurse for his wife, he will soon be staying in Smith's apartment; and if Joan will agree, they can have five straight days together there. They will pile into one bed: Faulkner, Joan, Benjy, Quentin, Caddy, Jake and Mrs. Murgatroid.[17]

Unfortunately, Faulkner's stay in Smith's apartment fell short of his expectations. In *The Wintering*, Joan recreates a scene in a borrowed bachelor's apartment in New York where Almoner is staying:

> As immediately as Jeff opened the door to the apartment, however, it seemed hostile and withdrawn. Like a sleeping porter, it did not want to be bothered.... He came across the stretches of quietude and soft carpet, holding out her glass.
> The hushed quality of everything irritated Amy. He seemed humble approaching, too eager to please her; so often, she wanted to tell him to be more assertive. Patience with her might simply be the wrong approach, she thought. She wanted really a man to drag her around by a hank of hair and tell her what to do. Jeff, by waiting to see what she was going to decide, made her often feel put on a spot.

Having persuaded Amy to spend the night with him, Almoner's tentative maneuverings compel her to assume the same hostile and withdrawn qualities of the apartment:

> She got in gingerly beneath the sheet; their heads turned instantly toward each other. For the first time, Amy did not look away from his close observation. But she was not stirred.... When his hand touched her, she stiffened. Behind closed eyes, she longed for some great emotion to take hold of her. She lay then wishful for love and staring into the darkness. Jeff's hand moved cautiously. Her brain became alert. If only she could stop thinking.... She cried silently, Don't! with her teeth gritted. Her soul and her spirit were unmanageable and ungiving.[18]

———

Such setbacks in their relationship would start Faulkner drinking again, or so he would tell Joan. He wrote her afterward that even though she has slept with him she has not *surrendered*. She has not said yes, yes, yes; she has not been able to give everything, to give completely, to not hold anything back.[19] While trying to handle the conflicting signals Joan sent him, and living day to day with his constant back pain, Faulkner turned to the usual remedies. Soon the alcohol debilitated him. Bob Linscott arranged for Dr. Ben Gilbert, known as Dr. Broadway, a famous physician who treated many Broadway stars, to care for Faulkner in Smith's apartment.[20] Dr. Gilbert managed Faulkner's care along with a nurse, and Joan also spent time with Faulkner during his temporary recovery. "I remember ... he was recovering from a drunk and a nurse was there with him and she called me up there and asked if I would have dinner with him. And I did. He ordered cheese cake in from Lindy's or someplace that was famous for their cheesecake."[21]

This interlude was merely a temporary respite. Faulkner was well enough to attend the National Book Award ceremony with Saxe Commins in early February where, even though he was not a recipient this year, he was quite the center of the literary buzz. At a small cocktail party following the ceremony, *The New Yorker* described Faulkner as "the lion of the afternoon ... very small and very handsome, with a voice that never rose above a whisper, [who] stood with his back to the wall and gamely took on all comers."[22]

His poise did not last long. Faulkner kept drinking and was soon in worse shape than before. When this episode escalated and Faulkner experienced a blackout, Dr. Gilbert decided a hospital stay was more appropriate. Joan and Commins took Faulkner to the Charles P. Townes Hospital on Central Park West where he was admitted[23]: "...we took him to this hospital on the Upper West Side. It was a private hospital for drinking. And when we left, Saxe said to the woman at the desk, 'Now I don't want you telling or talking to any newspaper people who come here' ... And the woman drew herself up and said, 'I certainly won't because I've never heard of William Faulkner. I don't know who that is.'

"Saxe said to me later, 'I'm glad this didn't happen in Princeton, my wife has never seen anything like that.' And I thought, God, what a privileged lady. You know. I was upset when he did this, but it was not like something I couldn't face or hadn't seen before or didn't think I understood. I had grown up with my father and mother going on binges."[24]

This hospital stay was under a week and when Faulkner returned to Smith's apartment, Smith informed him in a note slipped under his bedroom door that "he had behaved so badly he would have to go somewhere else." The Haases invited him to stay for a time in their home and then he moved to the Algonquin Hotel. That stay was interrupted by another alcoholic episode, after which for a brief time he recovered at the Commins home. These months in New York meant, for Faulkner, a series of doctor appointments and tests. Besides Dr. Gilbert, Faulkner saw Dr. Robert Melchionne and, for a time, Dr. S. Bernard Wortis, a psychiatrist and neurologist at the New York University Medical School. Dr. Wortis found Faulkner to be a "man with a strong need for affection, one who hoped for some sort of emotional equilibrium but was uncertain of finding it."[25]

———

An emergency situation in mid–April shifted the medical concerns from Faulkner to Estelle. He writes Joan that Estelle's son, Malcolm, called him with news that Estelle had suffered a hemorrhage and they were unsure if it was the stomach or esophagus.[26] Jill was meeting him in New York and they were flying to Memphis the next day. He is sorry not to be able to tell Joan goodbye and he asks her to take care of a few necessary details. He specifically asks her not to send the pictures (most likely those he took of her) to his Oxford home. At this point, Faulkner was subletting writer Waldo Frank's apartment in the Village.

Back in Oxford, Faulkner writes Joan in succession. In a letter noted as Wednesday, he reports that Estelle is better now but was almost gone after another hemorrhage.[27] Though there is nothing urgent for him to accomplish in New York, he wants to return by 1 June to see Joan. Their last phone conversation troubled him. She said come back but with such qualifiers as if, but, and only. He wants her to emphatically say come back. He is working at the big book though without the pleasure of seeing her almost every day and the freedom of New York. He thanks her for his ability to still work. Joan gave him that by restoring and renewing him at just the point he thought he was finished, done, empty. The few drinks he had he didn't enjoy, not without Joan. He believes he will go back to tomato juice.[28]

On Friday, he responds to Joan's letter, telling her it brought him much happiness. He admits he needs her, he who once took pride in needing no one. He is no longer the cat that walks alone and he is maybe glad of it. This may be better. He remembers Joan's eyes—all the remembering to remember—her sleepy face looking up at him from her pillow through a tangle of hair with the rising shape of her body beneath the covers. "Stay away from Wortis. I thought I had warned you. His bill was $450.00. I asked how come, he said he charges $50.00 a visit, made me 9 visits. I remember only 3, two of which I called at his office by his request, not mine. He is a psychiatrist; in my experience, psychiatrists will do anything. Stay with Melchionne, who is a simple doctor. He gave me a complete physical overhaul, charged $85.00, against Wortis' $450.00, out of which I got one bottle of seconal capsules."[29] If Estelle continues to improve, he plans to leave for New York and perhaps have one or two weeks before Jill's graduation.[30] He loves and misses Joan. Rowan Oak swiftly is closing in on him.[31]

During the next week, Faulkner writes Joan three long letters, noted as Wednesday, Wednesday night and Thursday. His mood vacillates from boastful to tender, from sensual to scolding. He misses Joan and asks her to wire him and let him know when he can reach her by phone. Though consistent with his other letters in style and subject, there is one other letter quite noteworthy for its frank and thoughtful appraisal of his own literary journal:

> I know now--believe now--that this may be the last major, ambitious work; there will be short things, of course. I know now that I am getting toward the end, the bottom of the barrel. The stuff is still good, but I know now there is not very much more of it, a little trash comes up constantly now, which must be sifted out.... And now I realise for the first time what an amazing gift I had: uneducated in every formal sense, without even very literate, let alone literary, companions, yet to have made the things I made. I dont [sic] know where it came from. I dont [sic] know why God or gods or whoever it was, selected me to be the vessel.[32] Believe me, this is not humility, false modesty: it is simply amazement. I wonder if you have ever had that thought about the work and the country man whom you know as Bill Faulkner--what little connection there seems to be between them....[33]

Two omissions from this paragraph, one in the middle and one at the end, noted by ellipses, unequivocally pronounce how important Joan is to his existence. The middle ellipsis substitutes for Faulkner's definition of himself at this time in his life: he is the man who loves Joan Williams; who wants to tell her his dreams and hopes; who wants to be with her; who loves her girl's body and wants to put as much of himself into it—physically—as possible. The closing ellipsis speculates that perhaps there is a close connection between the creator of the work and Bill Faulkner the country man—that all those years he was working toward the night Joan met his plane in Memphis and he at last found her.

He continues, writing that his thoughts recently have been dominated by memories of last summer and its beauty—how, after three years he touched her and she accepted him; and no matter what follows such a moment for a man and a woman, nothing ever replaces the first part, the strangeness—learning each other's secrets until none—even of the soul and spirit—remain. Then when the final, the physical one, is gone too, what remains is to thank the gods for his incredible and amazing fortune.[34]

On Wednesday night, he addresses their long-standing conflict of what Joan regards as pressure. She is troubled about his return to New York because the pressure will return with him. He promises to try and control himself. He feels relief that it is something within his control and not all of the Mississippi ties he carries with him; freedom from those family responsibilities will take time. He encourages her to continue with her writing until he can return to help her: "...put the novel and the story away, take something simpler, that you yourself are not so involved in, just for practice. Something you have seen—an anecdote—something you are not involved in, are on the outside of; do it just for practice, fun ... to show yourself what you can do with words, the tools of the craft which you love and believe in."[35]

The other writing will come later when Joan can let go and he believes, knows, she is trying. She has slept with him but she has not known total abandonment. And while he hopes this breakthrough will happen with him, he insists that the important thing for her is that it does happen. Returning to his writing advice, he again cautions Joan to try to write from the outside.[36] And then, in a curious transition, Faulkner raises his concern that Hal Smith will make a pass at Joan. He did it once before when Faulkner introduced him to a pretty young girl and then Faulkner left town. He imagines Smith thinking that if someone as battered as Faulkner can get to second base with a young woman, Smith may feel he should at least get to first. Yet, maybe he has wronged him.[37]

By Thursday morning, Faulkner's typing is erratic and there is a rough handwritten postscript. Joan is a poor baby who also may hate his pity. He thinks she needs him and that upsets him because he is not close to her. She needs to stop worrying about the novel and short story; when it is ripe, it will come. He knows once they are together again he can help her with it.

What he meant by Joan telling him to come back with the right spirit was not that she necessarily means come back and I will sleep with you whenever you want. It is that she wants him to come back because what they have together is too important to lose; to be destroyed by such things as the ghosts Faulkner carries with him or Joan's refusals of him. So by come back, he wants her to mean come back even when we fail each other. If she is not too afraid of his Mississippi ghosts, he believes she can say this and mean it.

His postscript assures her that he isn't unhappy, not with all he has to remember. He knows it will not be forever before they are together again without any pressures. Between loving her and having sex with her, he chooses loving her.[38]

———

Faulkner returned to New York on 9 May and decided to forego the sublet of Frank's Greenwich Village apartment. He moved back in with Hal Smith and worked sporadically on *A Fable*. During this month, Faulkner and Joan were together, though fitfully. Together they met E.E. Cummings and Joan introduced Faulkner to Dylan Thomas. The party with Cummings was in the Village and Joan remembered Faulkner especially wanted to go and meet the poet. According to Blotner, the two highly individualistic artists got on well and overcame their shyness to enjoy each other's company.[39]

Joan already knew Dylan Thomas through a friend. When she was introduced to Thomas, she recalled with amusement how he paddled her palm, and she thought to herself, "I can't be his girlfriend and Faulkner's." At the YM-YWHA Poetry Center on 24 May, Joan introduced Faulkner to Thomas and they had drinks later that night. Just six months later, on 9 November, a few days after his thirty-ninth birthday, Thomas was dead from "pneumonia brought on by acute alcoholic 'insult to the brain.'"[40] Joan accompanied Faulkner to the memorial service where she said a newspaper photographer asked Faulkner to stop so he could take his picture. Faulkner complied.[41]

———

On 1 June a deflated Faulkner, now back in Mississippi, writes Joan two letters. The first is a short note wondering about her whereabouts—"I dont know where you are"[42]—since his last communication with her was a hurried memo on 20 May saying she was rushing to catch a train for Bard. Then in a letter noted as "later," he shifts his attention to her writing and a bus trip around the country she proposed as a means of gathering material.

Don't expect suddenly to be a better writer when you step off the bus in San Francisco or when you quit your job at *Look* and dedicate yourself exclusively to writing. In his opinion, making a bus trip to see America in order to write is as foolish as attending a writer's conference. By learning to write he still means learning the craft so it will come easier and she will be able to make a living at it. Joan's trouble has never been what to say but how to say it, saying it so that it is fun at the moment and enjoyable later to read and remember afterward the way you did it. She should have been learning this from him the last six months instead of insisting she cannot learn from him because he wants to dominate. Her freedom will not be worth much if it only brings her more problems and indecision.[43]

The bus trip was one of those theoretical things Joan and Faulkner discussed, as well as a writers' colony he imagined creating. The colony seemed a good idea to him but he was always very discouraging of Joan attending anything like a writer's conference or even her living in Greenwich Village. Joan did not believe he communicated the craft and tricks of writing to her as he professed. "On the other hand, he said people were always writing him letters wanting to know the trick to writing like a dog would learn to sit and there wasn't any. He would say I should have learned such and such from him, but he never tried to teach it to me."[44]

Since Joan anticipated leaving her job at *Look* (which she did in July), she naturally was concerned about money even though her parents always had been financially supportive and continued to be so. Leaving her job suggested a greater commitment to her writing; and in many letters, like the following, Faulkner tries to convey more a state of mind—a mental approach to writing—than any concrete instructions. He begins emphatically; telling her to never, ever be afraid of anything, especially about money: "That is death to an artist."[45] They are alike, he writes, in that neither would ever accept money unless they gave something in return. He will help her find another job. He will send her money. Whom could she possibly accept money from who would be better than him? She means more to him than any mumble a j.p. or priest could ascribe, and he hopes she feels the same about him. He doesn't mean a few times in bed the past six months—that is important only at the moment—he means the need they had for each other during the past three years even when there was nothing physical involved; when holding her still, unresponding hand was like holding a child's.

The worry she feels now that she is without a job may be good for her. He believes her newfound worry will persuade her to take what he can give about the work, what he offers, and what anyone except a beautiful, stiff-necked, moralist like Joan W. gladly would have accepted. It is still there for her. She hasn't thrown it away. She has the talent and no one can teach her to write, but an expert like himself can teach her how to make a living at it.

He hopes that they can try again and have another time when they can be free together all day with no one to challenge, care or know. They must run on the same track with the same gait, the same craftsmanship. Before they were running the same race on two tracks. She must throw overboard her ideas about her work and not his; she must accept any and all help he offers, not because it is always right, but because he believes it is so.

Work on the big book has delayed his ideas about the writer's colony but her promises more on that subject later. Right now he feels the pressure of his own work would prevent him from doing justice to a group that relies on him. Such as problem would not exist if he was just working with Joan, the two of them, but a large group is out of the question now. The group must wait until next year when he is free of the big book.[46] "But not you. We can, must meet again."[47]

He will read her latest story that night and consider it, then write her a separate letter about it.

He loves her and knows she is strong. She doesn't need to prove her strength by refusing to accept what he offers—money, help, anything—because he gives it out of love. The damn Winchell thing is something he must decide to handle for Joan and Nora's sake.[48]

The colony he imagined starting, Joan believes, was out West, maybe in Taos, New Mexico, "where D. H. Lawrence and all those people were. He had always wanted to start one but he never did." The Winchell matter involved a friend of Joan's from Bard, Nora Stone. Walter Winchell, a well-known gossip columnist, had published a piece about Faulkner and Miss Stone taking a walking tour of Ireland together. "I don't know how they got linked together," Joan said. "I don't know how he got Nora Stone's name. I think he must have meant me." According to Joan, however, there was no truth to the story.

The stories Joan and Faulkner mailed back and forth after "The Morning and the Evening" was published (January 1952) "were stories that never got off the ground. One was about a plantation owner named Mr. Howard and a black man named Otis. I was telling the story from Mr. Howard's point of view." In this letter and others Faulkner uses the word "Doakes" to represent the reader.[49] Faulkner is instructive but scolding. Having recently given the commencement address at Jill's college,[50] he seems infected with a need to reach this younger generation. What continues to trouble him about Joan's work is point of view. He cannot seem to communicate what he sees as a critical issue with her fiction. Here, Howard cannot keep telling "Doakes" about himself, explaining himself, the reader must come to know Howard by seeing his actions and the reactions of the people in the story around him. Maybe he has overemphasized, even burlesqued, this point.

"But from this distance, I dont know how else to do it; I must write almost as many words explaining what I mean, as I would need to write the story itself, which would be much easier. And I hate to send the letter," he writes, worrying its effect may "discourage or depress" her.[51] They both know she has worked hard at this story but they do not agree on what she has accomplished.

> Where you didn't work hard enough was in using the time I was with you to learn from me the best point of view to approach a story from, to milk it dry. Not style: I dont want you to learn my style anymore than you want to, nor do I want to help you with criticism forever anymore than you want me to. I just want you to learn, in the simplest and quickest way, to save yourself from the nervous wear and tear and emotional exhaustion of doing work that is not quite right, how to approach a story to tell it in the manner that will be closest to right that you can. Once you learn that, you wont need me or anybody.
>
> I learned to write from other writers. Why should you refuse to? You could even do this: when I think you need help, take the help from me. Then, if your conscience troubles you because the story is, as you feel, not completely yours, just remember what you learned from that one and burn the story itself up, until you can use what you have learned, without needing to turn to me. The putting of a story down on paper, the telling it, is a craft. How else can a young carpenter learn to build a house, expect by helping an experienced carpenter build one? He cant learn it just by looking at finished houses. If that were so, anyone could be a carpenter, a writer.[52]

Even with Joan's hard work and Faulkner's precise attention—"The first sentence of the story should tell Doakes that something bad is going to happen. It should be such a sentence that Doakes has got to read it, then read all the rest of them, until he cannot put the story down until he finds out what happened. This is a story about violence. Therefore, the dialogue should be hard, explicit, bear down on it. Milk it dry"[53]—this story, like the others, was not published.

Though Faulkner accuses Joan of not taking the work seriously—"Of course this version is not the best you can do. I know that. So do you, you have proved it, not just this time, but before. So far, you don't take the work seriously. You take Joan Williams seriously, but not the work. You wont like that, because nobody would"[54]—she did carefully study Faulkner's letters of critique. Sometimes she would go back over a story writing his comments in the margin and noting whether or not she had failed to do what he suggested: "What about my first sentence? Was it wrong? And how do you milk dialogue dry?" This letter was returned with a few jottings of Faulkner's beneath a multitude of questions from Joan. At the end he appended a conciliatory note: "I may be completely wrong about the story.... It may be that, with one who is himself a writer, since his own work never quite is right, good enough, nobody else's can ever be.'"[55]

"I can't concretely say of anything he ever sat down and told me to try to learn. He never did."[56] "It was not, as I've said, technique that I learned from Faulkner but something harder about the task at hand, perseverance, belief in one's self, determination, the ability to stare solitariness in the face."[57]

And I don't think he ever did for me what Phil Stone[58] had done for him. I mean the books he told me to read were the hardest books anyone had ever heard of."[59] (Some of Faulkner's recommendations like Malraux's *Man's Fate* and Bergson's *Creative Evolution* probably did seem lofty for a twenty-one-year-old. Also, besides Housman, Faulkner stressed a close reading of the Bible and Shakespeare.) Joan remembered Faulkner saying of Bergson's *Creative Evolution* that "'It helped me.' But we never discussed [it] further, though inside on the flyleaf I found he had written something I'd forgotten about:

Don't work too hard at it
But read it"[60]

———

Faulkner was working diligently, though unhappily, at *A Fable* through the hot summer months of June and July. And he was missing Joan. In an early July letter from New York, Joan writes of her progress with her short story and her current reading list. The freedom she has captured appears to elicit the indecision Faulkner dreads, and a possible trip South remains uncertain:

Thur.

I am just sitting here, haven't written partly because I am trying to get the story done~in retyping have done a lot of rewriting~and think it is much better ... should get it to Ober[61] within the next 3 days or so, maybe. and haven't written also because I was waiting to hear from you in answer to my note and margin comments on your letter, but then when I didn't hear went on on my own rewriting and now am glad. I hope you will like it better too. I was disappointed when you had some reservations because as I wrote you I thought it was the best I could do altho [sic] I felt that disturbing but infallible feeling that there was something off and that it wasn't moving. I think it is more so now. It moves me to read it. I have gone fuller into each character. And it's nice to know I was wrong~it's not all I can do, even now.

It has its bad moments just sitting here, reading or writing. I find no enjoyment from going for walks on hot city streets and have hardly been out of the house in the daytime since I left Look last Wed. Read Cyrano~oh, god, bill~it is so wonderful, finished the Wild Palms ... Am going into a Dickens session when I finish H [The Hamlet].

Just received a check for $5.00 from the New Yorker for that fill in thing about being "tarty"~so at least I am still being published!

I have no plans. I would come on to Memphis except every time I think about it, I know there is no sense to it~just to be in a house like I am in an apartment here only there with frustrations, and etc. Will have to come sometime. But I don't want to keep using up my summers in Memphis. I've never been away from the place then except for the summer I was in Cal. I was wondering what plans you had made. I would love to come spend the summer in Memphis, yes, if Memphis was Oxford and outdoors. I don't even want to travel that highway from M. [Memphis] to H.S. [Holly Springs] anymore~sneaking etc. What are you thinking? Are you working on the big book? I was still thinking of the Colorado thing~just to be going for the scenery~and there's an after that? What would you be doing? And sometime there's got to be a Mexico~because I'm sick of never having been out of this country. Bill, what's happening to it. Book burnings etc. Is not McC.[62] a Hitler on the rise~the slow infiltration, the damn non-resistance or seemingly powerless non-resistance and the quiet voices of the would be thinkers and intellectuals of this country who it would seem to me would rise up and at least try to destroy this man, and what's happening to the country. write soon. I am sorry you were waiting, I was just waiting to hear from you.

> Blessed above all others be the hour
> When you remembered to remember me....

On 4 July Faulkner answers Joan, assuring her that he was not waiting to hear from her. He was waiting to hear where she was to know how to address the envelope. He would like to hear from her every day but has better sense than to wait for that. Memphis, he agrees, will not be much good for seeing each other. They deserve, need, more than having to meet in the woods now. Though that was beautiful it is now the past; and the past cannot be recaptured.[63]

"The expected happened, it ran dry after about two days, I was miserable, kept at it, the stuff was not good, I would destroy it every night and still try again tomorrow, very bad two weeks. But yesterday it began to go all right again, today was a good day."[64] If he had received a postcard saying come to me, Joan, he would be with her now. Instead he plans to keep at the big book until he hears from her again, and until, as he predicts, "it runs dry again."[65]

Faulkner emphasizes again his inability to work at home. There is nothing there for him to work toward except money. No one saying go on with it, I like it. He needs that just as all people do. He will see her whenever she lets him know the date.

Just a few days later he reports that his book is going well. "I just finished a section, chapter, this afternoon. It's good, it's all right."[66] It is too good for one person to contain. He needs Joan to read it and tell him it's all right, it's good. Then he will take hold of her elbows, hard, very hard, and say look at me, my face that looked at your azure eyes four years ago and will never get over it; the hands that are holding her hard; the heart that loves her heart; the body that wants her body—they made it.

Art is the only way on earth to say no to death. To create—to make something strong, fine and enduring. Some day, and probably soon, Joan will know this feeling too. She will know what it is to create something that doesn't just move her but that tears at her entrails. And maybe he'll be there to read it and tell her it's good, good, good. And then she will grip his hand or arm and say look at me, Bill—the azure eyes that looked at his face one day four years ago that he will never get over; the heart that loves his heart, the body her body wants—they made it.[67] In describing both scenarios—her ardent joy at his success and his ardent joy at her success—Faulkner concludes with the orgasmic joy of achievement. Their co-celebrations will be sexual gratification. This letter boldly asserts that Joan will want Faulkner as much as he wants her.

———

The long, hot summer almost was interrupted by a trip to Europe. Howard Hawks called Faulkner telling him that he and Gary Cooper were going to start on a movie in Paris and wanted him to join them. Faulkner, seeing an opportunity for them to be together, invites Joan to join him and even offers to pay her expenses. She wires him that she will not be able to go now, maybe later. He plans for them to spend a few days together in New York before he goes abroad. Sensing Joan's discouragement with her writing, he tries to motivate her. She has challenged the big time with the Bard prize-winning story, but that is in the past. To grow as a writer she must not sit like an empty vessel waiting for good stuff to flow from her fingers onto the paper. She must work to learn, work to do, and be willing to sacrifice and suffer emotional angst.[68]

When Hawk's movie was delayed by Cooper's illness, Faulkner's attention shifts to seeing Joan during her visit to Memphis. A short note welcomes her South again, though the 95-degree heat has him wishing to be elsewhere. He asks that Joan remember him to her father and mother and signs it Bill.[69] A long letter intended to explain the detached tone and innocuous content of the former follows. He is fretted with Joan because she did not seem to read the letter as she should have. He believes they both know Joan's mother is looking cross-eyed, so he wrote a foolproof letter that could be read by anyone should it be intercepted, but also one that would let her know he had heard nothing more from Hawks about Paris.

Responding to her unhappiness from a recent communication with Seymour Lawrence at the *Atlantic*, Faulkner tells her to expect as much if the editor is young, like Lawrence, and if he knows Faulkner and Joan individually and Faulkner and Joan together. Lawrence, he feels, read more into the story than was there because of their relationship. If he had been an older man, he would have been more detached.[70] (Joan does not remember exactly why Lawrence did not take the next story she sent him after "The Morning and the Evening," but she did not think Lawrence's age—he was a year and a half older than she—had anything to do with it.[71])

Lawrence came back into Joan's life in 1984 when they met again at a literary conference.[72] By then, Lawrence had his own imprint with Houghton Mifflin publishing many influential literary writers such as Kurt Vonnegut, Tillie Olsen, Jim Harrison, Richard Bausch, Tim O'Brien, Barry Hannah and others.[73] Lawrence, the editor turned publisher, found humor in the favors Faulkner asked of his editors and publishers at Random House. "Sam laughed one time from reading things [about Faulkner]. He said, 'Faulkner just treated all those people like flunkies. He would write and say Saxe, would you run over to such and such and send me some ... tobacco, and would you do this and that.' That's not the kind of thing most people did to their editors."[74] Lawrence surmised the writer/editor/publisher relationships with great acuity. Whatever boundaries suggested proper etiquette or a natural hierarchy, Faulkner disregarded. Today at the University of Mississippi, the William Faulkner Room and the Seymour Lawrence Room are centerpieces of the University's Special Collections Department.

This 1953 incident with Seymour Lawrence and the *Atlantic* illustrates how Faulkner's involvement in Joan's development as a writer was always a blessing and a curse. Certainly he opened doors for her with important introductions to editors and publishers, as well as referring her to the Harold Ober Agency, but all the while she lingered under his shadow. When Anne Tyler favorably reviewed Joan's short story collection *Pariah and Other Stories* in 1983, she wrote in error that "Rain Later" was influenced by Faulkner. That story, winner of the college fiction award for *Mademoiselle* and an honorable mention in *Best American Short Stories 1949*, predated Joan's introduction to Faulkner.[75]

After her marriage, Joan continued to worry about editorial comments she felt unjustly tied her work to Faulkner. She wrote him in 1959 about such concerns as she expanded her short story "The Morning and the

Evening" into a novel. Faulkner asks if she has already forgotten what he always preached: "Never give one goddam about what anybody says about the work if you *know* you have done it as honestly and bravely and truly as you could. I was in your life at an age which I think you will find was a very important experience, and of course it will show on you. But dont be afraid. There are worse people and experiences than me and ours to have influenced you. Dont be afraid. Do the work."[76] Of Course, he adds, some discerning person will holler Faulkner because there will be some Faulkner in it. That is simple. All writers are influenced by everything that touches them, from the telephone directory to God.[77]

All these years after her novel's 1961 debut, there is a sense that her oeuvre suffers because of her relationship with a literary behemoth. The critical attention it should have garnered in its own right was overwhelmed by Joan's being William Faulkner's protégée, even though her serious writing did not begin until she was married to Ezra Bowen. Looked at differently, one could argue that Joan's connection to Faulkner should actually accelerate interest. The substance of his letters of critique regarding her work is serious, thoughtful, and honest. There is no undeserved flattery. She is the only writer Faulkner ever mentored, something Faulkner recognized and acknowledged when he told her to remember that if he did not believe in the talent, he would not say it[78]: "If I did not take Joan Williams' work seriously, what a fool I would be not to turn it around and please Joan Williams."[79]

———

An airy but precise style, quiet subtlety, emotional resonance, and the Southern landscape are the signature marks of Joan's work. Her fiction easily matches that of Katherine Anne Porter, Elizabeth Spencer, Carson McCullers, Eudora Welty, Lee Smith, Ellen Douglas and Ellen Gilchrist, among others, yet her stature as a writer has been stunted by her connection with Faulkner. When Sallie Bingham considered *Southern Women Writers: The New Generation*, and other texts by and about Southern women writers in *Ms.* magazine, she cited Joan as an example of a woman writer who was "exploited" by her male mentor: "Important questions float, free of context: the influence of male mentors on a woman writer's success, for example. Faulkner seems to have exploited the young Joan Williams, in return for finding her an agent."[80]

Joan was angered by Bingham's comment. She did not believe it was justified or that it accurately described Faulkner's role in her life. Even at twenty-one years of age as she dealt with a figure of Faulkner's magnitude, Joan's letters to him make it clear she knew she had to write in her own way and assert her will when he pushed for collaborations and heavy-handed editing. Bingham's comment dismisses Joan's authorial independence and obvious talent.

The actual essay from which Bingham extrapolates that Joan was exploited does more fully address Joan's relationship with Faulkner. Judith Bryant Wittenberg writes in "Joan Williams: The Rebellious Heart" that "After Williams completed her first short story and before the honors accorded it were announced, she met William Faulkner, who would become an important figure in her personal life and who would have an impact on her career that was at once helpful and problematic.... For Joan, the relationship with Faulkner was also complicated artistically; he was, to be sure, a figure omnipresently *there* for any contemporary Southern writer— Eudora Welty compared him to a mountain always in the background—but he was far more important to Williams than to most comparable writers, playing a role in her life alternately that of father, Pygmalion, and ardent lover."

The essay also briefly considers Joan's five novels and short story collection, noting the themes of grief and of the lost chance as recurrent (the later theme appears in many of Faulkner's letters to Joan). She finds that Joan's personal life and her fiction "embody the problems of possessing a rebellious heart in a society that prizes tradition and conformity."

Since Joan's corpus is "small"; her personal life "somewhat turbulent"; and because she is "haunted by a powerful male mentor," Wittenberg believes it is more difficult to assess Joan's body of work. This statement illustrates a significant issue. It presupposes that a woman writer's personal life assumes a more potent force than it does for her male counterpart, or that it is more suspiciously appraised. This most certainly has been the case with Joan's literary career.

When Wittenberg suggests Joan's talent could sustain a reach well beyond her typical Southern landscape, and uses two stories without specific topography to illustrate her point, she is most useful. Both stories "could be set anywhere," and deal with issues facing middle-aged women. "Pariah" explores the pain of a middle-class alcoholic wife, and in "Vistas," a woman is startled to discover that her difficult relationship with her mother is mirrored in her own relationship with her son.

Though she lived most of her life in the North, Joan almost always looked to the South for inspiration, even spending summers in rural Mississippi to reclaim her landscape and recharge her imagination. Her childhood visits to relatives in Tate County, Mississippi, dominated her literary terrain and the pull this area had for her surpassed growing up in Memphis. "I am very moved emotionally," Joan said, "by Mississippi and the hills, and I write about that setting. It's just something about the country and the landscape as a background that makes me want to write."[81]

Had she felt motivated to explore the urban and suburban opportunities that surrounded her in New York City, Westport, CT, and Wilton, CT, Joan very likely would have expanded her subjects with perceptive and moving fiction that floats free of Southernness. Yet for all of her years as a Northern inhabitant Joan remained staunchly Southern. Joan once was asked after years of living in Connecticut when she would write a novel about Westport. She replied, "I'm never going to write about the East. And it's not because there's nothing to write about. It's just the Southern flavor that— just simply moves me."[82] Perhaps, as Wittenberg asserts, "Joan's Southernness has been at once an inspiration and a sort of psychic bondage."

Wittenberg acknowledges that Joan's work has been "more neglected than it deserves. The best of it documents the constrictions of small-town Southern life and individuals' moving realizations of loneliness, loss, and the limitations of the human condition. It also depicts those moments of imperceptible but significant inner change, when a rebellious heart comes into being. At such times, Williams's fiction speaks eloquently and memorably."[83]

———

At the time of publication, almost all of Joan's books received favorable reviews from other notable authors.[84] Doris Betts wrote in her review of *Old Powder Man* that "The excellence of style was expected; her remarkable skill at capturing complex human beings had already been demonstrated [*The Morning and the Evening*]. 'Old Powder Man' fulfills and advances her growing talent in both these areas. What is unexpectedly fine is the fullness of a strong male character, among chiefly male contemporaries, and the convincing details of a dynamite salesman's life blasting levees up and down the Mississippi river." *Old Powder Man*, Betts concludes, "is an illustration that the old-fashioned form of the novel can still be made to glow by the very talented."[85]

Robert Penn Warren's review "Death of a Salesman—Southern Style," for *Life*, is, if anything, more laudatory. "Like a water witch, Joan Williams can walk over the most unpromising territory and suddenly her willow wand bends toward the spot where the live spring lies hidden.... *Old Powder Man* might, however, be called a novel of anti-technique. But what in the beginning may seem a clumsy veracity emerges in the end with the dignity of a method. It is as if Joan Williams had said, 'Life isn't all a matter of focus, it's a matter of mist and drifting too, not a matter of controlled meanings but of a sudden, stumbled-on vision, and this is the only way for me to tell the truth about it.' ... My second observation has to do with the way Miss Williams regards her world. This is a Southern world, a part of the world immortalized by Wolfe, Welty, McCullers, Faulkner, Katherine Anne Porter, Flannery O'Connor and Tennessee Williams.

Irreconcilable differences are of course to be found among these writers, but there is one quality they all share—the need to seek intensifications, to lift life, to twist it, to shake it as a terrier shakes a rat, to make it reveal something beyond itself. Joan Williams asks only that it reveal itself."[86]

Old Powder Man found another fan in Joyce Carol Oates, who wrote that "'Old Powder Man' is the kind of traditional novel that affirms the intrinsic dignity and worth of the novel.... Frank Wynn's [the novel's protagonist] life story is told against a background of the American mid–South, the Mississippi Valley region, before, during and after the Depression, bringing us up, at the time of Frank's death, nearly to the present. Its mode is naturalistic in the highest sense of that word; there is nothing that is just statistical as in some American naturalists, but all detail is necessary and illuminating. One thinks of Flaubert, and this is the highest kind of praise. This is a novel recommended without qualifications both for those who enjoy good stories and for those who have an interest in the writing of these good stories."[87]

———

Joan published two short stories of significant length in 1995, "Happy Anniversary" (*The Southern Review*) and "The Contest" (*The Chattahoochee Review*), which was dramatized in 1997 by a Memphis theatre group, Voices of the South. The pieces beautifully address the issues of aging and the toll of maintaining long-term marriages as the partners evolve from youthful lovers to elderly spouses.

The settings for both stories are small, rural communities beset by modernity, with some characters, like Mary Virginia Abbot in "The Contest," resistant to change. Mary Virginia has been married fifty-five years to Aaron

> Who she looked after yea these many years was the bag of bones beyond. Aaron was the living dead, his pizzazz all gone. If he ever had any? If he sat fifty-five years later, like a bump on a pickle, dreaming of a younger woman, let him ... Infidelity was not part of country folks like themselves. That belonged in picture shows, books, and now on TV in your own living room. She expected to look up any minute and see the act completed before her eyes. Soap opera folks were the world's worst, the limit, and she could not think what else to call them.

The couple banters about attending the fair—among other subjects— where there will be a number of contests: a dance contest, the cutest couple contest, contests of all sorts. As the story advances, Mary Virginia's memories collide with her seemingly innocuous daily life and affirm the potency of the past:

> One memory surfaced of Aaron in bell bottoms their first evening together, buying her a rose on the way to his naval station in Pensacola, wearing the stupid, round hat gobs had to wear. The vendor was an old, old woman in a grey shawl: a crone in a fairy tale. She held up a flower while she~Mary Virginia~stood with her mouth agape thinking what age could do. That woman would have been young and pretty once, maybe even beautiful: with hopes and dreams. There were always those, weren't there?.... That night with Aaron over her, she reached out to touch the rose in its glass. "Ouch," she said when a thorn stuck her. And again later, "Ouch." The next morning a drop of blood on the sheet was the shape of a petal. "Good grief," Aaron had said raising up. He went on saying that for years till he quit. "Can I help it?" she had said. Her bones knit together, hardly a feather could pass. "It's not personal," she told him. Aaron kept on pushing, shoving, groveling inside for years till he quit that too.

At the fair, the husband, whom she considers "a sick old man," surprisingly wins the dance contest with his partner, Michele:

> Clearly they were old, familiar partners and had not just met. The others knew that. It was obvious from their stances and averted looks. Mary Virginia stood, knowing the greatest sense of humiliation and rejection only an older woman can feel. Wives of the men who met for coffee would have known behind her back because once Aaron was missing, the others would have found out why "Aaron's off again with that woman he's took up with." She heard the words in her head, the way they talked. And she was home, running the vacuum in a solitude she longed for.

Mary Virginia imagines them having met at the Wal-Mart near the woman's home where Aaron drove to do his shopping "at discount." "They might have met in the aisles, where Michele would already be dancing, shaking herself to canned music blaring all over the place."

The crowding memories rattle her stability and she understands that "it's never been death I've been afraid of, it's been living." A mental collapse causes her to huddle in the couple's walk-in closet. As she is taken away for help, Mary Virginia finally recaptures the missing words to a song that has haunted her all day. "I love you, baby. But your feets too big."[88]

———

Three perplexing letters arrived for Joan in late July with varied and forceful introductions. Faulkner goes from telling her he is fretted with her, to telling her she may make choices, not decisions, to addressing her as a pretty falcon—a girl hawk—middle sized and azure colored. Her lover is a peregrine, meaning distance, freedom, speed and faraway places.

Faulkner's anger in the first letter involves his impatience to see her again, either in Memphis or Holly Springs, and his belief that by this point in the relationship she should be more perceptive of his moods and needs. She is to remember that regardless of how odd or funny his behavior, she should be confident of his ongoing love. Very repetitive subjects surface. He asks that she get a passport; they are going somewhere. And also that she should never act again as she has. It makes him damn unhappy and undermines his concentration. She should know that any scrap from her elevates him. Finally, his work (A Fable) is going well but agonizingly slow because of his longing and remembering.[89]

There is a difference between decisions and choices at least where Joan is concerned. This fine distinction dominates his next letter. Since she drove in his yard four years ago one afternoon and said here I am, take me, Joan has not been in a position to make decisions. He will do the decision making and she may consider the various choices. Her choices, once she has had enough of Memphis, are to go to Linscott's farm in Vermont for an early fall month while Faulkner finishes his work and she works on hers. If they travel west, Mexico will be their destination.[90]

The pretty falcon letter registers an upbeat quality. Joan has agreed to meet him Tuesday. He likes the idea of Joan subletting her New York apartment and staying in Memphis for August. He believes that her novel is ready now and asks her to write it: "He said I had worried for a while because I was not doing it. Now it was beginning to worry and nag me saying, 'Come on, write me, make me. I want to stand up and breathe too. Which is as it should be. You're sunk, you might as well give up. There will be all sorts of pressures to try to make you be the other things first—put other things first before the writing. But you won't. You can't now. That comes first. After it, you will have everything.'"[91] The pressure to put other things ahead of the writing will come, according to Faulkner, because she is pretty and charming. A handwritten postscript in closing: Joan is to tell her father Faulkner will take care of her and her future.[92]

———

The discontent Faulkner felt at home was not lost on Estelle. She was coping with his bad temper and her own embarrassment over his alliance with Joan. She describes her summer to Dorothy and Saxe Commins as "hot and most trying." Estelle explains that Faulkner's success makes him the subject of envy and even malice. (A soi-disant friend of hers in Shanghai relishes sharing tales bound to upset her.) And if that wasn't enough, she heard Joan has come south again. Since this development might keep the cantankerous Faulkner at Rowan Oak, she and Jill decide on the own escape:

> Jill wants to go to the University of Mexico until Christmas~so I'll go down with her, take an apartment and play duenna! She decided against Europe this year because we had heard that *other people*[93] were planning a stay in France~
> Luckily I have managed a stiff upper lip~and retained my dignity.[94]

Somehow the couple muddled through most of August until Estelle and Jill left for Mexico on 25 August. Though initially feeling liberated and lighthearted, Faulkner eventually finds his days of bachelorhood more unhappy than happy.

———

Faulkner tries to arrange an early August meeting between Joan and Eudora Welty in Jackson, Mississippi. He wants Joan to tell her mother, whether or not he can confirm the date with Welty, that she is going to Jackson to meet with some Mississippi writers. He tells her that the meeting will be good for her and includes the City of New Orleans train schedule, times and dates, which she should use. "I know I was always going somewhere in his mind," Joan said. "He was always trying to think of some reason for us to go somewhere or meet somewhere. But we never did that [August trip to Jackson] either."[95] Later, Joan did come to spend time with Welty, once meeting her in a small Jackson coffee shop.

Faulkner continues with travel plans. He is looking to buy a used Nash[96] and if he has it in time he will meet Joan in Grenada;[97] if not, he also will take the train. Then an erotic paragraph follows where he stresses again his need to be with her continuously. A whole, free night. He wants to see her undergarments tossed over a chair, her shoes under it, and to lightly touch her hair and her sleeping shape under the sheets. He suggests they meet again soon.

His fourth paragraph is almost euphoric. Having finished the three temptations scene from *A Fable* he credits to Joan's effect on him, to touching her intimately (always her girl-hair) if only for a moment. After that he was able to come home and write the scene. He then closes with three sentences that are repeated almost verbatim in a letter to Saxe Commins.[98] "Damn it, I did have genius.... It just took me 55 years to find it out. I suppose I was too busy working to notice it before."[99]

Joan's reaction was to delay their next meeting and he agrees to wait. He is busy readying the family car for Estelle and Jill's trip to Mexico and still hopes to purchase another car by the time they leave. Encouraged she has been able to sublet her New York apartment, he tells Joan they can drive up there anytime after 25 August to clear out her things. He believes he will have a finished draft of A *Fable* by then.[100]

Still distracted with car details, Faulkner now pursues a Holly Springs meeting. The work is the only thing that helps him wait. "Am finishing another damn fine scene."[101] He mentions also paperback sales that Saxe said had gone well. He asks that Joan touch the bell he gave her before she goes to sleep at night to remind her of his feelings for her. The postscript promises a good fall and year ahead, full of hard, satisfying work and love.[102]

After their meetings in Memphis or Holly Springs (too few to suit Faulkner), Joan decides to take a trip to Florida. His disappointment is pronounced, having anticipated being with her while his wife and daughter were in Mexico. With his hopes dashed, his letter assumes a certain desperation.[103]

There were misunderstandings as Joan traveled back and forth to the beach in Florida. Even though she saw him en route coming and going, and spent one night at Rowan Oak, Faulkner was angry at Joan's unavailability when he was free. This conflict is a harbinger of the end, though the affair was briefly resuscitated when they travel to New York together in the fall.

"I spent one night at Rowan Oak and then he drove me to Birmingham to catch a plane to Florida." That night in Oxford Faulkner put on his RAF uniform for Joan, proud that it still fit. Yet while they waited for Joan's plane in Birmingham, an airport employee mistook Faulkner for Joan's father. [104]

Joan returned from the beach with a female friend and they met Faulkner at a café on the square in Holly Springs. "There was something about meeting him and something he was mad about."[105] Back in Memphis, Joan receives an angry letter, noted as 6:30, just home again. "One of the nicest conveniences a woman can have is someone she can pick up when she needs him or wants him; then when she doesn't, she can drop him and know that he will be right there when she does need or want him again. Only she should remember this. Sometimes when she drops him, he might break. Sometimes, when she reaches down for him, he might not be there."[106]

Still, despite these conflicts, he chooses to take her at her word, and unless he hears differently from her, he plans to drive to Memphis and bring her back to Oxford. He has needed her these last two weeks as he made an intense push on A *Fable* but she was not there for him. Being needed, he writes, is something she doesn't like—she calls it pressure—and she runs from it. He still needs her but he has sweated it out this far because the work is serious. She has let him down. "I love you. Don't (sic) lie to me. I dont know which breaks my heart the most: for you to believe that you need to lie to me, or to think that you can."[107]

The flowers he planned to send, he won't, since when he mentioned them she so quickly said no. They would not, he decided, help. He adds in closing he may go to Greenville to see Hodding Carter.[108]

———

Feeling abandoned by Joan but wanting to share his manuscript with someone, Faulkner arranged for a man to drive him to see Ben Wasson, an old friend now living in Greenville. Faulkner meets some of Wasson's friends, the Keatings, who invite him to stay on with them awhile. Unfortunately for all concerned, they do not sense that Faulkner's mood is too elevated and that a downward spiral is inevitable. They take him to a country-club dance, where it seems to his host that when they walked in "...everyone watched the small gray-haired man in the old-fashioned white pongee suit with the rosette in the buttonhole and the white handkerchief in the sleeve." The party continued at the Keatings' home until Faulkner decided it was time to show the guests his work. He then pulled out over 700 heavily revised typed pages. That moment of exhibitionism was followed by a fall during the night while he was trying to find the bathroom. Faulkner awoke with a gash over his eye and was talking of going to the Gulf Coast. His friends talked him out of traveling and drove him to Rowan Oak. Before Wasson left Oxford, he called to alert Estelle's son to Faulkner's weakened state. By 8 September, Jimmy Faulkner had taken him to Gartly-Ramsay where his chart read: "An acute and chronic alcoholic."

Faulkner gave into another round of depression and drinking shortly after Robert Coughlan's article "The Private World of William Faulkner" appeared in the 28 September issue of Life magazine. His recuperation this time occurred at Wright's Sanitarium in Byhalia.[109]

———

These last months of emotional turmoil were offset by a bit of good news for Faulkner. Joan, living again in New York, agreed to fly to Memphis and drive back to New York with him. "I flew to Memphis where Faulkner met me at the airport. I remember Faulkner walking into the airport and a man recognizing him."

They drove an old gray station wagon of Faulkner's with Joan doing most of the driving. She went off the road on a curve and badly scared them both. Joan's family did not even know she was ever in Memphis or driving to New York with Faulkner. "I felt very bad because I didn't tell my family.

My mother was in the hospital having her tonsils removed which was serious for someone her age and I wasn't able to see her."

For Joan to be so giving of herself and her time was a bit out of character. That was a long trip and guilt-ridden because she did not contact her parents. Her reflection of this episode—being in 2002 not only Faulkner's age but also alone herself—allowed for a new appreciation of his choices. There were many others to keep William Faulkner company, but not many he would seek for companionship. Joan's acknowledgement is a poignant reminder of their shared, almost unconquerable sense of loneliness. "Now that I am Faulkner's age, I understand his feelings of loneliness; that he chose solitariness over being with the 'wrong people.' I was someone with whom he felt comfortable."[110]

Once in New York, after a brief stay with Linscott, Faulkner settled at One Fifth Avenue where he worked diligently through October and where Joan came also to work at a typewriter he arranged for her. In fact, when he sent her a signed, first-edition copy of A Fable after its August 1954 publication, his enclosed note said her copy should be the first one off the press. If she had not been working hard at her writing then, he would not have been working hard to keep up, and would not have finished the book.[111]

———

Rather than the heady, fruitful fall his mid–August letter promised, full of creativity and love, it was a fall true to the sentiment of the season. It was a season of endings.

That September Joan met her future husband, Ezra Bowen, and while she does not remember a specific conversation with Faulkner about breaking up, there was a gradual drifting away. There were more and more appointments with Faulkner she failed to keep.

Melancholia settled over the author, and one night at her apartment he replicated in "nearly perfect form" a portion of Housman's A *Shropshire Lad*:

> Look, earth and high heaven ail from the prime foundation
> All thoughts to rive the heart are here, and all are vain:
> Horror and scorn and hate and fear and indignation
> Why did I awake? When shall I sleep again?[112]

———

Joan was now in a serious relationship with talk of marriage, a subject she and Faulkner mostly skirted over the past four years. There were Faulkner's letters telling Joan that marriage would not be good for her, that unless she married an artist her work would be compromised. Should she be careless or foolish enough to marry a champion of the middle class, moreover, her writing would most likely cease altogether. But what alternative did Faulkner hold for her? Besides the significant age disparity, Joan could not disregard her concern for Estelle and Jill. She never wanted or intended to be responsible for ending the Faulkners' marriage. These factors diminished the likelihood that she would insist upon or pursue a commitment of marriage from Faulkner.

In *The Wintering*, Joan introduces the idea of marriage through a conversation between Amy and Alex Boatwright, Almoner's editor:

> "Do you mind my asking, has he asked you to marry him?"
> "In a way, he has. I haven't thought about it, but I have to. I know he wants me able to make up my mind. Do you think I should marry him?"
> "I would," Alex said, "be very tempted if I were you."[113]

The actual conversation occurred during a lunch with Random House editor Robert Linscott. When Joan asked Linscott if she should marry Faulkner, he said, "I'd be very tempted. Has he asked you?"

"Yes," Joan answered, though Faulkner's actual proposal—"May I tell her [Estelle] we want to get married?"—seemed, in her opinion, less than ideal. "What kind of a proposal was that?" she asked.[114]

———

Bowen grew up in Bryn Mawr, Pennsylvania, and was far from a champion of the middle class. He was raised by his mother who was committed— perhaps overly so in Joan's opinion—to her writing. A tireless and prolific biographer, Catherine Drinker Bowen was fond of the French saying, "If you abandon art for one day, she will abandon you for three." Her one concession to Christmas was not going upstairs to her desk until noon.[115]

A magazine writer and editor, Bowen was a Northeasterner through and through. Joan remembers his astonishment at the spittoon in their hotel room in Memphis. "We spent our honeymoon night in a suite at the Peabody which my father had rented for us. And Ezra couldn't get over the fact that there was a brass spittoon in the room. For me that was normal. Everybody had a spittoon in their bedroom."[116]

Had Faulkner been willing to entertain the idea of Joan married to someone else, he might have chosen Bowen. "He really made me into a writer. He was very funny and very witty. I was never bored in fifteen years."[117] Bowen and Joan were close in age: she was twenty-five and he twenty-seven when they married. He told Joan if she wanted to write, to do it and quit talking about it. He helped her develop a strict writing schedule—his mother's in fact—working every morning without any interruptions, and saw to it that she always had live-in help with the house and children. They usually hired a young woman from Memphis or Mississippi. Mrs. Bowen's advice for writers, captured in her essay "Discipline and Reward: A Writer's Life," reflects many of the same ideas Faulkner expressed to Joan:

> Writing, I think, is not apart from living. Writing is a kind of double living. The writer experiences everything twice. Once in reality and once in that mirror which waits always before or behind him.... There is a channel down which your work pours. That channel must be kept clear, free running. At all costs it must be kept so. Unrequited love can loosen the dam and let the torrent down. These are the brief, rich experiences of life, the very stuff that flows and rolls through that channel, tumbling and roaring so the person can almost hear the noise.
>
> What clogs the channel ... is laziness, inattention, timidity, the propensity to lie to oneself, to avoid looking straight at a situation ... The most scrupulous honesty is necessary, in a writer. No matter on what level he operates, a total honesty is called for ... What the writer needs is an empty day ahead. A big round quiet space of empty hours to, as it were, tumble about in. Hours that must be filled, hours that force one to think, to get the words on paper. Oh, let the writer do his living in between books! And let him not be afraid, if he is young, that life will pass him by because he is alone in a room, thinking. If he fears that, he should take up some other occupation than writing.[118]

Having both individuals in her life was undoubtedly influential, possibly beyond Joan's immediate recognition. However, Joan determined after observing Mrs. Bowen's relationships with her husband and her sister-in-law that she would not emulate her mother-in-law's zealotry when it came to writing if it meant sacrificing time with her children. Joan often said the years of her boys' childhoods were the happiest of her life.

Every summer Joan traveled to rural Mississippi and rented a small cabin to gather material and write. During those absences, Bowen rented their home in Connecticut and lived with Joan's aunt in New York City. "After one of her summer sojourns, Ezra told Joan's mother, 'She's got to stop going to Mississippi every summer.' I guess he got tired of my going away for so long. But all my work came out of those summers!"[119]

———

Bowen's background impressed but intimidated Joan. In addition to a mother who was a prominent author, Bowen's uncle, Philip Drinker, along with Louis A. Shaw, is credited with developing the first iron lung in 1928 at the Harvard School of Public Health in Boston. "I was very glad to be with Ezra, who was highly intelligent and from the kind of background which scared me to death, but also glad that he didn't drink and act like [my father]. Mrs. Bowen didn't drink and she really disapproved of drinking. Ezra was very stringent about drinking, very disciplined.

"When I first knew Ezra in New York, he didn't see why I ever wanted to go back home. When I told him stories about things, he would always say, I was crazy to want to go back there. Well, it never occurred to me not to go back there ... The first story I told him was when I was about twelve and I was in a piano recital and I had a long dress, my first long dress, an evening dress. I went to show it to my father and when I walked in the room he said, 'Something else to spend money on.' Ezra thought that was just awful. I remember my mother saying, 'P.H., you ought to be ashamed.'

"He [P.H.] was so poor during the depression. He ran away from home when he was in the eighth grade. He never had over an eighth-grade education ... and he just had a horror of ever having to live like that again, of not having enough money ... I think that remark about the evening gown, [and] I only realized [this] later in life, that you learn some appreciation for yourself from your father. Most fathers are crazy about their daughters and I didn't have that. I didn't have somebody giving me self-esteem as a female."

She believes what she cultivated was determination, not self-confidence. "My parents undermined me all the time, telling me I couldn't do anything, that I was no good."[120] This was a part of Joan's past Faulkner trusted to give him a unique opportunity with her, since his age alone would make him a father figure. Even after their November separation, Faulkner's December letter from Switzerland emphasizes what he considers his dual role: lover and father.

"I am very happy to know that you are working, and that you know that nothing basic has changed with us. It never will" and no matter what course her life may take, "I believe you know that until I die, I will be the best friend you ever had." Anything he has is hers; anything he can give, he will. Nothing can break the bond between them. "I think I was—am— the father which you never had ..."[121] He knows this is true and beautiful, and that he is better for it. Some day she will know that she is better for it too.[122]

———

Joan thought that Faulkner felt a withdrawal on her part soon after she met Bowen in the summer while she was still at *Look*. "I worked at *Look* and he [Ezra] worked at *Esquire* and they were in the same building.[123] I met him at a party I had gone to with somebody from *Look* and they had gone to Amherst[124] together."

There were enough shared connections in their circles for Faulkner to have early news of Ezra's presence in Joan's life. "Somebody told me they were at Saxe Commins' house and Mrs. Bowen [Ezra's mother] was there and maybe Harold Ober. But Mrs. Bowen was very upset that her son was marrying the girl who had gone around with 'somebody' who wrote *Sanctuary*."

"When Saxe told him about the wedding, Faulkner said, 'Oh, she's already told me and even the date,' something like that. In fact, I have a telegram he sent me that says: 'Bless Ezra and keep him. If he makes you happy, he is the best friend I ever had.'"[125]

Faulkner, writing her in late November, allows his unhappiness to spill over to Joan's friends whom he describes as parasites and sophomores who don't even have to pass their courses to stay in school. Ironically, since he lived there when he was young, Faulkner even challenges her decision to live in Greenwich Village: "These people you like and live among dont want the responsibility of creating.... They go through the motions of art—talking about what they are going to do over drinks, even defacing paper and canvas when necessary, in order to escape the responsibility of living."[126]

———

Faulkner and Joan spent one of the two major holidays together when she joined him at the Commins home for Thanksgiving. By Christmas, Ezra Bowen would be staying with the Williamses in Memphis.

Besides participating in the usual traditions of Thanksgiving, Faulkner and Joan worked, sorting *A Fable*'s unwieldy manuscript pages into order. "For ten years he had just been throwing the pages into something. They were numbered so it wasn't that much trouble. He was very thrilled I would help him do that, as if I wouldn't have!"[127]

When Faulkner wrote at the conclusion of *A Fable*

December, 1944
Oxford–New York–Princeton
November, 1953

he ended a writing project that had dominated almost a decade of his life, with the intense and productive periods paralleling his relationship with Joan. She was his motivating source, his muse, and though he gladly would have kept her in his life indefinitely, Joan was looking for a fresh beginning with someone closer to her own age who shared her dream of starting a family.

In *The Wintering*, Joan portrays the parting between Amy and Almoner as difficult and uncertain. After breaking with Almoner, Amy wonders if she was wrong. Her self-doubt results in a silly and unsubstantial letter. Almoner finds her shallowness so insulting he merely responds with a note on the bottom of her letter:

> This letter is the only stupid thing you've ever done, Amy. That's because you wrote it out of your head and not from your heart. And this one is the one I never meant to write. I never intended to fall in love with you when all this began. I took you in only to shape you into what you wanted to be. But yours is the girl-woman face and figure I see when I close my eyes. No, I won't meet you again, for a ghost would be between us, as now I think when you are with him a ghost is between you, whether he knows it or not.[128]

The next four letters pouring from Faulkner in November, three of which are written on One Fifth Avenue stationery, are very much in character. Faced with loss and pain, he moves from anger to belittlement to a mocking assessment of Joan's new relationship to a letter of farewell that is not goodbye:

> I wont stop in. If this is the end, and I suppose, assume it is, I think the two people drawn together as we were and held together for four years by whatever it was we had, knew--love, sympathy, understanding, trust, belief--deserve a better period than a cup of coffee--not to end like two high school sweethearts breaking up over a coca cola in the corner drugstore.[129]

Joan may have tried to placate Faulkner after receiving this note, and in his next letter where Sunday morning is substituted for the date, he calls her dearest and tells her that telephoning will not do any good. He means exactly what the last letter said. He will see her again only on his terms. If she wants to see him badly enough to grow up and accept his terms, she should let him know before next Thursday when Random House will be closed and he may be out of town too.

Even if she doesn't care that much about seeing him, he still hopes she will grow up. He wants to believe in her and perhaps he still can even though she let him assume a lie. If she doesn't grow up, she is sunk. Two summers ago and last fall, she was a belated twenty-something trying to be older and wiser. Since that time she has gone backward and last spring she acted like a seventeen year old.

He spoke with Linscott on her behalf. Linscott assured Faulkner that all Joan needs to do is call on him and he will be there for her.[130]

———

Thursday night's letter begins with bullying veiled as concern. He is very worried about Joan because he will be far away when this one is over in a month or six weeks and she will need him. Naturally, he can't take this one any more seriously than the other four or five from Brandon, through the California one [Hardy Koch] ... and the one last summer, whom he has out-lasted. She won't like to hear this now but the time is short and he will soon be too far away. He will not be near her to be gentle and patient and wait-ing—to be available when she needs him. So call on Linscott. He has told him all about Joan's dreadful background, childhood—all that has hurt her so badly that she is in conflict with herself, vulnerable and confused. Trust Lin-scott to take his place while he is away. Unless he is wrong and then she won't need anyone, any help. But he has known her five years and he has seen her go through this before, and he believes she knows herself that this is not what she needs either. Maybe she knew the truth two years ago when she wrote him that she cried when she realized she would never find anyone to take his place—someone with the ability and desire to put her first, her happiness.

This advice should not be taken the wrong way too. He loves her and wants her to be happy. It breaks his heart to see her unhappy, to see her struggle and cry and believe each time that she is about to find something which possibly doesn't exist to her anymore than it does for him. Perhaps that is both their curses. If this is not so, forget it. If it is true, call on Lin-scott until he gets back and she can depend on him. He has heard Don[131] plans a farewell champagne lunch send-off on Monday. Will she come? He loves her. No one else will ever love her more. Someday she will know that.[132]

Faulkner was mistaken about the planned luncheon and he did not see Joan before he boarded his plane for Europe. The last letter from November she receives tells her this is not goodbye. He will probably see her when he gets back next year. By that time he hopes she will know that what they had, have, what they both need from the other, is too valuable to be treated this way.

Remember to call on Linscott if she needs anything, even if it is just to talk.[133]

———

When Faulkner boarded his plane on 30 November, Joan was not there to see him off. She already had shifted into plans for a new life. And if she was looking, as Faulkner wrote her, for something that did not exist, that was something for Joan to discover.

VI

1954–1962—
Blue Mississippi Hills

During the early months of 1954 when he was abroad, in Switzerland, Stockholm, Rome, and later in Egypt, Faulkner continued to write Joan, assuring her at one point that he would always let her know where he was.

On Howard Hawks' stationery, he writes to send his address in Switzerland. He has not yet decided whether to spend Christmas in England or Stockholm. He knows for sure he does not want to spend it in Switzerland at the Suvretta Hotel full of rich, American winter resorters.[1]

Then a letter about endings tempered by new associations: Joan's marriage and Faulkner's introduction to Jean Stein. Sounding more distant than usual, he writes of the changes between them. "Love" shifts to past tense. Their separation and division, though they have made him unhappy, have restored the vigor and intimacy of their letters. They are all right again. Joan is writing of her troubles and hopes. She knows he loved her completely and she loved him as she could, more than she loved anyone else. He compliments Joan on her emotional growth, not just toward him, but also her people (family). Such growth will help her writing that she, thank God, has not stopped—as he never for a moment thought she would.[2]

"Stockholm Xmas was pleasant; I had forgot how in Europe the artist is like the athletic champion at home. I tried to stay obscure, in a small hotel, but in two days reporters with cameras followed me, and every morning there would be gangs of schoolchildren, and older people in the snow at the hotel door, asking for autographs...."[3]

And then the surprise of the letter: "A curious thing has happened, almost repetition, her name is even Jean. She is 19. At a Xmas party of people nearer my age, the hostess told me that she had asked to be invited, the only young person there. It was a dull, stuffy party, so I asked her to go with me to a midnight mass at a Catholic church, which she did. I fetched her back home and left her, thought no more about it. Then when I got back here last Monday, she has sent me an Xmas gift, a leather carved traveling clock, much too expensive, also a letter, and by now a telephone call. I think an infatuation partly with my reputation and partly by the fact that I try to be gentle and serious with young people. It will run its course."[4] It could degenerate into intrigue but it won't because his heart is not in it. As he told Joan two—or was it four—years ago, what remained to him of this in his life, he already had given to her.

Enclosed with this letter are prints of pictures taken of Joan that he plans to enlarge when he returns home. He likes one and one he doesn't quite remember. Joan wears a pajama coat and doesn't seem to have washed her face.

He is not sure marriage is for her, but the only way to know is to try it. Naturally he doesn't want it to be anyone but him, but she must decide, and nothing she does will make any great difference between them.

She is still welcome to come to Europe and he will help with expenses. However, if she gets that close he may begin to hope again.

Keep at the work and don't let anything stop that.[5]

Clearly, he wants to keep Joan a part of his life, going so far as describing her marriage as insignificant. Like his earlier mention of Else Jonsson when he first met her, Joan assumed he was trying to make her jealous with his news of Jean Stein. "I heard, and I don't know if I heard it from Mrs. Commins or where, that when Mrs. Faulkner found out about Jean Stein she was furious because she thought I was it. It was over. And I guess she thought that at his age he ought to shape up."[6]

———

Faulkner's letter to Commins, composed eight days after Joan's wedding, is defensive. He chooses criticism of Joan and praise of Jean Stein over an acknowledgement of his own loss. The end of his romance with Joan resurrects some of Faulkner's earliest haranguing—art isn't enough for Joan; she isn't "demon-driven enough"; she is infected by her own middle-class background, "saying home, marriage, children." I was not free to marry her, even if I had not been too old. So I—we—expected this. This was my trouble last winter 1953: the art should have been enough. But it was not.

Faulkner continues as he describes meeting nineteen-year-old Jean Stein who holds none of "poor" Joan's stodgy Southern morals. He assures Commins that he probably will meet her in the fall, and even writes that had it not been for Jean's arrival in his life, the end of his affair with Joan would have hurt.

Jean is free of Joan's complexity and wants only a reciprocal love affair: "She came to me in St Moritz almost exactly as Joan did in Oxford. But she has none of the emotional conventional confusion which poor Joan had. This one is so uninhibited that she frightens me a little.... She is charming, delightful, completely transparent, completely trustful. I will not hurt her for any price. She doesn't want anything of me—only to love me, be in love.[7]

Most likely Commins took this news of Jean Stein in stride as he had before with Joan. "You just knew he [Commins] cared about Faulkner so much and he was very receptive to me. Of course, he probably had been through this a thousand times."[8]

———

In February, Bowen took a job with what was then a new magazine, *Sports Illustrated*, and after their 6 March 1954 wedding in Memphis, the couple lived on the Upper West Side in a three-room, one bedroom apartment on West 76th.[9] A period of silence between Joan and Faulkner followed her marriage, and when Joan and Faulkner resumed their correspondence it was sporadic and usually specific. He perhaps comments on a story Joan sent him to read, or they are going over the details of *The Sound and the Fury* manuscript. "As far as regular letters just to be writing letters, he didn't write to me after I was married. And I wrote him after my father died,[10] twice, I don't know why I was writing him, but I remember I wrote to Oxford and said, 'Did you know my father died?' And he never did respond to that, to those either." Yet she still received her birthday telegrams without fail.

Once, while Joan, her husband, and Robert Creamer, another editor from *Sports Illustrated*, were having drinks in the New Weston Hotel in New York they saw Faulkner in the hotel. "Faulkner was there eating by himself in the dining room. He was alone in New York and I always thought about his aloneness," Joan said. "Somebody at Random House said we always assumed he was with you, of course that was before I was married, but even when he wasn't with me and I wasn't married, he was alone a lot."

Faulkner sat down with them. This was sometime after the birth of Joan's first son,[11] Ezra Drinker Bowen, in October 1954. "I remember saying to Faulkner, 'I had a baby.' And he said, 'Yes, you look like you've been through the experience.'"

Robert Creamer vividly remembers the group's chance encounter with Faulkner who sat down with them directly across from Joan. "Faulkner was small, very neat, dignified, and gentlemanly. After a few initial hellos, Faulkner talked exclusively to Joan. While Joan talked animatedly to Faulkner, her husband glowered. Creamer said he took Ezra aside and said, 'Simmer down a little. After all, he is a great man.'

"And Ezra said, 'He may be a great man, but he sure as hell isn't a good one.'"

What a contrast the two men, Faulkner and Bowen, must have been. Creamer described Bowen as having a "macho look. He was very athletic, very patrician looking. He had been a first baseman at Amherst College and loved sports. He was also a good editor, and as a writer he had a deft, sure touch." Creamer remembers Bowen as "very proud of Joan's accomplishments."[12]

———

There are more letters from 1959 and 1960, usually short, with harmless stories of the horses Faulkner is riding and breaking, or a mention of *The Mansion*,[13] the last of the Snopes trilogy. The most significant correspondence of this time period involves Joan's publication of her first novel. Yet sometimes Faulkner's letters would lapse into the old yearning. He loves her. He wants to see her very much. There were occasional dates made for lunch in New York that frequently were broken.

In April he writes Joan from Oxford, "I still have one more book I want to write.[14] Now that I cant waste time with horses, I should get at it. Though I hope every day I can ride again."[15] The country is beautiful this spring and he would like to lie under a tree and drink beer with her.[16] By June of the same year, he has decided it is too painful to see her; she had nothing for him, and what he has for her can be delivered by mail. He loves her but can do with less pain.[17]

And there is one short note suspecting that Joan is intentionally missing him when he doesn't see her on his way through New York. He hasn't gotten over her yet and probably never will. Women are quite aware of the men who love them, so he assumes she is dodging him.[18]

In February 1960 he answers one of Joan's letters regarding the whereabouts of *The Sound and the Fury* manuscript. After he dies, its whereabouts won't matter to him, but while he is alive he will have to listen to whines and reproachments about where it is. The only female talk he wants to hear, likes to hear, is pretty girls saying yes. Though that won't worry him either when he is dead. He used to think that when he finally got to be sixty and seventy and eighty that he would quit walking in the woods or anywhere else and suddenly decide he just had to be in bed with her. Now it doesn't look like ninety will be old enough.[19]

———

The mixed blessing of Joan's association with Faulkner continued with the publication details of her critically acclaimed novel *The Morning and the Evening*. (At one point in the editing process, Joan asked the editor she was working with if he knew she knew Faulkner. He said, "Yes. I heard you showed up in his yard at thirteen. Barefoot."[20]) The Harold Ober Agency landed Joan's manuscript on the desk of Hiram Haydn of Atheneum Publishers. Faulkner initiated Joan's association with the Ober agency and it proved an invaluable alliance for her. Haydn pursued the book in part because of his respect for Joan's literary agent. Once he decided to take her novel, Haydn asked Faulkner for a book-jacket blurb. This innocent request became fodder for controversy and bewilderment.

Early in June of 1960, Joan shares with Faulkner word of her novel's acceptance. That is "splendid news," he writes her. "That not only justifies us but maybe absolves me of what harm and hurt I might have done you; maybe annoyance and exasperation are better words."[21] Joan's letter of response to Faulkner is typed on letterhead stationery from *Sports Illustrated*, where her husband worked as the sailing and skiing editor.

June 9, 1960:

Dear Bill:

Thank you for your letter--yes, it justifies everything if there has to be a justification--tho I always thought one only for that middle-class you are always talking about. I certainly don't think there was any harm or hurt.

Hiram Haydn is my editor--perhaps you knew him at Random House. It [*The Morning and the Evening*] will be published between Jan.--April--I want to know where you will be so I can have a copy sent to you....

Soon they are discussing the manuscript Haydn has asked Faulkner to read. Faulkner assures Joan that not only will he be glad to read the manuscript, but he also offers his forthcoming comments to her to use as she sees fit and best, to use freely any and all. He adds that she may even edit his remarks if it will help sales and suggests that she rely on Haydn's advice. In his closing paragraph he assures her that there is nothing wrong with friendship, but it is his problem to want much more. He still loves her, he writes, and wants a sexual union before he is too old, which, in relation to her, he believes he never will be. What would be terrible would be to remember how she looked and felt and to feel nothing.[22]

It must have been dispiriting for Joan to receive this 4 January 1961 letter from Faulkner. While her history with him assured her that "all right" was high praise from Faulkner, the novel at hand is practically dismissed as he elaborates on his expectations for her *next* novel.

When the manuscript form Haydn arrived Faulkner wrote that he greeted it with hope and expectation, and his reading of it dashed neither. It is a good first novel though she would be dissatisfied with it as her second novel. Her faults, all minor in his opinion, should dissipate the more she pushed herself and her writing. What he embraced in *The Morning and the Evening* was the story's concept. And, should Joan maintain such lofty goals, her next novel also will capture universal truths. Success will greet her the more she articulates emotions. She must love and hate not man's behavior but man's condition. So, as long as she rejects complacency and writes another novel as soon as possible, and takes care not to *rewrite* this novel, her accomplishment will be evident.

> It's a good first book and will be a bad last one. Not only because the more you write the more you will learn to correct the faults in this one, all minor in my opinion. It is a good story in concept because it is not regional nor topical. But universal. Next time, if you set your sights high, you will learn to milk dry the love and hatred you have to feel not for man but for a man in his condition. Dont write this one again. Write another one.[23]

Faulkner might have been writing this letter to himself. These are his goals, mostly achieved, but foisted on Joan. As he so often admonished, her writing, though better, has not found the emotional fire he believes crucial. Tacked on after his signature is his opinion that Joan even now has not let herself go. That she continues to save herself. Why, he asks, doesn't she realize that when you give all, there is still more to give?[24]

Though Joan had been married seven years by now, Faulkner's final, handwritten comments returns to his persistent theme of her inhibitions and how sexual reluctance adversely affects artistic development.

While far from effusive, Faulkner's letter expressed admiration for Joan's novel and faith in her future as a novelist. Mysteriously, his next letter assumes an angry, indignant tone as he conveys his outrage at Haydn's request for a book-jacket blurb. Faulkner's contrariness, which still seemed peculiar to Joan many years later, is captured in this previously unpublished January 1961 letter. Scrawled at the top of the letter is a handwritten note admonishing Haydn for his shabby behavior. Far from the glowing quotation Joan might have expected, the blurb Faulkner offers is more like damning with faint praise:

> This is not you, this is somebody else combing the bushes for plugs for your book ... How about this?
> QUOTE   This is a compassionate and hopeful first novel, hopeful in the sense that I dont believe Miss Williams will be satisfied until she has done a better one.
>   William Faulkner
> I will be here until about Feb 15th, go back to Va then until about April 1st, when the State Dept is sending me to Venezuela, unless by that time the new administration will have created an actual foreign policy, so that they wont need to make these frantic desperate cries for help to amateurs

like me who dont want to go, to go to places like Iceland and Japan and Venezuela to try to save what scraps we can. That will be a fortnight, then back to Va. until about July 1st. After that, likely back here. Though it looks like I am never anywhere alone, never again will be. At present an uproar with E.'s [Estelle's] daughter and her grand-daughter. Husband apparently at odds with both of them, and apparently I will now own them too.

I'm glad you are working, believe you will work, make a better one each time as you learn more, and how to tell it.

P.S. I cant say it's honest since no work of fiction is honest since fiction is a synonym for lying, which is why they call it fiction.

Bill [handwritten]

re above. I think any one who wants to be a serious and honest artist should get away from the entire east north of the Potomac and east of the mountains, and stay away until he or she is old enough to resist them.

P.S. The more I think of whoever it was cajoling, frightening, pressuring–whatever it was–you into swotting up plugs to sell one of his books, the madder I get. In my time, editors and publishers didn't do things like this to young writers, though maybe things have changed. Commins, Linscott, etc. not only wouldn't, they wouldn't have permitted it. Max Perkins too. Write another one, do one so true and moving that the old established people like Scribner's, Knopf, Random House, who dont treat inexperienced writers like this, cannot help but take and publish it.[25]

Never able to separate the personal and professional where Joan is concerned, Faulkner closes this letter with a frankly sexual remembrance—he loves her; he finds her physicality still fresh to him; he would like to rekindle their old intimacy—expressed in a most ungracious style. Faulkner's hope for Joan's book is that it stands on its own first and receives praise and recognition later. He wants to be proud of Williams knowing he has lost her.[26]

Since the early stages of their relationship, he promised to make a novelist out of her. Why, then, when she achieved their shared goal, did he overreact and essentially deny such an innocent request? "Of course I didn't ask him [for the book-jacket blurb]. Hiram Haydn asked him for it. He was my editor. It was obviously a very petulant kind of thing ... I never did understand why ... I thought it was a very mean kind of thing."[27]

Joan remembers discussing with Haydn the letters each received from Faulkner and their surprise at his indignation. "Faulkner wrote me this irate letter that when he was young publishers didn't beat the bushes to get statements and he hated me being exploited. He was funny that way. Why couldn't he have just given me a nice quotation?"[28]

Haydn may have been even more shocked than Joan. Faulkner

met Haydn in 1955 when Haydn succeeded Saxe Commins as editor in chief at Random House. In fact, Haydn's first day on the job involved sharing his new office (which had been Saxe Commins') with Faulkner for the next two weeks.

That awkward first encounter is chronicled in Haydn's memoir, *Words and Faces*, where he describes feeling like an intruder in Commins' office and sensing that Commins' colleagues saw him as such. He also had not been told that Faulkner was used to working there when he was in New York. "There were many useful telephone calls to be made, but how could I talk naturally to anyone when the greatest novelist in America was sitting a few feet away, working on a new book?" It was left finally to Faulkner to put Haydn at ease in his new surroundings. Faulkner assured him "whether he was home in Mississippi or here in Saxe's office, no amount of talk or noise affected his concentration," and that he never assumed Haydn wanted to usurp his friend and editor, Saxe.[29]

When Commins died, Albert Erskine took over as Faulkner's editor. Haydn recalls being in Donald Klopfer's office as Faulkner and Erskine met down the hall for their first editorial meeting. Faulkner burst in on Klopfer, telling him, "I got more help from Mr. Erskine in an hour than I have ever experienced." Haydn also described an enjoyable lunch arranged by Robert Linscott. Haydn brought William Styron to Random House when he left Bobbs-Merrill. This put the notion in Linscott's head that the two writers should meet. That afternoon when the four men dined together, Haydn noted Faulkner's "immediate courtesy and friendliness to Styron. Contrary to the stories about his aloofness and inaccessibility to other Random House authors, he was open and gracious."

In 1959 Haydn branched out, and along with two partners, Simon Michael Bessie and Alfred A. Knopf Jr., started Atheneum Publishers. Just one year later, Joan's manuscript arrived on Haydn's desk with a note from Ivan von Auw of the Ober Agency. "Little, Brown–Atlantic and Knopf have turned this down. I think it's fine."[30] His interest in the book was sparked in part because he respected Ivan von Auw. That very night he read *The Morning and the Evening* straight through and called von Auw the next morning promising to publish the novel. Haydn was rewarded as *The Morning and the Evening* received the John P. Marquand Award for the best first novel of the year and was a National Book Award finalist.

As her editor, Haydn was, Joan remembers, "very nice and very helpful." After dismissing Faulkner's unusable quotation, Haydn secured blurbs for *The Morning and the Evening* from William Styron and Robert Penn

Warren.[31] When Haydn moved to Harcourt Brace Jovanovich in 1964, Williams went with him and HBJ published her next two novels, *Old Powder Man* (1966) and *The Wintering* (1971).

Surely, given his knowledge of Haydn, Faulkner should have held him in higher regard. Why he went out of his way to insult both Haydn and Joan remains a curiosity. "I just think he had a sense of being used or was mad because I was married," Joan said. Yet she went on to add that she believes he did give book-jacket blurbs to other writers.[32]

His inability to compose a praiseworthy quotation for the one person he nurtured for years is much like his decision not to return *The Sound and the Fury* manuscript to Joan. Her marriage made her sexually inaccessible and Faulkner's interest dwindled accordingly. For a writer appreciative of irony he failed to see his own: after he derides the publishing world for its exploitation of a young writer in his January 1961 letter he closes with a vivid sexual remembrance—all this in what might have been a congratulatory letter on Joan's success.

———

During Faulkner's last year he appeared resigned if not reconciled to Joan's new life. When she was awarded a grant from the National Institute of Arts and Letters in May 1962 for her novel *The Morning and the Evening*, Faulkner sat on the stage with Eudora Welty. He appeared disinterested in what was occurring and reportedly kept asking Welty when the ceremony would be over. When she passed by him to receive her envelope from Malcolm Cowley, Joan was almost certain Faulkner was asleep.

While indeed a precipitous beginning, Joan's first novel was followed by four more: *Old Powder Man* (1966), *The Wintering* (1971), *County Woman* (1982), and *Pay the Piper* (1988); and many literary accolades, including a Guggenheim award for support while she wrote *Pay the Piper*. Louisiana State University Press reissued *The Morning and the Evening* (1994) and *The Wintering* (1997) as part of its Voices of the South Series. And there are uncollected stories: "Scoot" from *Southern Reader* (September/October 1991); "The Contest"; "Happy Anniversary"; an essay, "Remembering," from *Ironwood* (spring 1981); as well as speeches, book reviews and articles.[33] "The kinds of writers who influenced me," Joan said, "were Eudora Welty, Katherine Anne Porter, Carson McCullers, Faulkner. The kind of writers who, if they made any money, did so with a sense of surprise, literary writers."[34]

Besides treating her relationship with Faulkner in *The Wintering*, Joan's short story collection *Pariah and Other Stories* (1983)—which includes "The

Morning and the Evening"—is dedicated to the memory of William Faulkner. "The important thing," Joan once said, "is to be remembered."

—————

     Joan was in Memphis visiting her parents during the summer of 1962. And one day from her cousin Regina's home in Oxford, she called Faulkner to see about coming over. Estelle answered and she was very nice. She said Joan definitely should come to Rowan Oak. That July day Joan and Faulkner sat on the porch and talked. There was nothing terribly important or revelatory in what they said. He asked Joan if there was money in the envelope they gave her at the May award ceremony.[35] She said no, they gave her that later. They said goodbye and just ten days after Joan's visit Faulkner was dead.

     Still in Memphis, Joan traveled to Oxford for Faulkner's funeral. The Faulkner family plot was full and the author was placed alone at the bottom of a slight hill. Cards and wires flowed in from all over the world, including one from the president.[36] Writers like William Styron and Shelby Foote, Random House editors and publishers, including Bennett Cerf, and

Faulkner's office in Rowan Oak. The small dog on the top shelf was a gift from Joan purchased on Beale Street in Memphis. Below, Joan's first novel, *The Morning and the Evening*, occupies a prominent place on Faulkner's bookshelf (courtesy Arlie Herron).

a host of others descended on the small, Southern town that seemed as unsure of William Faulkner in death as they had been of him in life.

———

"This is what no one has picked up about Faulkner. He is talking about writing and he says, 'It is the only thing I have found maybe not to justify the breathing and existing but at least to make bearable the loneliness and solitude in which the breathing has to be done.' I think he is talking about how lonesome life is all the time," Joan said. "And I told you how in some other letter he said 'writing was the only thing he ever found to alleviate the boredom of living.' That is the vast truth to me about Faulkner. And maybe that is also why he ran from one affair to another."[37]

———

It would be difficult to dispute Joan's powerful and confident assessment, yet there was more to their union than Faulkner seeking distraction. Joan evoked from Faulkner strong romantic passions. Their years of involvement were a vast space of possibilities. In his mind, they were getting on planes for Europe or Egypt; they were spending months by the ocean at wintertime; they were walking in fallen leaves or lying in summer's grass. Her youth and appearance matched his sexual ideal, from white slips to a splashy girl-hand to an unwashed face. She was the child, infant, in need of his protection but also his love. He felt charged with liberating and fostering her artistic talent.

That a man at the very top of his profession should be so obsequious to a young woman, a coed at their first meeting, is not really all that mysterious. Again, it opened vistas for his imagination. If such a girl was unattainable to him in his youth, she would not be in his maturity. His pursuit, at times relentless, was necessary for his delicate self-esteem. The more Joan said no to him, the more challenged and determined he felt. Would he ever truly have disrupted his "real" life for her? Probably not. He was paralyzed by his domestic situation no matter how he railed against it. He loved his daughter, and most likely, in his own way, his wife. His marriage and Joan's tenuous availability allowed for fantasies, schemes, and intrigues—the world of the mind just that much richer and varied than the crumbs he accused Joan of giving.

Moreover, the substantial fabric of this relationship was evident through dialogue and context. "Thirty-one years in age separated us," Joan wrote, "but we had sprung from the same Southern middle class, the same part of the South. I grew up in Memphis, but the blue hills of North Mississippi were part of my family, my life, my heritage—the same earth as innate to me as that which eventually would hold him fast and find him breath as he wrote in *A Green Bough*."[38] He loved her as his "countryman" and she understood him as hers.

Joan came to know the life of a writer as she observed him living it. Even after seeing his pain, uncertainty, and solitariness, she still wanted it. Joan empathized with Faulkner's loneliness as a kindred spirit. Loneliness haunted her. She had an intrinsic fear of aloneness she never escaped. That she chose a profession of solitude confirmed Faulkner's belief that art indeed would overcome all obstacles.

The final image of Faulkner and Joan sitting on his front porch at Rowan Oak just days before his death, having their quiet, inconsequential talk, presents a lulling image—writer to writer. They seemed at peace finally with each other.

Appendix: Joan Williams' Critique of Faulkner's First Draft of *Requiem for a Nun*

After a ten-day New York visit in early February 1950 where Faulkner sees Joan, he mails her a three-page draft of the beginning dialogue for his play *Requiem for a Nun*. From the outset, Faulkner believed this collaboration beneficial to Joan's literary aspirations and a means of advancing his courtship. Joan, a Bard College coed at this time, felt overwhelmed when, especially as time went on, she would receive from Faulkner essentially completed sections of the play.

Faulkner's handwritten draft and personal note on Hotel Algonquin letterhead stationery is postmarked New York, New York, February 11, 1950.* Two pages into the draft of the dialogue, Faulkner instructs Joan to begin her work on the play. This passage from the letter appears in Joseph Blotner's *Selected Letters of William Faulkner*:

> You can begin to work here. This act begins to tell who Nancy is, and what she has done. She is a "nigger" woman, a known drunkard and dope user, a whore with a jail record in the little town, always in trouble. Some time back she seemed to have reformed, got a job as nurse to a child in the home of a prominent young couple. Then one day suddenly and for no reason, she murdered the child. And now she doesn't even seem sorry. She seems to be making it almost impossible for the lawyer to save her.
>
> So at the end of this act, everybody, sympathy is against her. She deserves to hang, a sentiment which reflects even on the lawyer defending her ... [298].

*The date referenced for the exchanged correspondence here and throughout this text reflects the postmark whenever possible.

195

Faulkner adds a personal note thanking Joan for a letter he received from her at the hotel and for the enclosed violet. (Upon his return to Oxford, he describes the violet as delicate, moving, and true, and comments that he is not surprised she thought of the gesture.) He closes with good-night and goodbye, at least for a bit.

Joan's long, single-spaced response primarily focuses on the play. Though she provides this earnest effort, Joan often remarked that she considered herself unprepared to "rewrite" Faulkner. Her valid and significant suggestions in this letter include ways to expand and develop Nancy's character. His encouragement aside, Faulkner appeared not to take Joan's contribution to heart; Nancy's character—enigmatic and diminished—remains a central flaw in *Requiem*:

> answer on feb. 13, 1950   monday
> your letter today. i will talk to you first about the play, and the best thing of all is the name nancy. i had been thinking and thinking about what to name the colored woman; i realized it had to be right and that is ... i like it all except I wonder how it is to be put across about the scene nancy and stevens have had about her pleading not guilty. by stevens actions? can he lean toward her and nod or something to indicate that he has told her, can he make a slight aside (that wouldn't be very good) and i don't like it when two characters talk together in indication that they are whispering simply because no one else takes notice of them. the thing then would have to be, it seems to me, that he makes some slight movement of the hand, a slight leaning forward in anticipation of her answer, almost continuing as tho she had said the not guilty then stopping abruptly in surprise as tho then hearing that she has not said what he thought she was going to. can this be done? or do you have some other way?
> can we have the judge's desk and the woman next [to] it and then to one side the railing seperating [sic] the place where the spectators sit from the participants in the trial so that stevens can turn to face them sometime when he says something so that the audience gets the feeling that just off stage is a group of people watching what they too can see. the jury may be facing the audience. temple's profile to the audience. i guess this is not too important and not yet anyway but it all came to me and i had to see it before i could think to write just as maybe we both had to know the negro's name. as i said i just got your letter this morning so i haven't written yet but i plan to tomorrow. i really have to sort of act as if i knew such a thing had happened, was going on, and then as you do i think i will hear someone say something. when the pandemonium breaks out the[n] maybe someone could say above the crowd's noise about steven's not expecting this. if all of act I is to be in the courtroom what we have is not enough to cover enough time for an act and yet I don't know what else should happen to cover time. is all of this about nancy to be brought out in this act: that she is a drunk, a dope fiend etc. or is that to come out only in the second when stevens goes to the governor. i think it should be in the first and the specific examples

in the II in flashbacks which show the concrete things that make the lawyer realize why nancy has done it. there should be perhaps some talk in the trial about why she took the job as nurse; stevens perhaps playing on the sympathy of the jury—here is a poor woman trying to reform, get along in the world against hard times and conditions and then some slow calm and yet sad and pitiful in its simplicity answer from nancy about why she took the job.* this could be the first glimpse of the part of her for which the play is named— a nun, and yet not too obvious yet, the kind of thing that at the end the audience will say "o yes, and remember in the first act when she made the speech in the courtroom..." he is trying to take some line of attack: that she had reformed when she took the job but something happened to make her kill, and this one incident must not be enough to make them want to kill a woman who is trying to act right for once, but nancy in her seeming stupidity will not let him make excuses for her, which of course makes her seem dumb to the audience, but also the audience must get the feeling that stevens is being rather pseudo about the thing, is just trying out his polished prose for the court's benefit and he doesn't care whether or not the case is lost, that is he wants to win for the glory of winning and not out of desire to save the woman. if she makes the speech i talked about the audiences sympathy will be with her but as you suggested it should really be at the end of the act with the others so something else must happen to make them turn their sympathy from her, something that will make then turn definitely although momentarily, at the time of the speech, they were with her; it will probably make them angry with themselves for sympathizing with her for a moment but then at the end of the play they will find they were right after all. is this all right, good, bad, or what.

the act could begin by the lawyer asking her questions: what is your name, profession, occupation, employers, how long etc. and from the way in which it is asked and answered obvious that it is rehearsed, then the next question guilty or not guilty and the expected, rehearsed answer he thinks is to come doesn't ... shock, surprise, etc. as you suggested. the only thing is ... in legal procedure is the question of guilty or not asked before the charges are discussed?...

*An excellent suggestion as it would have allowed Nancy a "voice" in the play. Instead, Nancy's story primarily is told through Temple Drake, mother of the murdered infant. Temple, who refers to Nancy as "a nigger dope-fiend," sympathizes with Nancy and understands her motives for the infanticide. (Nancy, like Dilsey in The Sound and the Fury, tries to keep a hopelessly fractured white family together.) Temple believes her own sinful past is the real cause of her baby's death and Nancy's tragedy.

Notes

Introduction: Middle Years

1. Joan Williams, interview with author, Holly Springs, MS, 14 October 1996.
2. Tom Dardis, *The Thirsty Muse* (New York: Ticknor and Fields, 1989), 85.
3. Elizabeth Mullener, "Joan Williams and William Faulkner: A Romance Remembered," *Times-Picayune, Dixie Magazine*, 19 September 1982, 8, 12.
4. Interview, 14 October 1996.
5. Mullener, 12.
6. Joan Williams, *The Wintering* (New York: Harcourt, Brace & World, 1971), 240.
7. Mullener, 13.
8. Joan Williams, "Twenty Will Not Come Again," *The Atlantic Monthly*, May 1980, 65.
9. Mullener, 16, 18.
10. Joan Williams, "Faulkner's Advice to a Young Writer," draft for Faulkner Conference, 1990, Oxford, MS.

I : 1949—An Afternoon Recalled

1. Ten years later, in a tragic mirroring of Quentin Compson in *The Sound and the Fury*, Orgill, then thirty-three years old, jumped to his death from the Memphis-Arkansas Bridge. His wife, Nancy Wilson Orgill, also a friend of Joan Williams,' followed her husband's suicide with her own, leaping from the same bridge twelve days later in February 1960. The Orgills left two small children, Kenneth W. Orgill III, five years, and three-year-old Elizabeth Orgill.
2. Patricia Lee Gauch, "Faulkner and Beyond: A Biography of Joan Williams" (Ph.D. diss., Drew University, 1988), 49.
3. Regina Holley, interview with author, Oxford, MS, 24 July 1997.

4. Joel Williamson, *William Faulkner and Southern History* (New York: Oxford University Press, 1993), 277.
5. Williams, "Faulkner's Advice," unpublished draft.
6. *Wintering*, 57–58.
7. Williams, "Faulkner's Advice," unpublished draft.
8. Joseph Blotner, *Faulkner: A Biography*, vol. 2 (New York: Random House, 1974), 1292.
9. Jay Parini, *One Matchless Time* (New York: HarperCollins, 2004), 316.
10. Joseph Blotner, *Faulkner: A Biography* (New York: Vintage, 1984), 504.
11. Joan Williams, "Advice to a Young Writer" (speech for the annual meeting of the Memphis Friends of the Library, Memphis, 21 April 1996).
12. Interview, 14 October 1996.
13. Williams to Faulkner, Annandale-on-Hudson, NY, fall 1949.
14. *Ibid.* Joan's letters are reproduced without corrections unless readability is at issue. In those cases, [sic] or brackets will be included.
15. Williamson, 277.
16. Blotner, 1984, 507.
17. *Ibid.*
18. Movie adaptation of Faulkner's novel *Intruder in the Dust.*
19. Memphis, Tennessee, afternoon newspaper.
20. *Requiem for a Nun,* a play, published in 1951, is Faulkner's next new work.
21. Her eye color.
22. Williams to Faulkner, fall 1949.
23. Joan Williams, interview with author, Memphis, 22 May 1997.
24. Blotner, 1984, 510.
25. *Ibid.,* 508–09.
26. Paul Gray, "Mister Faulkner Goes to Stockholm," *Smithsonian,* Oct. 2001, 59.

27. Blotner, 1984, 508.

28. Most likely *Knight's Gambit* published 27 November 1949.

29. Joan received an undated, one-sentence note from Faulkner stating simply that he wrote her a letter about a month ago but decided not to send it for a while, or perhaps not at all.

30. Blotner, 1984, 510–11.

31. Mullener,12.

32. Williamson, 278.

II : 1950–A Courtship of Letters

1. Joseph Blotner, ed., *Selected Letters of William Faulkner* (New York: Random House, 1977), 296.

2. Interview, 22 May 1997. See also Karl F. Zender, *Faulkner and the Politics of Reading* (Baton Rouge: Louisiana State University Press, 2002), 147–48.

3. Interview, 14 October 1996.

4. Mullener, 13.

5. *Ibid.*, 12.

6. Interview, 14 October 1996.

7. Mullener, 16.

8. Williams, "Faulkner's Advice to a Young Writer," unpublished draft.

9. James G. Watson, *William Faulkner: Letter and Fictions* (Austin: University of Texas Press, 1987), 145.

10. In discussing Faulkner's letters to Meta, Joan commented on the irony that she (Joan) one day would become Mrs. Bowen. In his letter to Meta, Faulkner used the names "Mr. Bowen" and Mrs. Bowen" to connote sexual organs.

11. See Watson, 145–146.

12. Interview, 14 October 1996.

13. Mullener, 13.

14. Interview, 14 October 1996.

15. Mullener, 16.

16. Hickman "William Faulkner: Dealing with his Demons," *Memphis*, Sept. 1993.

17. Faulkner, posing as a British citizen, joined the Canadian Royal Air Force as a cadet in July 1918. He served 179 days, received some flight instruction, but according to a 24 November 1918 letter to his mother and father, did not receive a pilot's certificate and was discharged as a second airman. After the November 1918 armistice, he ordered an RAF officer's uniform with the shoulder pips of a lieutenant and a pair of wings from the RAF's predecessor, the more glamorous Royal Flying Corps. Faulkner was very fond of his uniform, despite its dubious authenticity, and frequently wore it around the Oxford town square and at special occasions. See also *Thinking of Home: William*

Faulkner's Letters to His Mother and Father, 1918–1925, ed. James G. Watson (New York: Norton, 2000).

18. Interview, 14 October 1996.

19. Blotner, vol. 2, 1484.

20. Faulkner to Williams, St. Moritz, Switzerland, 14 December 1953.

21. *Wintering*, 306–307.

22. Joan Williams, "The Contest," *The Chattahoochee Review* 15, no. 4 (Summer 1995): 7.

23. Joan Williams, interview with author, Memphis, 21 March 1997.

24. Joan Williams, interview with author, Memphis, 28 May 1995.

25. Interview, 14 October 1996.

26. Williams, "Twenty," 61–62.

27. Interview, 14 October 1996.

28. Mullener, 12.

29. Interview, 14 October 1996.

30. *Ibid.*

31. Mullener, 12.

32. Joan Williams, "Faulkner's Advice to a Young Writer," in *Faulkner and the Short Story: Faulkner and Yoknapawtawpha 1990* (Jackson: University of Mississippi Press, 1992), 254.

33. Williamson, 279.

34. Williams, "Faulkner's Advice to a Young Writer," unpublished draft.

35. Blotner, vol. 2, 1302–3.

36. Watson, 147.

37. Williams, "Faulkner's Advice to a Young Writer," unpublished draft.

38. Frederick R. Karl, *William Faulkner: American Writer* (New York: Weidenfeld and Nicholson, 1989), 790.

39. Faulkner to Williams, Oxford, MS, 7 January 1950.

40. Most likely a reference to John Marcher, central character in Henry James' short story "The Beast in the Jungle."

41. Williams to Faulkner, Annandale-on-Hudson, NY, 17 January 1950.

42. Williamson, 279.

43. *Ibid.*

44. Faulkner to Williams, Oxford, MS, 23 January 1950.

45. Interview, 22 May 1997.

46. *Wintering*, 111.

47. Interview, 22 May 1997.

48. Mullener, 12–13.

49. Faulkner to Williams, Oxford, MS, 3 September 1950.

50. See also Meta Wilde Carpenter, *A Loving Gentleman: The Love Story of William Faulkner and Meta Carpenter* (New York: Simon & Schuster, 1976).

51. Interview, 14 October 1996.

52. *Wintering*, 110.

53. *Ibid.*, 113.

54. *Ibid.*, 106.

55. Faulkner to Williams, Oxford, MS, 3 March 1950.

56. Interview, 22 May 1997.

57. Karl, 792–793.

58. Faulkner to Williams, New York, NY, 11 February 1950.

59. Faulkner to Williams, Oxford, MS, 14 February 1950.

60. Interview, 22 May 1997.

61. See appendix.

62. Williams, "Twenty," 63.

63. David Minter, *William Faulkner: His Life and Work* (Baltimore: Johns Hopkins University Press, 1980), 217.

64. *Selected*, 299–300. In 1930 Sinclair Lewis was awarded the Nobel Prize for Literature and in 1938 Pearl Buck received the prestigious award.

65. Faulkner to Williams, Oxford, MS, 23 February 1950.

66. Interview, 22 May 1997.

67. Faulkner's *Go Down, Moses* was reprinted in 1949; Andre Malraux's *Man's Fate*. Faulkner also inscribed Malraux's *Man's Fate* to Phil Stone as a 1938 Christmas gift. Upon presenting the gift, Faulkner told Stone, "He's the best of us all." Blotner, 1984, 403.

68. February 1950. Joan typed at the top of her letter, "in answer to letter of feb. 23."

69. Faulkner visited Joan at Bard College and they walked in the snow near an old barn. Joan remembers them seeing a small beetle trying to crawl in the snow, and Faulkner pointed it out, saying it was the bravest thing he'd ever seen. A variation of this appears in *The Wintering*, 122.

70. A reference regarding how Faulkner might explain to Estelle his collaboration with Joan on *Requiem*.

71. Brandon Grove, a fellow Bard student whom Joan dated and whom Faulkner met while visiting Joan at Bard in the spring of 1950.

72. Karl, 794.

73. Faulkner to Williams, Oxford, MS, 22 March 1950.

74. Nelle Harper Lee, born 28 April 1926, from Monroeville, AL, author of *To Kill a Mockingbird*.

75. Interview, 22 May 1997.

76. Saxe Commins, Faulkner's Random House editor.

77. Interview, 22 May 1997.

78. Williams, "Faulkner's Advice to a Young Writer," unpublished draft.

79. Williams, "Faulkner's Advice to a Young Writer," 1992, 255.

80. Karl, 793.

81. Faulkner to Williams, undated, probably mid–February 1950.

82. Faulkner met Meta Carpenter in 1935 while writing scripts in Hollywood. Originally from Tupelo, Mississippi, Meta was employed as a script girl for Howard Hawks. Her off-and-on affair with Faulkner spanned twenty years.

83. Interview, 22 May 1997.

84. Blotner, 1984, 507.

85. *Requiem for a Nun* served a dual purpose in this regard. Ruth Ford, an accomplished actress, had asked Faulkner in 1943 to write a play for her. She was a friend of Faulkner's—some have suggested a romantic interest—and as an Ole Miss coed she had dated his brother, Dean Faulkner, who died in a plane accident in 1935.

86. Interview, 28 May 1997.

87. Interview, 22 May 1997.

88. Robert N. Linscott to Williams, New York, NY, 3 March 1950.

89. Temple Drake, the play's protagonist.

90. Karl, 794.

91. Faulkner to Williams, Oxford, MS, 22 March 1950.

92. Williams, "Faulkner's Advice to a Young Writer," unpublished draft.

93. Faulkner to Williams, Oxford, MS, May 1950.

94. Katherine Rosin's father, Harry Scherman, was head of the Book-of-the-Month Club. Faulkner pursued this contact for Joan and on 17 May 1950 received a note from Robert Haas who had contacted Mrs. Rosin on Joan's behalf. Haas assured Faulkner that Mrs. Rosin would be delighted to help Joan.

95. *Selected*, 303–04.

96. Faulkner to Williams, Oxford, MS, 6 May 1950.

97. William Faulkner, *Requiem for a Nun* (New York: Vintage, 1951), 132.

98. *Ibid.*, 137.

99. Blotner, 1984, 517.

100. Robert Coughlan, "The Private World of William Faulkner," *Life*, 28 September 1953, 133.

101. Coughlan, 134.

102. Hickman, *Memphis*, 88.

103. Faulkner to Williams, Oxford, MS, 9 May 1950.

104. Williams, "Faulkner's Advice to a Young Writer," 1992, 254.

105. Parini, 319.

106. Williams, "Twenty."

107. Interview, 22 May 1997.

108. Louis Daniel Brodsky and Robert W. Hamblin, eds., *Faulkner: A Comprehensive Guide to the Brodsky Collection, Vol. II: The Letters* (Jackson: University Press of Mississippi, 1984), 95.

109. See *Selected*, 303–04.

110. Faulkner to Williams, Oxford, MS, 9 May 1950.

111. A similar incident occurs in *The Wintering*, 119.

112. Interview, 22 May 1997.

113. Mullener, 13.

114. Interview, 14 October 1996.
115. Interview, 28 May 1997.
116. Blotner, 1984, 351.
117. *Ibid.*, 289.
118. See Brodsky, 116, 135, etc.
119. Joan's 1954 marriage to Ezra Bowen ushered in yet another connection to Harold Ober. Bowen's mother was the tireless biographer Catherine Drinker Bowen (1897–1973), who also was represented by Ober. She was in fact a close friend of the extremely taciturn and sometimes off-putting agent.
120. Parini, 320.
121. *Ibid.*
122. Interview, 22 May 1997.
123. Mullener, 14.
124. Faulkner to Williams, Oxford, MS, 17 June 1950.
125. Interview, 22 May 1997.
126. Williams, "Twenty," 62.
127. See Brodsky, 93.
128. Interview, 22 May 1997.
129. Faulkner to Williams, Oxford, MS, 9 July 1950.
130. See Lisa C. Hickman, "William Faulkner and A. E. Housman: A Writer's Poet," *Housman Society Journal* 26 (2001): 23–35. See also Zender, 146.
131. Parini, 321. Letter is actually postmarked 13 July 1950.
132. Faulkner to Williams, 13 July 1950.
133. Interview, 22 May 1997.
134. Interview, 28 May 1997.
135. Brodsky, 135.
136. Faulkner to Williams, Oxford, MS, 15 July 1950.
137. Faulkner to Williams, Oxford, MS, probably late summer or fall 1950.
138. Interview, 22 May 1997.
139. Faulkner to Williams, Oxford, MS, 19 July 1950.
140. Faulkner published *Doctor Martino and Other Stories* with Harrison Smith and Robert Haas on 16 April 1934.
141. Williams, "Twenty," 62.
142. Joan Williams, interview with author, Memphis, TN, 3 February 1998.
143. Joan Williams, *Pay the Piper* (New York: E.P. Dutton, 1988), 15.
144. Maude Williams (1903–1997) was born in Arkabutla, Mississippi; Priest or Priestly "P.H." Williams (1895–1955) was born in Humboldt, Tennessee. Joan dedicated her 1966 novel, *Old Powder Man*, to P.H. and Maude Williams.
145. Interview, 28 May 1997.
146. Maude Williams, interview with author, Memphis, TN, September 1996.
147. Blotner, vol. 2, 1327.
148. Faulkner to Williams, Oxford, MS, 14 August 1950.

149. See also Williams, "Twenty," 61.
150. Faulkner to Williams, 2 February 1952.
151. Blotner, 1984, 551.
152. Interview, 14 October 1996.
153. A friend of Joan's at Bard College whom Faulkner met while visiting.
154. Williams, "Faulkner's Advice to a Young Writer," 1992, 254.
155. Faulkner to Williams, Oxford, MS, 4 August 1950.
156. *Requiem*, 68.
157. Interview, 28 May 1997.
158. Blotner, vol. 2, 1327–28.
159. Faulkner to Williams, Oxford, MS, 20 August 1950.
160. Blotner, vol. 2, 1328–29.
161. Interview, 2 June 1997.
162. The correspondence, particularly an August 1952 letter from Faulkner, indicates he gave Joan the manuscript in the summer of 1952, not 1950. See *Selected*, 438–39.
163. Interview, 28 May 1997.
164. Interview, 14 October 1996.
165. Faulkner met Jean Stein 24 December 1953, at a party in St. Moritz, Switzerland. He would later compare Joan—unfavorably—to Jean Stein, writing Saxe Commins on 14 March 1954, "...she [Jean] has none of the emotional conventional confusion which poor Joan had." See Brodsky, 138.
166. Interview, 28 May 1997.
167. Faulkner to Williams, NA.
168. Interview, 2 June 1997.
169. *Wintering*, 170–173.
170. *Wintering*, 244–245.
171. Brandon Grove, telephone interview with author, 14 June 1998.
172. *Wintering*, 102–103.
173. Interview, 14 June 1998.
174. *Ibid.*
175. This afternoon on Faulkner's boat predated Joan and Estelle's lunch at the Peabody.
176. Interview, 22 May 1997.
177. *Wintering*, 165.
178. See page 47, Williams' letter to Faulkner, February 1950.
179. *Wintering*, 166.
180. Interview, 22 May 1997.
181. Interview, 14 June 1998.
182. Brandon Grove, letter to author, Washington, D.C., 15 June 1998.
183. Telephone interview, 14 June 1998.
184. Letter, 15 June 1998.
185. Interview, 14 June 1998.
186. Joan Williams, interview with author, Memphis, TN, 8 March 1998.
187. Williamson, 280–281.
188. Faulkner to Williams, Oxford, MS, 3 September 1950.

189. Karl, 802.
190. Faulkner to Williams, Oxford, MS, 29 September 1950.
191. Joan Williams, interview with author, Memphis, TN, 5 August 1997.
192. Interview, 28 May 1997.
193. Probably *Salammbô* (1863) by Flaubert.
194. Mullener, 16.
195. Williams, "Faulkner's Advice to a Young Writer," unpublished draft.
196. *Requiem*, 149.
197. *Ibid.*, 142.
198. Faulkner to Williams, Oxford, MS, 23 October 1950.
199. Faulkner to Williams, Oxford, MS, late October 1950.
200. Interview, 28 May 1997.
201. Williamson, 281.
202. Faulkner to Williams, Oxford, MS, 3 November 1950.
203. Williams. "Faulkner's Advice to a Young Writer." unpublished draft.
204. *Selected*, 308.
205. Interview, 28 May 1997.
206. Blotner, vol. 2, 1338.
207. *Ibid.*, 1344.
208. Interview, 28 May 1997.
209. Faulkner to Williams, Oxford, MS, 5 December 1950.
210. Parini, 329.
211. Blotner, vol. 2, 1352.
212. Michel Gresset, *A Faulkner Chronology* (Jackson: University of Mississippi Press, 1985).
213. Blotner, 1984, 54–55.
214. *Ibid.*, 56.
215. Watson, 52.
216. Blotner, 1984, 240.
217. Interview, 14 October 1996.
218. Interview, 22 May 1997.
219. Blotner, 1984, 245.
220. Interview, 14 October 1996.
221. Joel Williamson, *William Faulkner and Southern History* (New York: Oxford University Press, 1993), 276, and Tom Dardis in *The Thirsty Muse* (New York: Ticknor and Fields, 1989), 80–81.
222. Interview, 14 October 1996.
223. Interview, 22 May 1997.
224. Faulkner to Williams, London, England, 16 December 1950.
225. Interview, 28 May 1997.
226. Blotner, 1984, 531.
227. Faulkner to Williams, Oxford, MS, 21 December 1950.
228. Interview, 28 May 1997.

III : 1951—Other Loves

1. Theodore Weiss, telephone interview with author, 2 April 2001.
2. Faulkner to Williams, Oxford, MS, 9 January 1951. This short story was never published.
3. In a short, undated note, Faulkner writes Joan that his wife is drunk and threatening phone calls to Joan and her parents: he has tried to circumvent her by taking the telephone to pieces.
4. Faulkner to Williams, Oxford, MS, 15 January 1951.
5. Interview, 28 May 1997.
6. Faulkner to Williams, Oxford, MS, 21 January 1951.
7. Joan's home address, 1243 East Parkway South, in Memphis.
8. Interview, 28 May 1997.
9. Interview, 22 May 1997.
10. Faulkner to Williams, Oxford, MS, 28 January 1951.
11. Karl, 821.
12. No longer in operation.
13. Stewardess job Joan did not take.
14. *Selected*, 312.
15. Interview, 28 May 1997.
16. *Selected*, 313.
17. Karl, 822.
18. Faulkner to Williams, Beverly Hills, CA, 4 March 1951.
19. Faulkner met Meta Carpenter in December 1935. She was working as a script girl for Howard Hawks in Hollywood and she would transcribe Faulkner's handwritten scripts.
20. Faulkner's practice of bestowing such gifts predates both Meta and Joan. He saw to it that Joan received signed first editions of all his work.
21. Blotner, 1984, 538.
22. *Ibid.*, 369.
23. Joan Williams, interview with author, Memphis, TN, 6 June 1997.
24. Hickman, *Memphis*, 88.
25. Interview, 14 October 1996.
26. Hickman, *Memphis*, 87.
27. Interview, 28 May 1997.
28. *Life*, 28 September 1953, 127.
29. Hickman, *Memphis*, 87.
30. Blotner, vol. 2, 56–57.
31. Blotner, 1984, 559.
32. Stacy Schiff, "Terpsichore, Thalia and Yoko," review of *The Lives of the Muses: Nine Women and the Artists They Inspired* by Francine Prose, *The New York Times Book Review*, 22 September 2002, 9.
33. *Wintering*, 342.
34. "Faulkner Honors Bard with Sudden Visit," *The Bardian*, 15 May 1951.
35. *Ibid.*
36. Blotner, 1984, 146.
37. Joan Williams, "Personal Sketch," *The Bardian*, 15 May 1951.
38. Interview, 28 May 1997.

39. Interview, 22 May 1997.
40. Faulkner to Williams, Oxford, MS, 15 May 1951.
41. Joan's trip to California primarily was to visit Hardy Koch.
42. *Wintering*, 342.
43. He seemed to feel this would ensure greater security, although even after the P.O. box is obtained Faulkner still worries Estelle would gain access to the letters from Joan.
44. Interview, 28 May 1997.
45. Faulkner to Williams, 7 June 1951.
46. Interview, 10 June 997.
47. Blotner, 1984, 542.
48. Karl, 826.
49. *Selected*, 318.
50. Karl, 826.
51. Faulkner to Williams, Oxford, MS, 18 June 1951.
52. Interview, 28 May 1997.
53. *Requiem*, 128, 130.
54. *Ibid.*, 76–77.
55. Parini, 351.
56. Jay Tolson, ed., *The Correspondence of Shelby Foote and Walker Percy* (New York: Doubletake/Norton, 1997), 185.
57. Interview, 14 October 1996.
58. Williamson, 289.
59. Interview, 14 October 1996.
60. *Ibid.*
61. Blotner, 1984, 543–544.
62. *Ibid.*, 575.
63. *Life*, 28 September 1953, 133.
64. Robert Coughlan, "The Man Behind the Faulkner Myth," *Life*, 5 October 1953, 61.
65. *Ibid.*, 58.
66. Pine Manor College later moved to Chestnut Hill, Massachusetts.
67. Faulkner to Williams, Oxford, MS, 4 September 1951.
68. Blotner, 1984, 544.
69. Faulkner to Williams, Oxford, MS, 9 September 1951.
70. Minter, 223.
71. Interview, 28 May 1997.
72. *Ibid.*
73. This story was never published.
74. Faulkner to Williams, Oxford, MS, 29 October 1951.
75. Faulkner to Williams, Oxford, MS, 1 November 1951.
76. Blotner, 1984, 547, 550.
77. Karl, 834.
78. Faulkner to Williams, Oxford, MS, 29 November 1951.
79. Faulkner's letters to Joan, as they appear in *Selected Letters*, were edited to eliminate or minimize their personal nature.
80. Faulkner to Williams, Oxford, MS, 21 December 1951.
81. Williams, "Faulkner's Advice to a Young Writer," 1992, 256.
82. Watson, 148.
83. Interview, 28 May 1997.
84. *Ibid.*
85. Interview, 14 October 1996.

IV : 1952—Jacob Labored Seven Years for Rachel

1. Interview, 28 May 1997.
2. Hickman, *Memphis*, 90.
3. *Selected*, 337.
4. Blotner, 1984, 559.
5. Williams to Faulkner, New York, NY, July 1953.
6. *Selected*, 339.
7. *Ibid.*, 341.
8. *Ibid.*, 327.
9. Faulkner to Williams, Oxford, MS, 16 January 1952.
10. Pine Manor Junior College in Wellesley, MA.
11. Faulkner to Williams, Oxford, MS, 26 January 1952.
12. At this point in January, Faulkner is hopeful that *Requiem for a Nun* will be produced in Paris during the spring of 1952.
13. Williams, "Faulkner's Advice to a Young Writer." unpublished draft.
14. Joan Williams, interview with author, Memphis, TN, 2 June 1997.
15. Parini, 345.
16. Faulkner to Williams, Oxford, MS, 13 February 1952.
17. Blotner, 1984, 551.
18. Faulkner to Williams, Oxford, MS, 29 February 1952.
19. Interview, 2 June 1997.
20. Blotner, 1984, 552.
21. Faulkner to Williams, Oxford, MS, 14 March 1952.
22. Faulkner to Williams, Oxford, MS, 25 March 1952.
23. Parini, 346.
24. *Selected*, 331.
25. Most likely a reference to Else Jonsson.
26. Faulkner to Williams, Oxford, MS, 7 May 1952.
27. Parini, 346.
28. *Selected*, 7 May 1952.
29. Hotel New Weston, located at Madison Avenue at 50th Street in New York, was later demolished. In a 13 June 1997 phone interview with former *Sports Illustrated* editor Robert Creamer, he described the hotel as much like the Algonquin Hotel.

30. Faulkner to Williams, New York, NY, 17 May 1952. Joan was still living in New Orleans at this time. Faulkner never visited her there though he suggested it in letters.

31. Gauch, 77.

32. Williams, "Twenty," 64.

33. Joan Williams, "The Morning and the Evening," in *Pariah and Other Stories* (Boston: Little, Brown, 1983), 19–32.

34. Blotner, 1984, 555.

35. Faulkner to Williams, Oxford, MS, August 1952.

36. Faulkner to Williams, Oxford, MS, 29 April 1953.

37. Faulkner to Williams, Oxford, MS, 19 June 1952.

38. Blotner, 1984, 557.

39. Faulkner to Williams, Oxford, MS, 7 August 1952.

40. Faulkner to Williams, Oxford, MS, July 1952.

41. Faulkner to Williams, Oxford, MS, 2 July 1952.

42. Faulkner to Williams, Oxford, MS, 7 August 1952.

43. Parini, 349.

44. Certainly by this time Joan was sexually experienced: there was the annulled high-school marriage; fairly serious relationships while at Bard College; and her highly autobiographical novel *The Wintering* recounts an affair that primarily was sexual with a young man who also lived in Greenwich Village.

45. *Selected*, 336.

46. Gertrude Stein.

47. Interview, 2 June 1997.

48. Interview, 6 June 1997.

49. Interview, 2 June 1997.

50. Williams, "Twenty," 64.

51. Interview, 14 October 1996.

52. Faulkner to P.H. Williams, Oxford, MS, 23 July 1952.

53. Interview, 2 June 1997.

54. *Ibid.*

55. Faulkner to Williams, Oxford, MS, 31 July 1952.

56. Blotner, vol. 2, 1430.

57. See Williams, *Pay the Piper*, 31.

58. Interview, 2 June 1997.

59. Minter, 231.

60. Brodsky, 102.

61. Ezra Bowen, Joan's first husband, a writer and editor, was a member of the original editorial staff of *Sports Illustrated*. They were married from 1954 to 1970.

62. Letter to Saxe Commins, 9 December 1952.

63. Interview, 10 June 1997.

64. Interview, 14 October 1996.

65. Faulkner to Williams [Mrs. Ezra Bowen], Charlottesville, VA.

66. Interview, 14 October 1996.

67. Faulkner to Williams [Mrs. Ezra Bowen], Charlottesville, VA, 4 March 1957.

68. Faulkner to Williams [Mrs. Ezra Bowen], Oxford, MS, 10 August 1959.

69. Joan Williams, interview with author, 10 June 1997.

70. Joan eventually sold all the letters Faulkner wrote her to the University of Virginia.

71. William Thomas, "Literary Tale Will Be Tugged in Court," *Commercial Appeal* (Memphis), 2 November 1987, B1–2.

72. Interview, 10 June 1997.

73. David A. Maurer, "Longtime Friendship Developed Through Sound and Fury," *Daily Progress* (Charlottesville, VA), 23 January 2000, E1-3.

74. According to Dr. Donald M. Kartiganer, the Howry Professor of Faulkner Studies at the University of Mississippi, "Twilight" was Faulkner's working title for *The Sound and the Fury*.

75. Williams, "Faulkner's Advice to a Young Writer." 256–257.

76. Brodsky, 80–81.

77. Faulkner to Williams, Oxford, MS, undated, probably early August 1952.

78. Interview, 14 October 1996.

79. Watson, 14.

80. Faulkner to Williams, Oxford, MS, 7 August 1952.

81. Faulkner to Williams, Oxford, MS., 7 August 1952.

82. Blotner, 1984, 559. This signature line occurs in *The Wild Palms* [*If I Forget Thee, Jerusalem*] (1939; New York: Vintage, 1995), 273, and in letters to Meta Carpenter.

83. Interview, 2 June 1997.

84. Faulkner to Williams, Oxford, MS, 7 August 1952.

85. *Selected*, 338.

86. Faulkner to Williams, Oxford, MS, 8 August 1952.

87. Blotner, vol. 2, 1432.

88. Faulkner to Williams, Oxford, MS, 8 August 1952.

89. Faulkner to Williams, Oxford, MS, 10 August 1952.

90. Williams, "Faulkner's Advice to a Young Writer." unpublished draft.

91. *Selected*, 338–39.

92. Faulkner to Williams, Oxford, MS, 10 August 1952.

93. Williams, "Faulkner's Advice to a Young Writer," unpublished draft.

94. *Selected*, 340.

95. Faulkner to Williams, Oxford, MS, 21 August 1952.

96. Interview, 22 May 1997.

97. Ezra Pound, "A Virginal," in *Ezra Pound*

Selected Poems (New York: New Directions, 1926), 23.

98. Faulkner to Williams, Oxford, MS, 26 August 1952.

99. Karl, 843.

100. Faulkner to Williams, Memphis, 26 September 1952.

101. Hickman, *Memphis*, 93, 95.

102. Blotner, vol. 2, 1442.

103. Interview, 10 June 1997.

104. Blotner, 1984, 563–64.

105. Faulkner once wrote Joan that he carried the violet she sent him in his wallet in his pants pocket but he lost it—and his pants—when his sloop blew over. This appears to be a reference to the unusual location Faulkner chose for her letter.

106. Fleur Cowles' husband, Gardner Cowles, owned *Look* and *Quick* magazines. Fleur was the associate editor of *Look* and *Quick* magazines; founder and editor of *Flair* magazine (1953–1955); and the author of over ten books.

107. Faulkner to Williams, Oxford, MS, 9 September 1952.

108. *Selected*, 341.

109. Faulkner to Williams, Oxford, MS, 27 September 1952.

110. *Ibid.*

111. Located at 5th and Central Park South in New York.

112. William Inge (1913–1973), a playwright, enjoyed particular success in the 1950s with four consecutive Broadway hits: *Come Back, Little Sheba*; *Picnic*; *Bus Stop*; and *The Dark at the Top of the Stairs*. The year 1953 was notable for Inge, as *Picnic* not only debuted on Broadway but also won several prizes including the Pulitzer.

113. Faulkner to Williams, Oxford, MS, 27 and 29 September 1952.

114. Interview, 6 June 1997.

115. Parini, 350.

116. *Wintering*, 246.

117. *Ibid.*, 247.

118. The proposed names for *The Wintering*'s central characters.

119. Faulkner to Williams, undated, probably November 1952.

120. Brodsky, 82.

121. *Selected*, 341.

122. Another reference to the novel of letters about their relationship.

123. Faulkner to Williams, Oxford, MS, 29 September 1952.

124. The first seminar on Faulkner was held at Harvard University in 1948. This is perhaps Joan's way of further relating her character, Jake, to Ike Snopes in Faulkner's *The Hamlet*.

125. New York restaurant.

126. What would evolve into *The Wintering* (1971).

127. The idea for the bell comes in part from *Cyrano de Bergerac*. Faulkner quoted such lines to Joan as Cyrano had to Roxane. Faulkner identified with the besotted, but physically flawed poet, Cyrano. One day while walking in New York, Faulkner and Joan went into Tiffany's where he bought her a small, silver bell. See *The Wintering*, 229.

128. This letter includes Faulkner's notation at the top indicating his wife had this letter as well.

129. *Selected*, 342.

130. Saxe Commins to Joan Williams, New York, NY, 2 October 1952. On Random House, Inc., The Modern Library, stationery.

131. Williams to Faulkner, New York, NY, early October 1952. On Cowles Magazines, Inc. Publishers of LOOK and QUICK stationery.

132. Karl, 844.

133. Brodsky, 89–90.

134. Dardis, 83.

135. Brodsky, 91.

136. *Ibid.*, 96.

137. *Ibid.*, 93.

138. Faulkner to Williams, Memphis, 18 October 1952.

139. Interview, 2 June 1997.

140. Hickman, *Memphis*, 95, 115–116.

141. Faulkner to Williams, Oxford, MS, 24 October 1952.

142. Brodsky, 94.

143. Interview, 2 July 1997.

144. Brodsky, 97.

145. Seymour Lawrence.

146. Faulkner to Williams, Oxford, MS, 27 October 1952.

147. Faulkner to Williams, Oxford, MS, October 1952.

148. Blotner, 1984, 561.

149. Interview, 2 June 1997.

150. Faulkner to Williams, Oxford, MS, 2 November 1952.

151. Williams, "Faulkner's Advice to a Young Writer," unpublished draft.

152. Faulkner to Williams, Oxford, MS, 6 November 1952.

153. Interview, 2 June 1997.

154. Faulkner to Williams, Oxford, MS, November 1952.

155. Interview, 6 June 1997.

156. Interview, 2 June 1997.

157. Blotner, 1984, 563.

158. Faulkner to Williams, Princeton, NJ, 2 December 1952.

159. Interview, 2 June 1997.

160. Interview, 6 June 1997.

161. Interview, 22 May 1997.

162. Faulkner to Williams, New York, NY, 10 December 1952.

163. Faulkner to Williams, Oxford, MS, 17 December 1952.

164. Williamson, 286.

165. Robert Linscott was one of Faulkner's Random House editors.

166. Known as the master of the artistic pinup.

167. Faulkner to Williams, Oxford, MS, 28 December 1952.

168. Williams, "Faulkner's Advice to a Young Writer," 1992, 258.

169. Interview, 6 October 1992.

170. Williamson, 287.

171. Protagonist of a short story Joan was writing. It was never published.

172. Williams, "Advice to a Young Writer," 1996 speech.

173. Dardis, 85.

174. Faulkner to Williams, Oxford, MS, 31 December 1952.

V : One Fifth Avenue

1. Faulkner to Williams, Oxford, MS, 16 June 1953.

2. Gauch, 87.

3. Interview, 14 October 1996.

4. Williams, unpublished sketch.

5. Dardis, 85.

6. Williamson, 286–287.

7. A New York psychiatrist Joan saw who also treated Faulkner.

8. Mrs. Murgatroid was a short story Joan was working on at the time. Harold Ober talked about trying to sell it to *Good Housekeeping* but it did not sell.

9. Faulkner asked Hal Smith to leave a key to his apartment with Joan for his use when he arrived in New York.

10. Mr. Meeman was the editor of *The* [Memphis] *Press Scimitar*, the city's daily afternoon newspaper.

11. *A Fable*.

12. Williams, "Faulkner's Advice to a Young Writer," unpublished draft.

13. Blotner, vol. 2, 1445.

14. *Ibid.*

15. Faulkner to Williams, Oxford, MS, 8 January 1953.

16. Faulkner to Williams, Oxford, MS, 10 January 1953.

17. Faulkner to Williams, Oxford, MS, 17 January 1953.

18. *Wintering*, 239, 243–44.

19. Faulkner to Williams, Oxford, MS, 3 April 1953.

20. Blotner, 1984, 566.

21. Interview, 10 June 1997.

22. Blotner, 1984, 567.

23. *Ibid.*

24. Interview, 28 May 1997.

25. Blotner, 1984, 567–68.

26. *Ibid.*, 570.

27. Estelle received nine blood transfusions before she was stabilized.

28. Faulkner to Williams, Oxford, MS, April 1953.

29. Blotner, vol. 2, 1454–55.

30. Faulkner gave the commencement address at Jill's graduation from Pine Manor Junior College.

31. Faulkner to Williams, Oxford, MS, 25 April 1953.

32. Karl, 86.

33. *Selected*, 348.

34. Faulkner to Williams, Oxford, MS, 29 April 1953.

35. Blotner, vol. 2, 1457.

36. Joan found Faulkner's advice, to write from the outside, unsuited to her style. "Of course I never have. I can't help it." Interview, 10 June 1997.

37. Faulkner to Williams, 30 April 1953.

38. Faulkner to Williams, 31 April 1953.

39. Blotner, vol. 2, 1458.

40. *Ibid.*, 1475.

41. Interview, 14 October 1996.

42. Blotner, 1984, 571.

43. Faulkner to Williams, Oxford, MS, 1 June 1953.

44. Interview, 10 June 1997.

45. Karl, 861.

46. Faulkner to Williams, Oxford, MS, June 1953.

47. Blotner, 1984, 572.

48. Faulkner to Williams, Oxford, MS, June 1953.

49. Williams, "Faulkner's Advice to a Young Writer," unpublished draft.

50. On 8 June 1953, at Pine Manor Junior College in Wellesley, Massachusetts. Faulkner writes Joan in mid–June that the *Atlantic Monthly* paid him $250 for publication rights to his speech.

51. Williams, "Faulkner's Advice to a Young Writer," unpublished draft.

52. *Ibid.*

53. Williams, "Faulkner's Advice to a Young Writer," unpublished draft.

54. *Ibid.*

55. *Ibid.*, 259–260.

56. Interview, 6 June 1997.

57. Williams, "Faulkner's Advice to a Young Writer," unpublished draft.

58. Faulkner's long-time Oxford friend who shared his college reading lists (a B.A. cum laude from the University of Mississippi and a B.A. cum laude from Yale) with Faulkner and who was instrumental in helping him publish his first book, *The Marble Faun* (1924), a collection of poetry.

59. Interview, 6 June 1997.

60. Williams, "Faulkner's Advice to a Young Writer," 1992, 261.

61. Faulkner suggested Joan send Ober the short story with the Howard and Otis characters without relating to Ober Faulkner's critique of the story.

62. A reference to Joseph McCarthy (1908–1957), a controversial Republican senator from Wisconsin. He charged that Communists had infiltrated the U.S. government. Investigations during the 1950s of individuals later spread to agencies and organizations believed to be disloyal to America. Many were falsely accused and blacklisted. McCarthyism, the term attached to this movement, dissipated by 1954.

63. Faulkner to Williams, Oxford, MS, 4 July 1953.

64. Williams, "Faulkner's Advice to a Young Writer," unpublished draft.

65. Faulkner to Williams, Oxford, MS, 4 July 1953.

66. Blotner, vol. 2, 1461.

67. Faulkner to Williams, Oxford, MS, 9 July 1953.

68. Faulkner to Williams, Oxford, MS, 16 July 1953.

69. Faulkner to Williams, Oxford, MS, 18 July 1953.

70. Faulkner to Williams, Oxford, MS, 29 July 1953.

71. Interview, 10 June 1997.

72. Joan and Lawrence were together from 1984 until his death in January 1994. Over those ten years they lived part of the time in Wilton, CT, Key West, FL, and Oxford, MS, where Lawrence owned homes.

73. Other authors Lawrence published include: Rick Bass, Frank Conroy, Jayne Anne Phillips, Richard Currey, J.P. Donleavy, Tom Drury, Gish Jen, William Kotzwinkle, Thomas McGuane, Susan Minot, Dan Wakefield, Richard Yates, Thomas Berger, Louis-Ferdinand Celine, Robert Coles, Mark Helprin, William Humphrey, Robert B. Parker, William Jay Smith, Allen Tate, Katherine Anne Porter, Sean O'Faolain, Richard Brautigan, Jorge Luis Borges, Miguel Angel Asturias, Pablo Neruda, and Edwin O'Connor.

74. Interview, 22 May 1997.

75. Speech, 21 April 1996.

76. Williams, "Faulkner's Advice to a Young Writer," unpublished draft.

77. Faulkner to Williams, NA, later spring 1959.

78. Faulkner to Williams, Oxford MS, 4 July 1953.

79. Williams, "Faulkner's Advice to a Young Writer," unpublished draft.

80. Sallie Bingham, "Books: (Southern?) Women Writers," Ms. 1, no. 6 (1991): 69.

81. Hickman, "Joan Williams," Mississippi Writers Page, ed. John B. Padgett, University of Mississippi Department of English, 15 April 2005. http://www.olemiss.edu/mwp/dir/williams_joan/.

82. Ibid.

83. Judith Bryant Wittenberg, "Joan Williams: The Rebellious Heart," in Southern Women Writers: The New Generation, ed. Tonette Bond Inge (Tuscaloosa: The University of Alabama Press, 1990), 99, 106, 112–113.

84. See Louis B. Rubin, "Life and Death of a Salesman," Saturday Review of Literature, 21 May 1966, 32–33, and "Two True Sounds from Dixie," Time, 19 May 1961, 105.

85. Doris Betts, "There's Power in Powder Man," review of Old Powder Man by Joan Williams, Raleigh News and Observer, 19 June 1966, sec. 3, p. 3.

86. Robert Penn Warren, "Death of a Salesman—Southern Style," review of Old Powder Man by Joan Williams, Life, 20 May 1966.

87. Joyce Carol Oates, review of Old Powder Man by Joan Williams, Detroit Free Press, 15 May 1966, 2B.

88. "The Contest," 2, 4, 25, 28.

89. Faulkner to Williams, Oxford, MS, July 1953.

90. Faulkner to Williams, Oxford, MS, 30 July 1953.

91. Williams, "Faulkner's Advice to a Young Writer," 1992, 260–261.

92. Faulkner to Williams, Oxford, MS, 31 July 1953.

93. Faulkner's delayed trip to Paris for Hawks' movie. He had invited Joan to accompany him.

94. Brodsky, 116–117.

95. Interview, 10 June 1997.

96. A small station wagon.

97. Grenada, Mississippi.

98. Faulkner to Williams, Oxford, MS, 5 August 1953.

99. Blotner, vol. 2, 1462.

100. Faulkner to Williams, Oxford, MS, 8 August 1953.

101. Blotner, vol. 2, 1462.

102. Faulkner to Williams, Oxford, MS, 13 August 1953.

103. Faulkner to Williams, Oxford, MS, 20 August 1953.

104. Interview, 14 October 1996.

105. Interview, 10 June 1997.

106. Karl, 864.

107. Parini, 351.

108. Faulkner to Williams, Oxford, MS, 4 September 1953.

109. Blotner, 1984, 573–75.

110. Joan Williams, interview with author, 4 February 2002.

111. Faulkner to Williams [Mrs. Ezra Bowen], New York, NY, late summer or early fall, 1954.

112. See A.E. Housman, *A Shropshire Lad* (New York: Dover, n.d.), 34. See also Lisa C. Hickman, "William Faulkner and A.E. Housman: A Writer's Poet," *Housman Society Journal* 27 (2001): 23–35.

113. *Wintering*, 278.

114. Interview, May 1998.

115. Interview, 10 June 1997.

116. Interview, 22 May 1997.

117. Joan and Ezra were married 6 March 1954. Their divorce was final in May 1970.

118. Catherine Drinker Bowen, "Discipline and Reward: A Writer's Life," *The Atlantic Monthly*, NA, 88–89.

119. Interview, 3 February 1998.

120. *Ibid.*

121. Blotner, vol. 2, 1484.

122. Faulkner to Williams, St. Moritz, Switzerland, 14 December 1953.

123. *Look* and *Esquire* shared a building at 488 Madison Avenue.

124. Amherst College in Amherst, Massachusetts.

125. Interview, 22 May 1997. See also Williamson, 291.

126. Williamson, 289–290.

127. Interview, 2 June 1997.

128. *Wintering*, 329.

129. Brodsky, 126.

130. Faulkner to Williams, New York, NY, November 1953.

131. Don Klopfer, one of the three partners at Random House along with Bennett Cerf and Robert Haas.

132. Faulkner to Williams, New York, NY, November 1953.

133. *Ibid.*

VI : *1954–1962—Blue Mississippi Hills*

1. Faulkner to Williams, Stresa, December 1953.

2. Faulkner to Williams, St. Moritz, Switzerland, 11 January 1954.

3. *Selected*, 358.

4. Parini, 359.

5. Faulkner to Williams, St. Moritz, Switzerland, 11 January 1954.

6. Interview, 10 June 1997.

7. Karl, 875.

8. Interview, 22 May 1997.

9. Gauch, 107.

10. Joan's father suffered from emphysema and died in 1955.

11. Joan's second son, Matthew Williams Bowen, was born in 1956. *The Wintering* is dedicated to her sons.

12. Telephone interview with Robert Creamer, 13 June 1997.

13. Published 13 November 1959.

14. *The Reivers*, published 4 June 1962.

15. Blotner, 1984, 666.

16. Faulkner to Williams, Oxford, MS, 26 April 1959.

17. Faulkner to Williams, New York, NY, 12 June 1959.

18. Faulkner to Williams, NA.

19. Faulkner to Williams, 4 February 1960.

20. Speech, 21 April 1996.

21. Blotner, 1984, 689.

22. Faulkner to Williams, Charlottesville, VA, 19 June 1960.

23. Speech, 21 April 1996.

24. Faulkner to Williams, Charlottesville, VA, 4 January 1961.

25. *William Faulkner: The Carl Petersen Collection Catalogue* 48 (Berkley: Serendipity Books, 1991), 33.

26. Faulkner to Williams, Oxford, MS, January 1961.

27. Interview, 10 June 1997.

28. Interview, 14 October 1996.

29. Hiram Haydn, *Words and Faces* (New York: Harcourt Brace Jovanovich, 1954), 88, 92.

30. *Ibid.*, 318.

31. Interview, 30 August 2001.

32. Interview, 10 June 1997.

33. See Mississippi Writers Page, http://www.olemiss.edu/mwp/dir/williams_joan/

34. Speech, 21 April 1996.

35. National Institute of Arts and Letters, May 1962.

36. John F. Kennedy. Blotner, 1984, 716.

37. Interview, 14 October 1996.

38. Williams, "Faulkner's Advice to a Young Writer," unpublished draft.

Joan Williams
Selected Bibliography

Fiction: Novels

The Morning and the Evening. New York: Atheneum, 1961. Reprint, *Voices of the South.* Baton Rouge: Louisiana State University Press, 1994.

Old Powder Man. New York: Harcourt, Brace & World, 1966.

The Wintering. New York: Harcourt, Brace & World, 1971. Reprint, *Voices of the South,* with an afterword by Joan Williams, reprint, "Twenty Will Not Come Again." Baton Rouge: Louisiana State University Press, 1997.

County Woman. Boston: Little, Brown, 1982.

Pay the Piper. New York: Dutton, 1988.

Fiction: Short Story Collection

Pariah and Other Stories. Boston: Little, Brown, 1983.

Teleplay

Co-author with William Faulkner. "The Graduation Dress," General Electric Theatre, CBS, 30 October 1960.

Selected Short Story Publications

"The Contest." *The Chattahoochee Review* 15, no. 4 (Summer 1995): 1–28.

"Daylight Comes." *Saturday Evening Post.* Reprint, *Pariah and Other Stories.* Boston: Little, Brown, 1983; Avon, 1985.

"Going Ahead." *Saturday Evening Post,* December 1964, 58–60. Reprint, *Pariah and Other Stories.* Boston: Little, Brown, 1983. Reprint, *Southern Christmas Literary Classics of the Holidays,* edited by Judy Long & Thomas Payton, 95–105. Athens, GA: Hill Street Press, 1998.

"Happy Anniversary." *The Southern Review* 31, no. 4 (Autumn 1995): 907–934.

"Jesse." *Esquire,* November 1969. Reprint in *Pariah and Other Stories.* Boston: Little, Brown, 1983.

"The Morning and the Evening." *The Atlantic Monthly,* January 1952, 65–69. Reprint, Chapter One, *The Morning and the Evening.* New York: Atheneum, 1961.

"No Love for the Lonely." *Saturday Evening Post,* 19 January 1963, 48–51. Reprint, *Pariah and Other Stories.* Boston: Little, Brown, 1983.

"Pariah." *McCall's,* August 1967, 80–81, 121–126. Reprint, *Pariah and Other Stories.* Boston: Little, Brown, 1983.

"Rain Later." *Mademoiselle,* August 1949, 331–338. College Fiction Award Winner,

Mademoiselle, 1949. Reprint, *Pariah and Other Stories*. Boston: Little, Brown, 1983.

"Scoot." *Key West Review* 3.1 & 2 (Fall and Winter 1989): 146–163. Reprint, *Southern Reader* 3, no. 2 (September/October 1991): 16–17, 23+.

"Spring Is Now." *The Virginia Quarterly Review* (Autumn 1968): 626–640. Reprint, *Pariah and Other Stories*. Boston: Little, Brown, 1983. Reprint, *Crossing the Color Line*, edited by Suzanne W. Jones, 97–107. Columbia, SC: University of South Carolina Press, 2000.

"Vistas." *Pariah and Other Stories*. Boston: Little, Brown, 1983. Reprint, *Homeworks: A Book of Tennessee Writers*, edited by Phyllis Tickle and Alice Swanson, 35–38. Knoxville: University of Tennessee Press, 1996.

Nonfiction

"'You-Are-Thereness' in Fiction." *Writer*, April 1967, 20–21, 72–73.

"Remembering." *Ironwood* 17 (Spring 1981): 107–115.

"In Defense of Caroline Compson." In *Critical Essays on William Faulkner: The Compson Family*, edited by Arthur F. Kinney, 402–407. Boston: G.K. Hall, 1982.

"Faulkner's Advice to a Young Writer." In *Faulkner and the Short Story: Faulkner and Yoknapatawpha, 1990*, edited by Evans Harrington and Ann J. Abadie, 253–262. Jackson: University Press of Mississippi, 1992.

"Personal Sketch [William Faulkner]." *The Bardian*, 15 May 1951, 1, 4.

"Twenty Will Not Come Again." *The Atlantic Monthly*, May 1980, 58–65.

Speeches and Addresses

"Advice to a Young Writer." Memphis Friends of the Library. Racquet Club, Memphis, Tennessee. 21 April 1996.

"Faulkner's Advice to a Young Writer." Faulkner and the Short Story: Faulkner and Yoknapatawpha Conference, Oxford, Mississippi. July 29–August 3, 1990.

"The Purpose of the Novel." A speech.

"The Southern Writer in the Vanishing South." A speech.

"Waiting for Inspiration." A speech.

"Writing Fiction as a Paradox." A speech.

Memorial Remarks for Seymour Lawrence (1994).

Dramatizations

Odle, Jenny, and Alice Berry. "Twenty Will Not Come Again." Voices of the South. Circuit Playhouse, Memphis, Tennessee. 8–22 March 1997.

Odle, Jenny, and Alice Berry, and Joan Williams. "The Contest." Voices of the South. Circuit Playhouse, Memphis, Tennessee. 21 & 22 March 1997.

Odle, Jenny, and Alice Berry. "Twenty Will Not Come Again." Voices of the South. Faulkner and Yoknapatawpha Conference, Oxford, Mississippi. 27 July 1998.

Odle, Jenny, and Alice Berry. "Vistas." Voices of the South. TheatreWorks, Memphis, Tennessee. 17, 18, 23, 24 and 25 March 2006.

Televised Interview

"Talks with Authors" Memphis Friends of the Library. 4 March 1996.

Seminar

Key West Literary Seminar: Spirit of Place. 17–21 January 2002.

Bibliography

Betts, Doris. "There's Power in Powder Man." Review of *Old Powder Man* by Joan Williams. *Raleigh News and Observer*, 19 June 1966, sec. 3, p. 3.

Bingham, Sallie. "Books: (Southern?) Women Writers." *Ms.* 1, no. 6 (1991): 68–70.

Blotner, Joseph. *Faulkner: A Biography*, vol. 2. New York: Random House, 1974.

_____. *Faulkner: A Biography*. New York: Vintage, 1984.

_____, ed. *Selected Letters of William Faulkner*. New York: Random House, 1977.

Bowen, Catherine Drinker. "Discipline and Reward: A Writer's Life." *The Atlantic Monthly*, NA, 87–92.

Brodsky, Louis Daniel, and Robert W. Hamblin, eds. *Faulkner: A Comprehensive Guide to the Brodsky Collection, Vol. II: The Letters*. Jackson: University Press of Mississippi, 1984.

Carpenter, Meta Wilde, and Orin Borsten. *A Loving Gentleman: The Love Story of William Faulkner and Meta Carpenter*. New York: Simon and Schuster, 1976.

Coughlan, Robert. "The Man Behind the Faulkner Myth." *Life* (5 October 1953): 55–68.

_____. "The Private World of William Faulkner." *Life* (28 September 1953): 118–136.

Dardis, Tom. *The Thirsty Muse*. New York: Ticknor and Fields, 1989.

"Faulkner Honors Bard with Sudden Visit." *The Bardian*, 15 May 1951, 1.

Faulkner, William. *The Marble Faun and A Green Bough*. New York: Random House, 1924, 1933.

_____. *Requiem for a Nun*. New York: Vintage, 1951.

_____. *The Wild Palms* [*If I Forget Thee, Jerusalem*]. New York: Vintage International, 1939.

Gauch, Patricia Lee. "Faulkner and Beyond: A Biography of Joan Williams." Ph.D. dissertation, Drew University, 1988.

Gray, Paul. "Mister Faulkner Goes to Stockholm." *Smithsonian* (October 2001): 56–60.

Gresset, Michel. *A Faulkner Chronology*. Jackson: University of Mississippi Press, 1985.

Haydn, Hiram. *Words and Faces*. New York: Harcourt Brace Jovanovich, Inc., 1954.

Hickman, Lisa C. "Joan Williams." *Mississippi Writers Page*, edited by John B. Padgett. University of Mississippi Department of English. 15 April 2005. http://www.olemiss.edu/mwp/dir/williams_joan/.

_____. "William Faulkner and A.E. Housman: A Writer's Poet." *Housman Society Journal* 26 (2001): 23–35.

_____. "William Faulkner: Dealing with His Demons." *Memphis* (September 1993): 36–40, 85–95, 115–116.

Karl, Frederick R. *William Faulkner: American Writer*. New York: Weidenfeld and Nicolson, 1989.

Maurer, David A. "Longtime Friendship Developed Through Sound and Fury." *Daily Progress* (Charlottesville, VA), 23 January 2000, E1–3.

Minter, David. *William Faulkner: His Life and Work.* Baltimore: Johns Hopkins University Press, 1980.

Mullener, Elizabeth. "Joan Williams and William Faulkner: A Romance Remembered." *Times-Picayune, Dixie Magazine* (19 September 1982): 8–10, 12–14, 16, 18.

Oates, Joyce Carol. Review of *Old Powder Man* by Joan Williams. *Detroit Free Press,* 15 May 1966, 2B.

Parini, Jay. *One Matchless Time.* New York: HarperCollins, 2004.

Pound, Ezra. "A Virginal." In *Ezra Pound Selected Poems.* New York: New Directions, 1926.

Schiff, Stacy. Review of *The Lives of the Muses: Nine Women and the Artists They Inspired* by Francine Prose. *The New York Times Book Review,* 22 September 2002, 9.

Thomas, William. "Literary Tale Will Be Tugged in Court." *Commercial Appeal* (Memphis, TN), 2 November 1987, B1–2.

Tolson, Jay, ed. *The Correspondence of Shelby Foote and Walker Percy.* New York: Doubletake/Norton, 1997.

Warren, Robert Penn. "Death of a Salesman—Southern Style." Review of *Old Powder Man* by Joan Williams. *Life,* 20 May 1966.

Watson, James G. *William Faulkner: Letters and Fictions.* Austin: University of Texas Press, 1987.

William Faulkner: The Carl Petersen Collection Catalogue. 48. Berkeley: Serendipity Books, 1991.

Williams, Joan. "The Contest." *The Chattahoochee Review* 15, no. 4 (Summer 1995): 1–25.

_____. "Faulkner's Advice to a Young Writer." In *Faulkner and the Short Story: Faulkner and Yoknapawtawpha, 1990,* edited by Evans Harrington and Ann J. Abadie, 253–262. Jackson: University of Mississippi Press, 1992.

_____. "The Morning and the Evening." In *Pariah and Other Stories.* Boston: Little, Brown, 1983.

_____. *Pay the Piper.* New York: E.P. Dutton, 1988.

_____. "Personal Sketch." *The Bardian,* 15 May 1951, 1, 4.

_____. "Twenty Will Not Come Again." *The Atlantic Monthly* (May 1980): 58–65.

_____. *The Wintering.* New York: Harcourt, Brace & World, 1971. Reprint, *Voices of the South,* with an afterword by Joan Williams, reprint, "Twenty Will Not Come Again," 371–389. Baton Rouge: Louisiana State University Press, 1997.

Williamson, Joel. *William Faulkner and Southern History.* New York and Oxford: Oxford University Press, 1993.

Wittenberg, Judith Bryant. "Joan Williams: The Rebellious Heart." In *Southern Women Writers: The New Generation,* edited by Tonette Bond Inge, 97–113. Tuscaloosa: The University of Alabama Press, 1990.

Zender, Karl F. *Faulkner and the Politics of Reading.* Baton Rouge: Louisiana State University Press, 2002.

Index